LAUGHTER IN A GENEVAN GOWN

The Works of Frederick Buechner
1970-1980

MARIE-HÉLÈNE DAVIES

WILLIAM B. EERDMANS PUBLISHING COMPANY
Grand Rapids, Michigan

*To my parents
and
to my mentors*

Copyright © 1983 by William B. Eerdmans Publishing Co.
255 Jefferson Ave. S.E., Grand Rapids, Michigan 49503
Printed in the United States of America

Library of Congress Cataloging in Publication Data

Davies, Marie-Hélène.
Laughter in a Genevan Gown.

Bibliography: p. 193
1. Buechner, Frederick, 1926-   —Criticism and interpretation. 2. Buechner,
Frederick, 1926-   —Religion and ethics. I. Title.
PS3552.U35Z64 1983   813′.54   83-14205
ISBN 0-8028-1969-9

Table of Contents

Throughout my life, I have been blessed with a number of mentors. Parents, teachers, friends, my husband, and writers of various schools of thought have led me in turn on the way. An eager disciple, I have always found it sad when our paths diverged, when I had to change from follower of a mentor to dissenter. Whether our relationship has remained friendly or whether we have parted has depended on the emotional maturity and the degree of *agape* on both sides.

Such *agape* I have found particularly in my husband, Horton Davies, who inspired me to undertake this task because of his respect for Buechner. I owe him many thanks for his understanding, advice, and support.

Whatever the trend of my recent thought, as follower or as dissenter, I owe it to Frederick Buechner. I have read his works avidly, and they have definitely changed my attitude toward life.

I am grateful to have worked in the libraries of Princeton University and Phillips Exeter Academy. Both have some of Buechner's writings in manuscript. I also wish to thank the Huntington Library, San Marino, California, where the gestation of this book took place. The warmth and kindness of the staff, their willingness to accommodate my needs as a reader and provide me with isolated offices or cubicles, have largely facilitated my work. As a token of gratitude, I have promised the library my annotations of the changes Buechner made between the first edition of his tetralogy and its second appearance under the title of *The Book of Bebb*, as well as, whenever appropriate, some letters from the author.

Among the Huntington Library senior research associates, Dr. Hallett Smith read and criticized part of my work and provided encouragement. To him and to all those who have proved true friends, I wish to extend my gratitude.

It is my privilege to thank the following loyal friends of Mr. Buechner who willingly granted me interviews: Mr. James Merrill, the poet; Mr. Douglas Snow of Exeter, New Hampshire; and

Messrs. Hlavacek and Thurber of Princeton. I also appreciated the opportunity to talk with Dr. McLellan, headmaster of the Lawrenceville School, who gave me insight as one of Buechner's former colleagues in the English department.

Last, I wish to thank the Hun School of Princeton for giving me a year of freedom to bring this book to term, and my editor, Ms. Hietbrink, for serving as midwife.

                                              M.-H. D.

*Society demands [that] each must stand at his post,
here a cobbler, there a poet. No man is expected to be
both. . . , that would be queer. Such a man would be
'different' from other people, not quite reliable . . . in
short, he would always be suspected of unreliability and
incompetence, because society is persuaded that only the
cobbler who is not a poet can provide workmanlike shoes.*

Carl Jung, *Two Essays in Analytical Psychology*

A lady was once introduced to Sabine Baring-Gould, minister
of the Church of England, author of the hymn "Onward, Christian Soldiers," novelist, and antiquarian. She asked: "Are you the
good Mr. Baring-Gould who writes such beautiful sermons, or the
other Mr. Baring-Gould who writes novels?" This suspicion of
writers engaged in some other occupation not pertaining to their
art is fairly recent. The Renaissance was used to those who were
involved in the political world and were mathematicians,
philosophers, and theologians as well. They admired most of all
the omnicompetent Leonardo da Vinci—sculptor, painter, architect,
anatomist, and thinker—as *l'uomo universale.* In contrast, the modern
industrial world tends to rely on the specialist and the expert who
has spent years in the same occupation.

Frederick Buechner, both clergyman and novelist, has suffered
from our modern narrowness. He began his career as a writer with
the highly acclaimed *A Long Day's Dying,* but met difficulties when
he published his fourth novel, *The Final Beast.* At that point, critics
assumed that the writer had metamorphosed into a full-time clergy-

man who could no longer write a serious and realistic novel. The ''good'' Christians, on the other hand, were shocked by novels in which the pastor did not appear as a cardboard character, a Mr. Goody-Goody, and discarded Buechner on this account.

The more sophisticated, however, praised Buechner for his grappling with evil while suggesting the presence of mystery and the response of wonder, and delighted in his marvelous craftsmanship. James Dickey, Cynthia Ozick, Reynolds Price, and, in *The Times Literary Supplement,* James Idema, have all in turn acclaimed his work for its particular sensitivity, humor, and freedom from sensationalism. Others, like Julian Moynahan, have been turned off by the lack of direct message which they expect in a novel, unable to understand that Buechner, like Kierkegaard and many modern writers after him, proceeds by indirection.

In writing this book, it was my intention to show both facets of Buechner: the lover of life, inhaling the scents of the earth, and the mystic with eyes turned toward heaven. Both sides of his personality blend because Buechner is no dichotomizing Platonist. Heaven can be reached only through the earth, he believes, which accounts for his particularly chthonic brand of Christianity. On the other hand, ever since his conversion, Buechner's art has been permeated with Christianity, which accounts for his particular form of imagination.

One might call this my ''angle,'' except that it is not an angle in the narrow sense of the word, a revisionist slant that tries to render all previous approaches outdated. A one-sided view would be appropriate for an author who has already been much debated. But apart from doctoral dissertations, this is the first book on Buechner, and it must suffer the fate of pioneering work: it digs the ground and reveals treasures, but cataloguers and other archeologists will have to come and label each item with care and precision.

I have limited myself to the corpus of a decade: 1970-1980. In Buechner's earlier works one can trace many of his recent themes, but those relevant to the duality that I have emphasized began to appear after Buechner committed himself to being an exponent of Christianity. It is in those that the sacred and the profane best interlock.

The first half of the book deals with religious themes: it stresses Buechner's relationship to his mentors, covers his very diverse and protean religious production, and traces four main themes developed in his novels. The second part deals with the earthy side of our writer: his struggles with and absorption of modern existentialism and psychology, the working out of some modern themes in his novels, and the craftsmanship peculiar to his imagination. What I try to show is how Buechner's artistry and themes blend to make a harmonious corpus worthy of further study.

This sort of approach required numerous readings of Buechner's works. Like a camera, the critic needs to shut off parts of himself to take angled shots of an author's literary creation. Thus I had to summon my religious, psychological, literary, and cinematic selves in turn to give sample pictures of the multi-faceted Buechner. Each interpretation required isolating well-interwoven threads, exposing them, and in some way impoverishing them, for "We murder to dissect," as Wordsworth knew only too well.

In my analysis, I have tried not to push my own prejudices, yet however objective a critic tries to be, some will always emerge. My French love for clarity and pattern, for instance, leads me to prefer *Telling the Truth* to *The Alphabet of Grace*, which I have heard praised by many a reader less averse to romanticism. My Catholic background certainly predisposes me to favor the Eucharist as *the* sacrament, even if the hearing of the Word has lured me toward Protestantism from a very early age. And all of us, including me, relate to characters according to our own peculiar chemistry, especially at a time when the novel is no longer dictatorial in its conclusions. Still, the critic must try to be objective, for his task is, at least as much as the author's, to hold a mirror up to reality. This time, however, the critic holds a mirror to the reflection of reality. At its worst, this mirror will present a picture distorted by the mercurial flecks of its background. At its best, like the mirrors in Van Eyck's paintings, it will disclose another corner of the room, otherwise hidden.

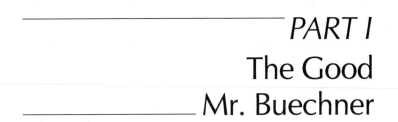

PART I
The Good
Mr. Buechner

Religious Background and Convictions

Lord, how can man preach thy eternal word?
 He is a brittle crazie glasse:
Yet in thy temple thou dost him afford
 This glorious and transcendent place,
 To be a window through thy grace.
Herbert, ''The Windows'' in *The Temple*

From Princeton, New Jersey, to Pasadena, California, from the verdant hills of Vermont to the lowlands of Florida, in Episcopal, Presbyterian, and Methodist churches, pulpits resound with quotes from the good Mr. Buechner. In the largest Benedictine abbey in the United States, the silence of the monks at table is broken while a lector reads selections from Buechner's medieval novel, *Godric,* for, like him, they count the world well lost for God.[1] But Buechner is not so good as to be dull. His phrasing is chosen specifically because he, like the seventeenth-century metaphysical preachers, combines wisdom with wit, learning with the experience of life.

Every theologian is God's man and his own man. To understand Frederick Buechner, one must know the media through which the divine influences have come. The Bible, theological teachers, and his musing on the events of his own life, traumatic or salvific, have accelerated Buechner's ''Sacred Journey.''[2]

---

1. Information conveyed by Father Godfrey Diekmann, O.S.B., monk of Saint John's Abbey, Collegeville, Minnesota.

2. *The Sacred Journey* (New York: Harper and Row, 1982) is the first part of Buechner's autobiography.

I asked Buechner's old friend Mr. Gerrish Thurber if he was surprised at Buechner's conversion. Thurber, the former librarian at
Lawrenceville School who watched the boy's and the young man's
development, gave this answer:

> Yes; it was unexpected, and the parties following the success
> of the first novel, *A Long Day's Dying*, and his picture in *Life* maga-
> zine did not prepare us for this. Also, he was not brought up re-
> ligiously. He must have felt that the life of parties and the in-
> tellectual life were not fulfilling. . . .[3]

However, he and other people interviewed, like the present headmaster of Lawrenceville, Dr. Bruce McLellan, noted the particular
sensitivity of the young man, his concern for his fellows and his
compassionate response to social injustice.

Looking at Buechner's early manuscripts, now in Princeton University Library, provides some more clues to the undercurrents in
the young man's life. Among the doodles in the margin we find
concern with life-and-death issues, theological questioning, draw-
ings of people's heads, and the endless scribbling of the alphabet.
All of these reappear in Buechner's theological works as well as in
his novels. Thus, if Buechner in later years did in fact learn to fly,
he was more consistent in his metamorphosis than is the caterpillar
who becomes a butterfly.

Between 1970 and 1980 Buechner wrote seven non-fictional works
devoted to various aspects of Christianity—if one is to include *The
Faces of Jesus*, a rambling commentary on visual depictions of
Jesus—and seven works of fiction, four of which form the tetralogy
The Book of Bebb. * Different as the techniques employed may be,
they all show indebtedness to the major theologians who influenced
Buechner and whom he thanks in the prefaces to *The Magnificent
Defeat* and *Wishful Thinking*.

Chronologically, the first strong influence on Buechner's life was
George Buttrick, the senior pastor of Madison Avenue Presbyterian
Church in Manhattan, who served as a catalyst to Buechner's con-

---

3. Personal interview with Mr. Thurber at his home in Princeton on
January 4, 1980.

* *The Book of Bebb* comprises *Lion Country* (1971), *Open Heart* (1972), *Love
Feast* (1974), and *Treasure Hunt* (1977).

version. Having entered the church one Sunday for no specific reason, Buechner heard Buttrick preach a sermon on Christ being crowned with tears and great laughter. At this point Buechner felt ''as if the great wall of China had tumbled down,'' as if he was being infused with new life. He discussed the impact of the sermon with Buttrick, who immediately drove him to Union Theological Seminary at 120th Street on Broadway; there arrangements were rapidly concluded for his admission.[4]

At that time Union Seminary shared with Yale Divinity School the reputation of being the most distinguished institution of higher theological education in the United States. Among the men there who influenced Buechner was Paul Tillich, who correlated Christian existentialism with culture in its psychological, sociological, and aesthetic dimensions. Another was Reinhold Niebuhr, professor of applied Christianity, whose *Notebook of a Tamed Cynic* demonstrated the malaise of a society in Detroit which in its assembly lines reduced human beings to disposable objects. Yet another influential teacher was James Muilenburg, a man who wrote little but to whom Buechner dedicated *The Magnificent Defeat* and whom he portrayed in the character of Kuykendall in *The Return of Ansel Gibbs*. He brought the Old Testament prophets back to life in Union's largest lecture room. His final lecture in the course, which drew students from all confessions and backgrounds, including Jews and Columbia University graduates, testified to how highly he was esteemed. The students took their shoes off before entering the auditorium, as if they were on holy ground.

Other men who earned Buechner's gratitude include John Knox (professor of New Testament) and Paul Sherer (professor of homiletics), who were his teachers, and R. R. Wicks, the Dean of Princeton University Chapel, who later taught with Buechner at Phillips Exeter Academy in New Hampshire. Later influences were C. S. Lewis; W. T. Stace, Princeton philosopher; and David Read, a literary minister who succeeded Buttrick at Madison Avenue Presbyterian Church. He also learned much from Agnes Sanford, who was running healing seminars for the Episcopal Church in New

---

4. Buechner, *The Sacred Journey*, pp. 109-111.

York State. (She was the model for the character of Lillian Flagg in *The Final Beast*.)

The reigning religious philosophy at the time that Buechner attended Union Theological Seminary was neo-orthodoxy. Its creed was wittily summarized as "Thou shalt love the Lord thy Dodd with all thy Barth, and thy Niebuhr as thyself." It is therefore not surprising that one of the major sources of inspiration in Buechner's theology is indeed Karl Barth.

The theology of the Word of God is at the center of Buechner's thought, for the Scriptures are the records of divine encounters with humanity. Since man is subject to the law of time, to live is to change. Theology often comes to man at a time of crisis, at the turning point of an illness or a change in his thinking. Because our human world is broken, the last word in theology cannot be pronounced—that would mean bringing infinity within the range of finite concept. Then, too, a man will not view theology in the same way at every stage of his life. Thus theology must proceed dialectically, not with the dialectics of Hegel but with the existential dialectics of Kierkegaard. In the same way, Buechner always insists on the importance of moving on, of burning one's bridges and getting on with the new.

The paradox of paradoxes in Christianity—of the sinner being pardoned, of time entering eternity, and of the finite participating in the infinite—is all resolved in the person of Christ. Theology for Barth and for Buechner is therefore the service of God's Word trying to clarify the basis and the norm of the preached message of the Church. It is an act of faith that follows the Anselmic pattern, *credo ut intelligam* (I believe in order to understand).

The minister, then, must direct all his efforts to the exposition of Scripture after praying for the inspiration of the Holy Spirit.[5] The theological truth is personal and is learned through obedience. Though Barth insists on the importance of both preaching and the sacraments of the Word (baptism and the Lord's Supper), Buechner mainly retains the former. Like Barth, he rejects Catholicism, ecclesial tradition, and Liberal Protestantism with its dilutions and

---

5. Most of this summary of Karl Barth's theology is derived from H. R. Mackintosh, *Types of Modern Theology, Schleiermacher to Barth* (New York: Scribners, 1937).

faddism. He relies on the Holy Spirit, who gives the ears and the eyes to faith.

Barth believes that natural religion is unbelief and that the true locus of religion is in the Church. But the Church is constantly challenged by Scripture, which limits its authority. It has authority only insofar as it is obedient to the Word of God and translates it anew in modern terms. Man has a covenant with God and can enjoy the creation only insofar as he obeys God's Word. Though he has freedom, he was predestined to obey the commands and laws of God. Man should not see himself as dichotomous but as an inextricable unity of body and soul. Insofar as he is in history, man participates in the history of salvation according to the covenant God gave to man and the promise accomplished in Jesus Christ that death would be robbed of its sting. Therefore we must trust that God in his providence will preserve and sustain us if we cooperate with him. He will save us from nothingness, which is evil: sin, sickness, hunger, and death. Disobedience leads to nothingness, but since it has been annihilated on the Cross, nothingness can now drive us to God rather than from God.

Buechner also borrows his belief in angels from Barth. Angels do not do what God does, but they bear testimony to what he does. They are his emissaries, and they obey his will faithfully. When God mediates himself, they are there as his ambassadors and witnesses. But if God works directly, why does he need ambassadors? God does not delegate authority, but he delegates the tasks to be achieved. Thus all angels have a protective function to serve toward men, though Barth rejects the Catholic idea that every individual has a guardian angel assigned to him. Angels are opposed by the demons, the creatures of nothingness, who must not be granted the reality of God's world in case they might thus gain strength.[6] Thus, following Augustine and Calvin, Barth affirms the ontological reality of evil but denies it ultimacy. Demons will finally destroy themselves and the creation will be affirmed.[7]

---

6. See Geoffrey W. Bromiley, *An Introduction to the Theology of Karl Barth* (Grand Rapids, Mich.: Eerdmans, 1979).

7. For a good analysis of the historical ways of considering evil, see Theodore Plantinga, *Learning to Live with Evil* (Grand Rapids, Mich.: Eerdmans, 1982).

Finally, we must hope, for we are those that stand expecting the resurrection. We are saved by hope, and we gain peace in God and await the day when death shall finally be vanquished.

Barth's influence is easily recognized in Buechner's theology and his novels. The priority given to obedience and listening to the Word of God, the importance of evangelism, the belief that God sustains us and sends us his messengers in the form of angels, the subordination of Church and ministry to God and Scripture, an Augustinian approach to the problem of evil—all this shapes the thought of Buechner. But he was also influenced by two other major writers: Kierkegaard, that great Dane of a nineteenth-century philosopher, whose ideas he taught as a chaplain at Phillips Exeter Academy, and the modern theologian Paul Tillich.

From Kierkegaard as well as Barth, Buechner borrows the notion of paradox, but it is mainly with Kierkegaard that he shares the notion of passionate commitment. Man cannot be a spectator in life's struggles; he has to roll up his sleeves and participate (many pictures on the jackets of Buechner's books show him with rolled-up sleeves on his farm in Vermont). Faith is responsibility to God expressed in personal decision. Buechner also shares Kierkegaard's belief in indirect communication, which for Kierkegaard took the form of pseudonyms. In his novels Buechner fabricates characters who represent various aspects of contemporary life. He lets them all work out their own views and pay for the consequences of them, in order to awaken the reader to the truth and make him examine his own life.

Like Kierkegaard, Buechner also insists on the fact that faith is a risk, and that man progresses through three stages: the aesthetic, the ethical, and the religious. (This is particularly obvious in *The Book of Bebb.*) Man is therefore a sinner and a pilgrim on the road to God, and even though religion is usually linked with morality, it always lives in tension with it. Faith is paradoxical, and the true believer gives up having a system about the world and trusts himself to God, knowing that he is looking at God's image through a broken world and that he can thus get only broken concepts. God cannot be known directly but only through the revelation of Jesus Christ. This anti-intellectual and anti-systematic position is very much that of Buechner, who hates being called a theologian, though of course, insofar as he has written theological books and delivered sermons and written novels either serving an evangelical purpose or pervaded with the love of God, he *is* a theologian. But anything systematic or rationalistic makes him cringe, and in this respect he is very near to the existentialist approach of Kierkegaard.[8]

Buechner was particularly struck by the story of Abraham and Isaac in *Fear and Trembling*, and Kierkegaard's interpretation of the theme of religion conflicting with morality and the fact that the comic and the tragic there touch each other at the point of infinity. From that book Buechner also takes up the idea that the knight of faith renounces the universal in order to become the individual who translates himself in terms of the universal. The true knight of faith rides alone and is a witness to God. He knows that what is truly great is accessible to all. He cannot always reveal the purpose of God or the purpose of his own actions insofar as he is directed by God because they would not be understood in terms of either aesthetics or ethics.[9]

Although there is no common measure between God and man, man is strengthened by the grace of God as Paul was strengthened when he was in prison. Man cannot strengthen himself because testimony is a gift from God. Both Buechner and Kierkegaard insist that adversity helps to strengthen the inner man, and that the injured man tends to be more open to the mercy of God, from whom he awaits his salvation.[10]

To sum up Buechner's indebtedness to Kierkegaard, one can say that Buechner derives from him the idea that faith is a passion and a paradox, that man goes through three main stages in his life—the aesthetic, the ethical, and the religious—and that the knight of faith always goes his way alone to salvation.

The third great inspiration for Buechner was Paul Tillich. Buechner would agree with him that all beings who have ultimate

---

8. For Kierkegaard's anti-intellectualism, see particularly the preface to *Fear and Trembling*, trans. Walter Lowrie (1941; rpt. New York: Anchor Books, 1954), p. 24.

9. Kierkegaard, *Fear and Trembling*, p. 40, pp. 89 ff., pp. 97 ff.

10. Søren Kierkegaard, *Edifying Discourses* (New York: Harper, 1958), pp. 107-115.

concern are religious, and all faiths coincide as ultimate concern, but Jesus Christ is the New Being after whom we should be modeled. Tillich links religion and psychology and is strongly influenced by Jung. Man's unconditional concern is the acceptance of his justification by faith amidst doubt and questioning. He is given a new quality of the self, a trans-self, which is the very ground of the self. Faith breaks through the estrangement in human life. Since man is always the subject as well as the object of the introvert's analysis, there is no way of getting down to the whole truth about oneself; therefore grace is the belief that one is accepted and pardoned and that, in relation to God, man is always wrong.

It is also from Tillich that Buechner gets the idea that sin is estrangement or alienation, and that faith is expressed by all men according to their ability and to what has been revealed to them. Objective statements of faith merely point to the truth, which we cannot apprehend except through the revelation. Man does not open himself up to the revelation until he has reached the rock bottom of despair. The symbol of the Cross is the best symbol there is because it is a self-denying positiveness and represents the trust that the Kingdom of God will solve the ambiguities of history. Jesus is the picture of ''a personal life which is subjected to all the consequences of existential estrangement but wherein existential estrangement is conquered in himself and a permanent unity is kept with God.''[11] There nature is redeemed by the transcending of it, through self-negation.

But Buechner and Tillich do part company at a certain point. Tillich ultimately believes that the God of Abraham, Isaac, and Jacob is the same as the God of the philosophers, whereas Buechner's anti-intellectualism makes him radically opposed to this idea. Buechner is not primarily interested in philosophy, though he is interested in what the Eastern religions, especially Buddhism, offer. He would also take a different approach to history than Tillich does. Though Buechner refers to historical events in his sermons, he does not hold any systematic view of the history of salvation through historical time. But he does allude, as Tillich does, to the

---

11. Paul Tillich, *Systematic Theology*, II (Chicago: University of Chicago Press, 1951-63), 135.

difference between *kairos*, the critical quality of time, and *chronos*, the succession of events.[12] Christ is at the center of time for both men, but Buechner believes in the historical character of Jesus—that Jesus actually lived on earth—which Tillich doubts.

On the subject of de-mythologization, on which Bultmann has written cogently, Buechner also goes only so far. He would gladly re-interpret the Descent into Hell and the Virgin Birth. He also believes in re-mythologizing in modern terms the Genesis account of the creation, something he has done in *The Alphabet of Grace*.[13]

The last clear influence on Buechner's books is that of C. S. Lewis. Though Buechner objects to his neo-Thomistic system as being too packed, too rigid, and therefore contrived, he still great-ly admires Lewis's ideas. *Mere Christianity, The Great Divorce,* and *Till We Have Faces* he acknowledges as strong influences on his thought. In *Mere Christianity*, Lewis affirms that the law that man can disobey is also the law which separates him from plants and animals. The moral law is fundamentally different from the herd-group mentality, though it is universally humanly applicable. Chris-tianity speaks only to people who realize that there is a Power behind the law and who, having broken the law, have repented. It cannot speak to those who are unaware of it all. Buechner uses Lewis's argument against atheists in *Wishful Thinking*.

Buechner and Lewis also share a dislike of reductionism in modern Christianity, which some would approach from a merely psychological or sociological standpoint. They both believe that, in the modern world adverse to religion, Christians form a secret society on enemy territory. Each and every one of the saints is, in Protestant terms, "listening in to the secret wireless from our friends."[14] Evil is seen as rebellion, disobedience to God's will. Man

---

12. Frederick Buechner, *The Hungering Dark* (New York: Seabury Press, 1969), pp. 104-105. For further considerations on time, see also *Godric* (New York: Atheneum, 1980), pp. 57-61.

13. Frederick Buechner, *The Alphabet of Grace* (New York: Seabury Press, 1977), p. 101.

14. C. S. Lewis, *Mere Christianity* (New York: Macmillan, 1957), p. 36. One will recognize this as the inspiration for Bebb's activities in the fireproof building in *Love Feast* as well as for those of the magician Babe in *Treasure Hunt*.

is free to rebel at his own risk, as he is free to saw the branch on which he is sitting. But the laws of God and of the creation cannot be broken with impunity.[15] Pride and the unruly self are the root of all evil, the cause of the Fall. Christianity is a free and unexpected gift, since Christ forgives the sinner as if he was himself the offended party. Christianity cannot be the product of man's wishful thinking, because it defies all human reason. It is absurd for the Greeks and for the Jews.[16] Morality is harmony on a personal and interpersonal basis and is in line with the general purpose of human life. All this Buechner subscribes to. For him, as for C. S. Lewis, Christianity is more than mere morality, but morality is the direct consequence of an orderly vision of the universe. They have the same attitude toward sex in marital relationships, although, as far as sex in general is concerned, Buechner is the more modern and permissive of the two. Faith consists in discipline and praying every day; its result is attempting to lead a moral life.

Yet experience dictates against Pelagianism. Morality is not within the reach of man unaided by God. Trust in God is the essence of religion, and the rogues who put their faith in their savior stand a better chance of salvation than all the do-gooders. In *Peculiar Treasures*, Buechner defies human reason to account for God's choice in election. Man's duty consists in not resisting God's will. The purpose of the Christian is to become a little Christ,[17] something he can achieve through habit: by putting on Christ, he gradually trains himself to act and think like Christ.[18] Although the French

---

15. Lewis, *Mere Christianity*, p. 38.

16. Lewis, *Mere Christianity*, pp. 40-41.

17. Lewis, *Mere Christianity*, p. 138. For Lewis, as for Buechner, the cost of being a Christian is immeasurable. Both men believe it entails becoming perfect or facing destruction. In *The Great Divorce*, Lewis points out that people resist God's will by hanging onto their pet sins; in *Till We Have Faces*, God works on Orual's face until it becomes as beautiful as that of her sister Psyche, who has surrendered to the Great Lover.

18. This belief was also shared by the Greek writer Kazantsakis, who, in *The Greek Passion*, has his shepherd hero carve a face of Christ and wear it until he has become like it. But unlike Lewis, Kazantsakis has the mask of judgment prevail over the mask of love, for this is the face that the mature shepherd carves and espouses.

saying "L'habit ne fait pas le moine" still holds true, for Buechner and Lewis the habit contributes to shaping the monk.

Last but not least, Buechner and Lewis have in common their tremendous sense of humor. The later Buechner, like Lewis, is often witty and amusing, sometimes even flippant in the coining of aphorisms.[19] For both men this can be traced back to the pulpit tradition of metaphysical preachers, striving to keep their audience awake by shaking them out of their torpor.[20] Both rely heavily on their literary talent and explain the Creation in terms of literary creation,[21] as Dorothy Sayers did in *The Mind of the Maker*.

If Buechner relies heavily on the works of these masters of theological thought to inspire his own meditations, he opens even more frequently the book of his own life to be illumined and interpreted in the light of The Book of the revelation of the Word of God. *The Alphabet of Grace* includes this statement: "At its heart most theology, like most fiction, is essentially autobiography." The concept implies a number of consequences.

---

19. Buechner's constant reference to the minister as lover and lunatic echoes C. S. Lewis's reference to Christ: "We are faced, then, with a frightening alternative. This man we are talking about was (and is) just what He said or else, a lunatic, or something worse" (*Mere Christianity*, p. 42).

Or compare Lewis's and Buechner's satires of the fundamentalists who interpret the Bible only literally. Lewis says: "All the scriptural imagery (harps, cords, gold, etc.) is, of course, a merely symbolical attempt to express the inexpressible. . . . People who take these symbols literally might as well think that when Christ told us to be like doves, He meant that we were to lay eggs" (*Mere Christianity*, p. 106). In *Wishful Thinking* (New York: Harper & Row, 1973), Buechner writes: "If somebody claims that you have to take the Bible literally, word for word, or not at all, ask him if you have to take John the Baptist literally when he calls Jesus the Lamb of God" (p. 11).

In the seventeenth century the witty Thomas Fuller fought the same fight to interpret Christ's claim that he was "the Door": "Hee who is so sootish as to conceive that Christ was a materiall Doore showeth himself to be a Post indeed" (from *The Collected Sermons of Thomas Fuller D.D., 1631-1659*, I [London: Unwin, 1891], 144).

20. See Horton Davies' forthcoming volume *The Witty Preachers: The English Metaphysical Divines*. Sir Thomas Browne and John Donne are favorites of Buechner.

21. Lewis, *Mere Christianity*, p. 138. See also Buechner, *The Alphabet of Grace* and *The Sacred Journey*.

First, for Buechner, our vision of God is essentially subjective, although there is an object of faith which is essentially unknown to us.[22] We can serve only as pointers to a truth that escapes us. The only reason to believe that we have part of the truth is that we are taken by surprise—not by our own choosing but by God's choosing. *Peculiar Treasures* is an attempt to console all those who feel unworthy by showing precisely this: that God chooses the most unlikely people, those who, so to speak, do not have a leg to stand on and therefore fall into the "everlasting arms" of God.

The second consequence of this concept is that theology, like life, changes as one grows in the faith. The young theologian holds part of the truth that the old theologian will sneer at. This change in Buechner's own theology is best shown in the evolution of the major religious characters in his novels. In *The Final Beast*, Nicolet is a minister but is also a man struggling to overcome his own doubts about faith. In *The Book of Bebb*, Bebb is totally committed to the preaching of the Gospel, but seems to fail with people; nevertheless, he remains obedient and listens more carefully to the word of God. Godric is entirely committed to the worship and praise of God, no longer busy interfering with anyone, but he offers the record of his life as a witness to the works God has performed in him. This reveals a shift in emphasis from the second to the first commandment. In interviews and letters Buechner gives the same impression of change and growth in his faith. He says, for instance, that the part of the Apostles' Creed that is particularly alive to him just now is the communion of saints,[23] but that in his younger days he would have cringed at the idea of praying with and for people.

In this, Buechner is a man of his time. He allows for relativism. But unlike process theologians, he believes that the truth is there, that it has been mediated once and for all by Jesus Christ. A man of faith is called to witness, for his time and age and in its language, that God has revealed part of the eternal truth to him in personal encounter.

---

22. Frederick Buechner, *The Magnificent Defeat* (New York: Seabury Press, 1966), p. 23. Hereafter, where appropriate, this work will be cited parenthetically in the text.

23. In a letter received from Frederick Buechner, August 20, 1981.

Buechner's reluctance to be called a theologian results from epistemological questioning. The mystery of God is deeper than his creatures can ever fathom, so it is arrogant to try to corner him. Even Barth at the end of his life wondered about the validity of his multi-volume *Church Dogmatics*, erected like a medieval cathedral, and he left it unfinished. Buechner does not attempt to build cathedrals. He is a pointillist theologian, a translator of the divine truth as it comes into focus. For him the Bible is the story of all these people, the saints, pointing to truth.[24]

Buechner's existentialist attitude also precludes in his writing the reference to or study of traditional literature with which he must have become acquainted at the seminary. Rarely, for instance, does he mention the Church Fathers or the long corporate experience of Christianity through twenty centuries. It seems that his readings are limited to modern interpretations of the faith, apart from those of a few mystics to whom he is particularly attracted. For him revelation is a private affair. Since God will translate himself to the man of any time, we might as well watch for his signs in our contemporary civilization.

Buechner is indeed watching for signs here and now. In *The Magnificent Defeat*, he insists that God, through crisis and even through daily trivia, speaks to us about ourselves and what he wants . us to become (*MD*, p. 47), and that this is the miracle that we are vainly searching for in the stars. The same idea pervades the whole of *The Alphabet of Grace*, a description of a day for Buechner with its marvelous and terrifying realizations. If we do not see the miracles in everyday life, it is because, like Gloucester in *King Lear*, we have eyes but do not see, because we resist God's grace. A good example of people seeing only what they want to see is the program "Candid Camera"; the participants ignore the truth and substitute instead their own truths (*MD*, pp. 136ff.). We do the same thing in our lives: because we overlook daily miracles, the image of truth is blurred.

---

24. From an interview in *The Wittenburg Door*, Jan. 1980, p. 19. Buechner also believes that real beauty and truth cannot be studied, but is "best seen on the run, out of the corner of the eye—to look at it too long and too hard is to disfigure it" (*The Magnificent Defeat*), p. 131.

Like Kierkegaard and Barth and many other theologians and literary men, Buechner is aware of the frailty and wretchedness of human beings who grope their way blindly toward the truth as they are swayed by the storm and tossed upon the sea of life. He is aware of the incommensurability of the natures of man and God and of the infinite distance that separates man from his Maker. Grace therefore comes as surprise and relief. ''Amazing Grace,'' in fact, is the theme that pervades Buechner's works, for human beings, though blundering fools, have been saved from utter destruction through the agency of grace.

Buechner's concept of grace is very Tillichian. Grace amounts to being supported by the Ground of Being; one feels that it is not altogether indifferent to whether one swims or sinks in the sea of troubles.[25] Grace is a gift from God, and Buechner, like Tillich, affirms that the ability to recognize and accept grace is also a gift of the Holy Spirit.[26]

This brings about the problem of election, on which Buechner is not clear. He talks about it in *Wishful Thinking* under the rubric ''Israel'' (*WT*, p. 44). To him election means to be chosen to suffer for the world and to be able to recognize God's glory and the necessity of sacrifice. The elect are chosen neither for their strength nor for their virtue—this is the whole point of *Peculiar Treasures*—but are picked by God despite their crookedness to be witnesses for him.[27] With Origen and Barth, Buechner believes in the election of all, that sooner or later we shall come to our salvation because it is God's plan to make Christs of all of us.[28] He affirms this in *The Magnificent Defeat* and even more vividly in *Peculiar Treasures*:

---

25. See the preface to Buechner's *The Book of Bebb* (New York: Atheneum, 1979).

26. *The Magnificent Defeat*, p. 115. See also *Wishful Thinking*, p. 34. Hereafter, where appropriate, this work will be cited parenthetically in the text.

27. *Peculiar Treasures* (New York: Harper and Row, 1979), pp. 57-58. Hereafter, where appropriate, this work will be cited parenthetically in the text. See also ''Follow Me'' in *The Magnificent Defeat*.

28. *The Magnificent Defeat*, p. 115. See also *The Hungering Dark*, p. 79, and *The Alphabet of Grace*, p. 11.

> . . . The basic plot of the whole True Romance of History seems
> to be just that Love will have us lovely before he's through, or
> split a gut trying. He will badger us, bulldoze us, clobber and
> cajole us till in the end we all make it. . . . (*PT*, p. 178)

In another sermon in *The Magnificent Defeat*, Buechner defines
saintliness, which is to live in perfect obedience to the Creator, "the
way the grass grows." It is the concern of the elect whether they
know that they have been chosen, like Buechner himself, or whether
they do not, like Camus, for instance. These are people branded
by God. To be a saint is to have surrendered everything to God,
who "before giving us life . . . demands our lives—our selves, our
wills, our treasure" (*MD*, p. 18).

Being elected, being chosen by God, does not consist in shutting
God up in oneself but in letting his life flow through oneself like
a cleansing stream. Thus it follows that, for Buechner, all believers
are priests who let the voice of God move their feet. The priest does
not differ from the laity in status, only in tasks. The priest who
clings to his status sometimes impairs the flow of God's grace rather
than encourages it. (Buechner's anti-institutionalism, evident here,
is similar to that of Kierkegaard.[29]) On the other hand, people's
idolatry encourages the priest to be prideful about his function. At
the same time they make impossible demands of the priest, forget-
ting that he is merely the mediator of God's Word, not the epitome
of morality; by wearing vestments, he plays down his folly and frailty. God chooses all sorts of odd creatures for his ministers. Buechner
holds the Pauline view that they are treasures in earthen vessels:
the Gospel, not the man, is the jewel; the man is the clay casket
that contains it. To worship either a church or a minister is to attempt to lock God in earthen urns and to manipulate or limit him
in the process.

Buechner's attacks bear on the alleged superiority of the priesthood, of the World Council of Churches, of the women's
temperance movement, of the Baptist Church, and of all rigorous-
ly judgmental conservative groups. They are uncharitable in excluding those who do not belong and pharisaic in their approach

---

29. *The Magnificent Defeat*, pp. 16, 46, and 77; *Peculiar Treasures*, pp. 47,
70, and 121.

to life. The true priest of God is willing to follow Christ and feed all the lambs of God's pastures.

When asked whether he could say the Apostles' Creed in its entirety, Buechner acquiesced, though he would not be limited by it in matters of doctrine and he would re-interpret the Virgin Birth and the Descent into Hell. The de-mythologization of the Virgin Birth appears both in *Wishful Thinking* and in *Peculiar Treasures*.[30] For Buechner the Virgin Birth is "matter indifferent," to use a term employed by Richard Hooker, the Elizabethan apologist. Jesus was born of country people. *How* God was in Christ does not matter; what does matter is that he indeed *was* in Christ. The birth of righteousness is always virgin, miraculously new (*MD*, p. 65).

Buechner makes no particular reference to Jesus' descent into hell in his theological writing, but one might infer that in this matter he takes a psychological approach. The despair that overtook Jesus on the Cross can be translated in terms of hell. Hell for Buechner cannot be an everlasting torment. It is the agonizing sense of the loss of the divine presence, the contemplation of the misery one's cruelty or insensitivity has inflicted on others and of one's tragically wasted talents or years. Jesus' hell was his experience of atheism expressed in his cry of dereliction on the Cross, induced by the agony of suffering and overcome in his final commitment to God in his dying words: "Father, into thy hands I commend my spirit."

Buechner adheres basically to the Apostles' Creed. He believes in God the Creator and believes that the creation was good until it was marred by man's disobedience. The disobedience resulted from man's wanting to usurp the Godhead, whereas he should have been content to be as God made him, and be full of joy at the marvels that were given him. The power of God is to heal our brokenness, to restore our zest for the life that is given us (*MD*, pp. 131-135). Buechner sees God as a Father and us as God's children. What is striking about children is their capacity for wonder and trust, a constant theme in Buechner's writings. A child lives for the moment. He knows that he is forgiven and loved, and he

---

30. *Wishful Thinking*, pp. 94-95; *Peculiar Treasures*, p. 18.

goes on with the business of his life without losing track of the essential components of life: to get food, to take time to love and be loved, and to go about his games with utmost seriousness, knowing that they are games and do not ultimately matter.[31] Our business is really to recover Paradise in the belief that through Christ's intercession we are saved. Therefore, as salvation starts here and now, we can again enjoy the world as God's good creation, even if we have to undergo the tribulations that our sin has brought upon us. In Buechner's own terms, we can live as lovers and drunks, can recover a reeling sense of joy.

Like the religion of his masters, Buechner's religion is essentially Christological. Jesus is the Son of God, and Buechner would not try to enclose this truth in a limiting concept any more than C. S. Lewis would. Christ is the one who let God's grace flow through him at whatever cost, even that of his death. He is the one who rejoiced with those who rejoiced and wept with those who wept, whose life was always full though he kept giving. His is the life and Cross we should follow (*MD*, p. 120).

Buechner has the most touching words to say about Jesus, the reassurer. In *Peculiar Treasures*, particularly, he feels that all the words we have used to refer to Jesus have never expressed the true love we have for him and his true nature. And in a beautiful though paradoxical sentence, part of a description of Jesus sleeping in the disciples' boat, Buechner expresses his particular tenderness for him:

> And even if you are not religiously inclined, you can see why it is you might give your immortal soul, if you thought you had one to give, to have been the one to raise that head a little from the hard deck and slip a pillow under it. (*PT*, p. 64)

Though Buechner speaks very tenderly about Jesus, he is not sentimental about him. He recalls the times when Jesus was angry about that lot of dummies, the disciples, who always kept missing the point—angry as an artist would be about his critics failing to understand his message—and yet he always forgave them. Jesus had to have a sense of humor, and Buechner is grateful to Luke

---

31. See also "All's Lost, All's Found" by Buechner in *The Christian Century*, March 12, 1980, pp. 282-285.

for having recorded his jokes (*PT*, pp. 94-95). He insists on Jesus' concern for the poor, though he does not think that the Gospel should be reduced to humanitarianism or communism. He shows him as constantly unsheltered and on the move. These are aspects of the teaching and life of Jesus that are left out of the Apostles' Creed and which Buechner emphasizes.

And yet Buechner does not omit the sufferings of Jesus. The Cross is present in his writings, and so are Jesus' frustrations, unnecessary torments, and his last temptation to renounce God at the time of trial, since God seemed to be absent from the universe. In *Peculiar Treasures*, as in most of his novels, Buechner shows extraordinary compassion for the agnostic—in this case Pontius Pilate. In *The Magnificent Defeat* as well as in *Peculiar Treasures*, he is depicted as an overworked bureaucrat who would gladly have saved Jesus if he had not been so pressured to have him executed. Since Pilate did not know that the truth to fight for was right in front of him, Buechner feels that he is to be pardoned like most of the rest of the agnostics.[32]

As a neo-orthodox man, Buechner believes that the central doctrine of Christianity is the Resurrection. In *Wishful Thinking*, Buechner explains that God and nature are totally opposed when it comes to life processes. In the Resurrection, God will give us a new life, just as he gave us life in the beginning. The Resurrection is not a natural recycling process nor the expression of the indomitable spirit of man, but a sheer gift from God.[33] It is interesting to note that Resurrection is not treated separately but as part of the rubric "Immortality." Buechner's ideas about the Resurrection also appear in "The Road to Emmaus" in *The Magnificent Defeat*. Although belief in the Resurrection cannot rest on proof, many witnesses have shown that Jesus, the continuing love of God, walks down not only Paul's road but many Damascus roads into the present. For Buechner this doctrine is extremely important but is surrounded by a penumbra of mystery. It cannot be pinned down

---

32. *The Magnificent Defeat*, pp. 74 ff.; *Peculiar Treasures*, pp. 137-139.

33. See "Immortality" in *Wishful Thinking*, pp. 41-43. See also *The Magnificent Defeat*, pp. 77-79.

any more than Christ could be pinned down on the Cross (*MD*, pp. 84-89). And yet Thomas was granted his wish to touch Christ and was finally convinced (*PT*, pp. 165-166). Inexplicable mystery though it may be, the Resurrection is a fact.

In *Peculiar Treasures* (under the rubric "Thomas"), Buechner says that when Christ came among the defected apostles, he breathed his Holy Spirit upon them. The Holy Spirit is the inspiration from God, the breath of God that transformed a figure of clay into Adam. It is the power that makes one drunk with the love of God. To him this is the experience of life and communication, the Holy Spirit being the communication channel (*WT*, pp. 91-93). This shows that Buechner is decidedly Trinitarian in his religious outlook.

Though Buechner is anti-institutional, believing that denominational labels are limiting libels, he affirms that there is a Church of God. Until recently he rather missed the communal aspect of salvation insofar as he persisted in seeing people as islands rather than as communities of love under Christ. He is critical of the institutional Church and prefers to believe in the invisible Church, where God alone knows who are his true servants. This is a matter beyond the human capacity to judge. The Church has only a limited temporal use; indeed, it will no longer exist in the New Jerusalem, for the brotherhood of men will have been perfected (*WT*, p. 15).

Buechner's anti-institutionalism also overrides his possible appreciation of historical progression in the Church. Buechner reminds his readers that Christ was crucified by the Church and that he preferred the company of sinners. As a human institution, the Church, taking its truth for The Truth, becomes a destructive force. Yet at its best the Church expresses the mystical union of the individual with God in Christ, and the concern of human beings for each other.[34]

Like Jesus' role, the minister's role is to extend the peace and the pardon of God to his flock and refocus their vision. God and their neighbors should be their primary concerns. Unlike those who have given up on God because of the pain they see in the world, the wise minister knows that "whichever side of the grave you are

---

34. *Peculiar Treasures*, p. 70; *The Magnificent Defeat*, p. 101.

talking about, life with God apparently involves growth and growing pains'' (*WT*, p. 76). Pain is the price man has to pay to be made like Christ, the true unfallen man.

The enlightened minister does not preach the Gospel as if it was an academic subject. He shows with discretion how God's will was realized in his own life. Buechner applies this principle to both his preaching and his writing. *The Alphabet of Grace* retraces one day of the author's life in those ways in which it is relevant to faith. *The Sacred Journey*, like Saint Augustine's *Confessions*, is another of Buechner's attempts to show how often God beckoned him to the path of life and how he resisted until he could no longer do so.

Life is sacramental. The sacraments of the Church give only a sample of what all life is about. Buechner therefore insists on the importance of the preacher as the translator of the Word of God rather than as a dispenser of the sacraments. Like Richard Baxter, the seventeenth-century Puritan who said that he preached ''as a dying man to dying men,'' Buechner feels the urgency of preaching the good and reassuring news and of pressing people to repent in order to re-establish the right relationship to God.[35]

Here is expressed both the individualism and the universalism of Buechner's thought. Each one of us is meant to be like Christ, and therefore God speaks to and saves each of us in our individuality. On the other hand, since we are all meant to be Christs for ourselves and to each other, we are unified in this one God-man, who is to be the model for us all. Yet it is only recently that Buechner has expressed his awareness of the communion of saints. Until now, in his novels and his theological works, the communion of saints is something to be striven for, something not already in action, like the Resurrection of the body and the life in the world to come.

Though he shows little concern for the sacraments of the Church, Buechner has somehow shifted his position on the Eucharist. In *The Magnificent Defeat*, he seems to have a high respect for this sacrament. Despite different theological interpretations of its meaning, all recognize its power of transformation and its capacity to give new life. Buechner recognizes that the bread that is broken is more

---

35. *The Alphabet of Grace*, pp. 39-40.

than bread; it symbolizes the willingness to die for others and obedience until death to the will of God. Through this ritual Christ commissions us to go and live as he has done. Finally, he acknowledges that Christ is with us because we do this for love of him. However, in *Wishful Thinking*, Buechner sees Communion as sacred only because of the human joy and honesty induced by the meal; furthermore, he regards the sacrament as only a species of "make-believe" (*WT*, pp. 82-83, 51-52). And in *Love Feast*, he inadequately expresses the symbolism and sacrificial action in this sacrament by replacing the bread and wine with pretzels and Coca-Cola, which do not represent Christ's broken body and shed blood. Buechner, one concludes, greatly prefers the Word preached in the pulpit to the Word dramatized in the sacrament.

For him, baptism is also symbolical rather than instrumental. He believes in infant baptism, because the child knows the importance of faith, love, and forgiveness, but he also believes that the child needs to be redeemed from selfishness. Yet he would agree with the Baptists that being immersed under water is a better expression of the symbol of the dying and rising again with Christ, the rebirth, than the sprinkling or dabbing performed during infant baptism (*WT*, pp. 5-6).

Buechner also minimizes the importance of worship. For him it is less divine communication than it is an expression of human gratitude offered to God. To Buechner it seems foolish to think that God will appreciate worship any more than hairshirts; rather, worship is a token of love. Whichever way it is performed is, for him, "matter indifferent" (*WT*, pp. 97-98). In this way, too, Buechner shows his contempt for ecclesiology and his sole interest in individual piety.

One can easily see how Buechner, despite his hatred of tags, fits in the Protestant tradition rather than in the "Mother Church." He emphasizes the preaching of the Word rather than the performing of the sacraments, the imitation of Christ rather than the perfecting of worship. His approach to religion is individualistic rather than corporate, in the tradition of mysticism. In the last few years, however, one can perceive a change in Buechner's thought. He now places contemplation and the adoration of God above action in the life of the believer. The character Godric illustrates this change:

at the end of his life, he becomes a hermit and dedicates his life to prayer and the worship of God. It will also be interesting to see if Buechner's new awareness of the communion of saints manifests itself in his preaching, his theological works, and his fiction.

Buechner would agree with Flannery O'Connor that God takes us by storm even if he is the God of stillness.[36] Buechner is particularly sensitive to the born-again, those who have had the Pauline experience along the way, the lightning that strikes at midnight, for this was his own experience. He has little to say about those born into the faith—those who, like Mauriac (whom he admires), have always belonged to the Christian faith, moving steadily from dawn to noon.

A passionate man himself, a man quick to react and gifted with great power for work and sensitivity to joy and sorrow, Frederick Buechner projects his personality in his theology. Anti-intellectualism (an amazing attitude for an intellectual), anti-fanaticism, concern for contemporaneity and relevance, and a proper respect for the sacramental quality of daily life—these are the main features of his theological outlook. Buechner, however, warns us against himself. Over and over again he tells us that he is only one of those who point to the truth, and that in the long run anything ever written is tainted by subjectivity. In this way Buechner is his own watchdog, alerting us to the limitations of his virtues.

---

36. Horton Davies and Marie-Hélène Davies, ''The God of Storm and Stillness: The Fiction of Flannery O'Connor and Frederick Buechner,'' *Religion in Life*, Summer 1979, pp. 188-196.

II

The Theological Works

Laugh where we must, be candid where we can;
But vindicate the ways of God to man.
Alexander Pope, An Essay on Man

"Let the preacher tell the truth," says Buechner at the end of *Telling the Truth*, the truth in all its outrage and illogicality. And let him tell it in modern terms, making the word that was written some nineteen centuries ago speak to the modern world; in the words of Donne, let him "update the Bible." If the three different theological genres of Frederick Buechner have one thing in common, this is it. It is this willingness to present to us life as he perceives it from a point of view which is not systematic but existential, not intellectual but emotional, not rationalistic but romantic. Buechner sees the supernatural within the helter-skelter of everyday life. He senses the mystical union of the creation and man in God the Creator and in his Son, the new Adam, who is the perfect man, the opposite of the old Adam, the fallen man. He views the whole world from a universalistic perspective: the history of one is the history of all. Consequently, there is no minute detail which does not deserve attention, and nothing human that is foreign to any man. The world should be listened to and looked at. The primary function of the man of God and the evangelist is to show this to those who might pass by, indifferent, to put the spotlights on one or another corner of the existential truth. This is common to all of Buechner's theological writings, this sense of being at a great show in which each actor is given the chance to have his say, or sing her aria, all of which points to their grasp of life and their vision of the greater truth.

Buechner says the same things in two different modes: the novel and the theological work. Similarly, one can divide the theological works into approximately three categories according to genres. First come the meditations, which were in fact sermons preached to a young audience of students at Phillips Exeter Academy in New Hampshire, where Buechner was the school minister. The works in the second category have entries arranged in alphabetical order: *Wishful Thinking* is a biblical *What's What*, and *Peculiar Treasures* is a biblical *Who's Who*. Finally, the third category is composed of the lectures Buechner gave at Harvard and Yale. In them he attempts to show the tragedy and the comedy of life as well as the grace of God that turns everything ultimately into a fairy tale. Insofar as all these works bear the distinctive mark of Buechner's style and are influenced by his preaching technique, it is artificial to study them separately, but insofar as they belong to different genres, they deserve individual attention.

What follows, then, concentrates on each genre in turn, and pays attention to the techniques and imagery of Buechner common to all three.

The theological bias always affects the use of cultural material in a sermon. Buechner does not endorse the tradition that requires a sermon to have a systematic intellectual content, in favor, for instance, in eighteenth-century preaching. His meditations often follow the type of exposition and exhortation that was typical of early Jewish sermons. His preaching imitates that of Jesus, using pithy sayings and interesting stories. He does use amplification and rhetoric, but he downplays these techniques. And though he does make moral points, his point is not morality but the saving of souls by God's grace. Buechner persuades his audience by holding life up to them; he does not attempt to convince them. His modern theological outlook can be perceived in the light that he sheds on his material and the examples that he chooses. Yet since he thinks that neither man nor God can be pinned down, he does not use much logical invention. Because he believes the truth to be plain, he suppresses his natural tendency toward scholarship and aesthetics, and chooses increasingly the rhetorical devices most likely to hammer the truth home and to move his hearers' feet on the right path.

In *The Magnificent Defeat* and *The Hungering Dark*, each meditation is preceded by a text from the Bible. This usage goes back to the post-

Babylonian synagogue. It inclines people to piety and holiness and is consonant with the Reformed emphasis upon the Word. *The Hungering Dark* (unlike *The Magnificent Defeat*) contains prayers Buechner delivered after the sermon. These also illuminate the point made in the sermon and the conclusion drawn.

In both collections the beginnings of the sermons are varied. Buechner does not always reveal the point of the sermon at the start— as shown by ''The Road to Emmaus'' in *The Magnificent Defeat* and ''The Monkey-God'' in *The Hungering Dark*—but it can be inferred from the story told. Sometimes it is left completely up to the listener to construe, as in ''The Birth,'' a very unusual sermon, written like a short story, which shows three different reactions to the birth of Christ as the innkeeper, the wise men, and the shepherds all express their joy and regrets.

Sometimes Buechner begins with anecdotes. The biblical story is used in ''The Road to Emmaus,'' and Indian Buddhist legends appear in both ''The Tiger'' and ''The Monkey-God.'' Some anecdotes are derived from personal experience: the joy of being in the Vermont mountains, killing time in the waiting-room of a station or a hospital, the ringing of the telephone, the frustration of speaking to the hard-of-hearing or to those who see only what they want to see. Because such stories are common to everybody's experience, they help the younger listeners to prick up their ears and wonder what will come next.

At other times the sermon starts with references to biblical or secular literature. James Weldon Johnson's own version of the biblical story paraphrases and illuminates the biblical text in ''In the Beginning,'' and Donne's ''No man is an island'' introduces ''Pontifex,'' a sermon on Christian unity. In addition, Buechner does not neglect movie classics like *La Dolce Vita*, with its view of a statue of Christ soaring over the corrupt city, or television shows like ''Candid Camera,'' most likely to be relevant to a young audience.

Buechner may also begin with historical criticism, which was so much in favor in the late nineteenth century. In ''The Two Battles,'' he indicates that the authorship of the text is doubtful, and in ''The Power of God and the Power of Man,''[1] he stresses the difference in

---

1. For another example, see ''Confusion of Face'' in *The Hungering Dark* (New York: Seabury Press, 1969).

outlook resulting from different authorships. In "The Me in Thee," he recalls the various ways in which the doctrine of the Atonement has been interpreted. Occasionally Buechner starts with philosophical criticism: he recalls the Tillichian difference between *kairos* and *chronos* in "The Rider," and Anders Nygren's distinction between *eros* and *agape* in "The Two Loves."

In "Message in the Stars," the accusing words of man challenging God to show himself in the heavens provide a more dramatic beginning. At other times, as in "The Breath of Life," Buechner takes the point of view of the atheist, for whom the Christian language is dead. The preacher then agrees that Christianity is a dead metaphor before he proceeds to show that the Christian myth is the best way of approaching the reality of life.

Often Buechner will begin by updating the Bible, translating it into a language students can understand and showing its relevance to modern hearers. He then proceeds either by evocation and impressionistic or pointillist techniques,[2] or by analysis and delineation.[3]

The two collections differ little in their indications of the methods Buechner prefers. He obviously believes in fighting his audience's inclination to doze off. The beginnings of the sermons are all varied and startling; there is no telling what the magician will pull out of his hat. Sometimes Buechner intentionally does not make the exordium plain in order to keep the audience guessing. He does not usually enunciate the divisions of the sermon, though they are there and plain to see. Buechner's sermons are structured, but the wires that hold the puppets are carefully hidden. He leaves little to the spontaneous overflow of powerful feelings fashionable in the Nonconformist churches of today.

Most of Buechner's sermons can be divided into two categories. His explicatory sermons analyze the biblical text and provide observations with exegetical remarks. His propositional sermons, their counterpart, discuss dogma without being restricted to the biblical statement,

---

2. See "The Road to Emmaus" and "Follow Me" in *The Magnificent Defeat* (New York: Seabury Press, 1966); "A Sprig of Hope" and "The Wedding at Cana" in *The Hungering Dark*.

3. See especially "The Birth" and "The End Is Life" in *The Magnificent Defeat*; "Confusion of Face" in *The Hungering Dark*.

taking the text as a mere starting point. One can see a distinct evolution from *The Magnificent Defeat*, in which the sermons tend to be more propositional, to *The Hungering Dark*, in which Buechner is more exegetical and relational, producing biblical tone poems.

Two different logical patterns appear, though both can occasionally be blended. The first is inspired by Hegelian dialectics. "Pontifex," a sermon on Christian unity, is constructed in the following fashion: (1) No man is an island (thesis); (2) All men are islands (antithesis); (3) Therefore, all men are alike (synthesis). The Kingdom of God consists in bridging all these islands and making them into an archipelago. In "The Power of God and the Power of Man," Buechner prefers another type of dialectics, more Kierkegaardian perhaps: God heals, man destroys (thesis); Does God have power? Man can create (antithesis); Man has only coercive power, whereas God has internal power (conclusion).

In "The Two Battles," Buechner follows a similar pattern, but he subdivides each section. Life is a battle which man must fight; here are its adversaries against whom armor and force must be employed. In the struggle for power, the armor of God puts the Christian at a real disadvantage. But in fact the real fight is God's fight; we have different enemies and need a new armor and strength to win the spiritual struggle, for which the battle for conquest does not prepare us. This is the only fight worth winning, and all can win it. Buechner uses this more subtle subdivided pattern again in "The Two Loves." It also appears, with variations, in "Come and See" and "The Killing of Time."

The second method Buechner usually prefers is that of a progressive deductive crescendo, which he uses in "Message in the Stars": (1) God should give us a sign to assure us of his existence; (2) If he did, later generations would not understand the relevance of the revelation; (3) It is in our daily life that we need God; (4) But God *is* present in our daily life; (5) Let us listen to him and to his miracles. In "Follow Me," Buechner uses the analytic procedure taught in English class: Why follow? Whom do we follow? (The "whom" is repeated twice for proper emphasis.) Students would have recognized the familiar questioning and responded positively to this rhetoric.

In "Confusion of Face," Buechner proceeds by increasingly deep analysis: (1) All are confused, including the preacher; This is true (2) psychologically and (3) historically; (4) God's idea of us is not confused. We are meant to be Christs.

Last, let us examine "A Sprig of Hope," which states the various stages of conversion in the story of Noah. God despairs over the human race; so do we, though we try to escape from the fact. God calls Noah, and he reacts with surprise and doubt; he then changes paths, accepts the role of fool for Christ's sake, goes his lonely way, and obediently surrenders to God with the hope of final salvation. The hope turns out to be realized.

These logical patterns are sometimes blended with another pattern: that of putting logic aside to let the biblical story talk. Buechner then uses his remarkable capacity to live in another person's skin and translate feelings into words. I have already mentioned "The Birth," which is a pure example of this method. In "The Rider," Buechner recreates Palm Thursday, Good Friday, and Saturday of Holy Week in this fashion. The pattern is even more evident in "The End Is Life," in which Buechner dramatizes the feelings of Pontius Pilate when the Pharisees ask him to make the tomb secure. He also recalls the contradictory feelings of the Jewish elders, who fear a religious hoax and are also afraid that they might have made a mistake and killed the real Messiah. Buechner then lets the Bible speak for itself by updating the biblical language. He relates the feelings of the man of yesterday to those of the men of today in the hope that each will feel personally concerned. As with Kierkegaard, the audience is to react as if they were watching a play; they take sides and see their own iniquity as they condemn a protagonist who, like Pilate, looks strangely like themselves. Buechner thus uses a method very similar to that of the psychodrama.

It would be difficult to divide Buechner's sermons into three parts—doctrine, reason, and use—as was customary in Puritan sermons, because of his careful artistry. Yet the pattern is largely there. Buechner is a biblical preacher and does not deviate from the Word. He strongly disapproves of preachers who use the biblical text as a pretext to express worldly concerns, be they social or political. Buechner sticks to doctrine. His talent is showing how doctrine is, in fact, the best possible way to express the reality of life and how the Christian faith is in man's best interest. To be saved from the valley of despair man has to turn to Christ. Conversion is at the center of his thoughts, as it was for Saint Paul.

The sermons are arranged so that they build to a climax and leave us at an emotional peak. The endings are as varied as the beginnings. Sometimes Buechner finishes with a question: "In the Beginning" asks whether we are joyful in the face of transience. Sometimes he concludes with the application or the intellectual clarification. "The Me in Thee" leaves us with the clarification of the sacrament of the Lord's Supper. "The Breaking of Silence" assures us that prayer is not for the wise but for those who are fools for Christ's sake. "The Two Loves" declares that *eros* and *agape* are ultimately one and the same thing. Many sermons end on this seemingly rational note, which does not give the hearer any choice except the right one: conversion.[4]

Sometimes Buechner leaves the reader on a prophetic note. "The Annunciation" ends with the vision of the Second Coming, and "Pontifex" finishes with the evocation of the Kingdom of God being realized, when all separate persons, like islands, will have united to form an archipelago. "The Magnificent Defeat" ends on the paradox expressed in the title. Buechner repeats the point in the body of a second sermon, "The Two Battles."

Buechner's two favorite endings, however, are exhortation and assurance. Exhortation brings the audience to an emotional peak by stressing the urgency of conversion. *The Magnificent Defeat* tends to address the audience directly: "Go to him," Buechner says, or "Listen to him" or "Go and kiss the earth." *The Hungering Dark* uses the inclusive "we" more often: "Let us praise God" or "Let us open our arms" or "We must commend ourselves." In "The Wedding at Cana," the ending is almost a prayer, exhorting the bride and groom to grow in love for the world as they strengthen each other and are able to face the storm.

Though his function as a minister is to coax and exhort people to travel on the right path, Buechner also realizes that the twentieth-century world and teenagers in particular need soothing and reassur-

---

4. For other explicatory endings, see "Journey in Search of a Soul," "Follow Me," "The Me in Thee," and "The Breaking of Silence" in *The Magnificent Defeat*; "Confusion of Face," "The Calling of Voices," "The Sign by the Highway," and "The Two Loves" in *The Hungering Dark*.

ance. This may be what accounts for the number of sermons ending with the assurance of the peace of God or of the fulfillment of the divine purpose in *The Magnificent Defeat*. They say: we shall overcome, or God loves us, or we shall be made into Christs or be destroyed for our own sakes, or miracles are at our doorstep and we just need to see them. All assure us of the loving care of a concerned God. The sermons in *The Hungering Dark* indicate that Buechner later thought that clarification was what his students most needed. These sermons tend to end on a more intellectual note.

This difference of outlook might also account for the different approach to theological themes in each book. It appears that *The Hungering Dark* concentrates more on doctrine as such. It focuses on the great biblical truths and uses less material from the world of private experience without excluding it. "The Power of God and the Power of Man" is illustrative of the irremediable gap between God and man (as explored by Barth).

Sin for Buechner is illustrated by killing and death, confusion and blindness, as in John 1:4-5; by hardness of hearing and unwillingness to talk and communicate. Communication is one of our modern obsessions. Its study is part of the curriculum in our schools as opposed, for instance, to the mere study of rhetoric or eloquence. A man of his age, Buechner tackles this problem in eight of his sermons.[5] He considers sin more in terms of sickness and brokenness, death and darkness, than in terms of bondage. Man's real need is for wholeness and love through atonement (three sermons in *The Magnificent Defeat* deal mainly with this theme).[6] God is the Creator but he is also the Healer and the Recreator of men, who need to be broken in order to be remade (seven sermons center on this theme).[7] God is therefore the light that

---

5. See "The Magnificent Defeat," "Message in the Stars," "The Breaking of Silence," and "The Miracles at Hand" in *The Magnificent Defeat*; "Confusion of Face," "Come and See," "The Sign by the Highway," and "The Killing of Time" in *The Hungering Dark*.

6. See "The Magnificent Defeat," "The Two Battles," and "The Tiger."

7. See "In the Beginning," "The Breath of Life," "To Be a Saint," and "The Breaking of Silence" in *The Magnificent Defeat;* "A Sprig of Hope," "The Sign by the Highway," and "The Monkey-God" in *The Hungering Dark*.

dispels the darkness, and he calls us to the joy of his creation and of his recreation of man in the Resurrection.[8]

Buechner also uses his sermons to express traditional views on the Christian life. In "The Two Battles," he explores the idea that life is a battle, though for him it is mainly a journey. We go on our pilgrimage with dragging feet because we never know our destination and have to travel on trust.[9] For this similitude Buechner has biblical authority: Hebrews 11:13-16, for instance, I Peter 2:11, and John 14:6. The Christian is therefore to trust in God like a child. In this comparison Buechner follows the tradition of Matthew 18:3, Mark 10:14-15, and Romans 8:15-17. Only one sermon, "Become like Children" in *The Magnificent Defeat*, treats the subject at length. Other sermons allude to the sense of wonder that children have, to their willingness to go and see whether what they have been told about exists. They do not have the preconceived ideas of older people, and they are eager to explore; finally, their sense of sight is better than ours. This theme becomes stronger as Buechner grows older; in these sermons, written earlier, it is only budding. Trust also consists in talking to God to restore the communication broken by sin; prayer is thus one of the essential components of the Christian's life.[10]

Many of Buechner's sermons deal with Christian unity, the realization of the Kingdom of God. They can all be gathered together under the various headings of "Fellowship" or "Communion of Saints," and they tell of Buechner's great concern for his fellow-man—something that all the people interviewed about him attested to. Compassion is one of the central features of his writing.

The Christian Year is not one of Buechner's main considerations. Yet he has one sermon on the Annunciation (with that title), two on Christmas ("The Birth" and "Come and See"), one on the Passion

---

8. See "In the Beginning," "The Birth," and "The End Is Life" in *The Magnificent Defeat*; "Come and See," "The Killing of Time," "The Wedding at Cana," "The Monkey-God," and "The Rider" in *The Hungering Dark*.

9. See "Journey in Search of a Soul," "Follow Me," and "To Be a Saint" in *The Magnificent Defeat*.

10. "The Power of God and the Power of Man" and "The Breaking of Silence" in *The Magnificent Defeat*.

and Holy Week ("The End Is Life"), and two on Easter ("The Road to Emmaus" and "The Killing of Time"). The theological virtues become particularly important for him in *The Hungering Dark*, which starts and finishes with sermons on faith, which is linked to hope and charity in "A Sprig of Hope" and "The Hungering Dark."

And last there come two sermons that Calvin would have approved of, which relate the Bible and poetry. The Bible as metaphor is one of the striking themes of Buechner's later works. Though he follows Tillich in considering that myths should be explained, he thinks that one of the tasks of the modern preacher is to re-mythologize the Bible in modern terms. The importance of the Bible as poetry is already expressed in "In the Beginning," "The Annunciation," and "The Me in Thee."[11] *Telling the Truth* will fully develop this theme.

Although Buechner very consciously rewrote these meditations for readers,[12] he designed them primarily for an audience, a congregation. Buechner mainly geared the illustrations of his sermons to young people, but he also had a number of older people in his audience at Phillips Exeter. He attracted crowds from the area, and the school chapel welcomed them in the way that Princeton University Chapel welcomes townspeople. When asked to summarize the sermon, most listeners will recall the illustration, the anecdote. Interestingly, personal anecdotes in Buechner's meditations are rather few. For him the Bible is predominantly narrative, and provides most of the necessary anecdotes. We find the story of Jacob the con man

---

11. See also "The Calling of Voices," p. 30, in *The Hungering Dark.* Other passages underline the metaphoric importance of the Bible (a theme that Buechner takes up again in *The Alphabet of Grace* and *Telling the Truth*). In "The Face in the Sky," for instance, Buechner expresses sadness for those who consider the Nativity merely the birth of another child born to die and then to be no more, when they could see that it is "poetry that points beyond itself to the very heart of reality, which is beyond the power of time and change to touch" (p. 15).

12. One should also note the logical progressions of the sermons in *The Hungering Dark.* Each meditation includes a point from the preceding one, and then moves on a step further. This is the artistry of the novelist at work, who never leaves a loose thread in his tapestry.

fooling his father and then struggling with the angel; the story of Jesus telling the taxpayer that he will come and eat at his place; the story of Sarah laughing because she is going to have a child at the age of ninety. These are some of Buechner's favorite passages.

Other anecdotes he derives from literature. From Indian Buddhist literature, Buechner tells the story of the tiger who has lived among goats and upon encountering one of his own kind discovers his better nature. We hear of the monkey-god, a symbol of vanity, business, and stupidity in both Indian and African literatures, who tries to impress Buddha by his feats and findings, whereas Buddha holds up his fingers to the sky to symbolize the marvel of the creation. Buechner also retells Frank Baum's fable, *The Wizard of Oz*, in "Journey in Search of a Soul," not only to show the difference between the Pelagian and the Christian concepts of salvation, but to underscore their unity as he affirms that, for both, home is the here and now. In "The Me in Thee," Buechner also uses the end of Hemingway's novel *For Whom the Bell Tolls* to illustrate the meaning of Christ's words at the Last Supper: the man who is going to die commissions his beloved to go and live her life for both of them, for he will be with her in spirit after he dies.

Buechner takes some anecdotes from everyday life. Most striking are those of the boy who killed his father and is heard calling for him in prison (in "The Annunciation"), and of the woman at the store who remarked that one life is more than enough to suffer through (in "The Killing of Time"). Another interesting story, which Buechner uses in "The End Is Life" and again in other works, is that of the sailor who told him how to see lights on the horizon. Equally alluring is the story in "The Hungering Dark" about the Pope in Rome, whose face was intent as he searched for Christ in the midst of the people assembled.[13] Finally, the world of television provides a most vivid example of "Miracles at Hand," when a man in a restaurant moves to another table to avoid looking at the rose drinking unexpectedly from his glass.

Another way of holding the audience is to use surprising effects.

---

13. The same story is retold in a different manner with a different interpretation in *Godric*.

Buechner, who was an unbeliever for so long, always preaches with the agnostic and the worldly in mind. The audience is surprised to hear the minister grant the atheist's point of view before he pushes his own, that of the Word revealed. He mainly uses this technique in *The Magnificent Defeat*; we learn that dishonesty is not a bad policy for getting on in the world, that no proof can be given that the creation was not an accident, and that religious words mean nothing nowadays.

Buechner also takes his young audience by surprise by reviving dead metaphors which have become curses, like "God knows" or "Heaven knows" or "who in Hell." The most striking example comes from *The Magnificent Defeat*:

> If this is indeed all the power that God has—the power of an idea—then who in Hell is interested in him? In Hell—just there— who is interested in a God without power. . . . In fact Hell might be described as the place or condition where men find God interesting and where this is all that they find; where they look at the Cross and are interested.[14]

"For God's sake" and "for Christ's sake" also appear often as revived metaphors in "The Calling of Voices" in *The Hungering Dark*.

In most of Buechner's sermons one can see the mark of the conscious stylist. He uses the weaving technique most effectively, leaving no loose threads. For instance, at the beginning of "The Face in the Sky," he recalls the statue of Jesus in *La Dolce Vita*; at the end of the sermon, the image reappears. The weaving technique is particularly obvious in "The Tiger," in which visions of the tiger being himself and feeling joyful are intermingled with visions of the sadness of the tiger's attempt at adjustment, at escapism, and at dull moral rearmament. Another striking example occurs in "The Calling of Voices," in which Buechner describes the various voices that call to us and the possibility of having missed the right voice; these ideas call to each other throughout the sermon.

Buechner also uses amplification and the cinematic technique of panning. In "Confusion of Face," he focuses his invisible camera

---

14. "The Power of God and the Power of Man," p. 31.

on different faces, sometimes stopping at one and going deeper and deeper into the secret furrows of that face. In "A Sprig of Hope," he travels from Noah's face to Noah's feet.

Repetition is of the essence of the rhetorical persuasive technique, which consists in letting the penny drop, and the device is so common that it is not worth quoting in Buechner's work. But sometimes worth quoting are some of the finer balanced sentences, which grow shorter as Buechner matures in the homiletical technique. In "In the Beginning," for instance, one reads, "The gods are dying. The gods of this world are sick unto death. . . . And we all shudder at the sound because to witness the death of gods is a fearsome thing."[15] Many examples of incomplete sentences used for the sake of emphasis can be found in "The Power of God and the Power of Man." And a fine example of delayed information appears in "The Two Battles": the other war that we fight—the one that is "not a war against flesh and blood"—is announced on page 39, but it is only expounded at the bottom of page 40, a good five minutes, one would guess, after the audience has been alerted to it.

The Hungering Dark tends to use more of the all-in-all technique, found in both Emerson and Kierkegaard. For instance, "The Face in the Sky" tells us that we are not safe from God and that God is not safe from us. Later in the collection one reads that ever since God gave Moses his name, He has never had a peaceful moment, nor have we.

I could go on and on about the various subtle techniques Buechner uses in both collections, and I could stress his artful use of imagery. But since these are not peculiar to the sermons, I shall explore them in another section. What remain to be considered are Buechner's own thoughts about preaching. They are expressed most clearly in the Beecher lectures, but they appear already in *The Magnificent Defeat*, and Buechner's convictions have not changed. In this early work Buechner mainly reiterates the anti-clerical view already expressed by Kierkegaard. We learn that preachers are not always honest and often trifle with the biblical text to suit their own prejudices. They tend to do away with mystery and make the Bible

---

15. "In the Beginning," *The Magnificent Defeat,* p. 31.

safe instead of letting the miracles of God speak. Buechner reminds us that in the story of the Good Samaritan, both the priest and the Levite were blind.

But the fiercest attack of all appears in ''The End Is Life,'' where Buechner accuses ministers of thinning out the Word of God. They are afraid of miracles. They reduce the Bible to fiction, to a superb example of the human spirit, or to a book of human values, instead of letting the Word of God speak in all its poetry. *Telling the Truth* shows that the preacher is neither a poet nor a humanist, nor is he necessarily a moral man, but he is there to tell the truth in the most un-reductionist kind of way. His function is not to dilute the Word of God into a cordial that man can swallow, but to proclaim the Bible as tragedy, comedy, and fairy tale that proves true: ''With his fabulous tale to proclaim, the preacher is called in his turn to stand up in his pulpit as fabulist extraordinary, to tell the truth of the Gospel in its highest and wildest and holiest sense.''[16]

Buechner goes on to express the highly emotional purpose of preaching:

> And finally let him preach this overwhelming of tragedy by comedy, of darkness by light, of the ordinary by the extraordinary, as the tale that is too good not to be true because to dismiss it as untrue is to dismiss along with it that catch of the breath, that beat and lifting of the heart near to or even accompanied by tears, which I believe is the deepest intuition of truth that we have.[17]

If anyone were to deny the romantic tendency in Frederick Buechner, he would encounter it larger than life in these words. As for the wildness of the preacher, Buechner proves to be an example of it himself in his later works. But the collections of sermons are still very tame and solemn, though never pompous. As Buechner has grown older, the great laughter that drove him to the seminary has asserted itself more and more in his works, as it did in the C. S. Lewis of *The Screwtape Letters*.

This is certainly the case in part of his alphabetical works: in *Wishful Thinking* and mainly in *Peculiar Treasures*. In both works

---

16. Frederick Buechner, *Telling the Truth* (New York: Harper and Row, 1977), p. 91.

17. Buechner, *Telling the Truth*, p. 98.

Buechner proves to be a lexicographer, something he had expressed a desire to be in *The Magnificent Defeat*:

> And when I ask myself, as I often do, what it is that I really hope to accomplish as a teacher of "religion," I sometimes think that I would gladly settle for just the very limited business of clarifying to some slight degree the meaning of four or five of these great, worn-out Christian words, trying to suggest something of the nature of the experiences that I believe they are describing.[18]

In *Wishful Thinking,* Buechner is trying to make words come alive, whereas in *Peculiar Treasures* he shows these words enfleshed in the bodies of those chosen by God to be the proclaimers of his truth. Both works are geared toward the modern agnostic, and both try to elucidate the ancient truth and wisdom in modern terms.

Wishful Thinking, as I have said, is a *What's What* of the Bible. In this book it seems Buechner is betraying himself and leaning toward systematic theology—and in a way he is expressing thoughts as abstract as he is likely to venture. Yet out of the 147 entries, eight concern biblical characters, thus announcing *Peculiar Treasures.* Abraham's name appears under the heading of "Faith," and Adam and Eve's names under "Man." Buechner also includes his own name and that of Jesus, Job, Mary, Paul, and Zaccheus. God is given two entries, "God" and "YHWH." So even in the midst of abstract terms and concepts, Buechner cannot resist including some of his favorites.

The entries can largely be divided into three categories: doctrine, worship, and discipline, with the lion's share given to doctrine. Under the heading "God" can be put glory, grace, healing, holy, life, ubiquity, predestination, omniscience, revelation, and sanctification. "Christ" and "Jesus" also comprise Cross, divinity, Word, Gospel, Incarnation, Messiah, Resurrection, and sacrifice. There is an entry for Spirit and one for Trinity. Under "Sin" one can find conversion, repentance, devil, evil, guilt, and justification. Other doctrinal entries are angels, Bible, Church, covenant, creation, doctrine, election, superstition, theology, toleration, and man. Eschatological themes include the Annunciation, eternal life, eter-

---

18. "The Breath of Life," p. 111.

nity, heaven, hell, immortality, judgment, the Kingdom of God, purgatory, salvation, time, and Resurrection. Worship could comprise Church mysticism, ministry, baptism, bread, confession, the Lord's Supper (under various names), ritual, sacrament, wine, meditation, prayer, and worship. The moral life is defined in morality, principles, pacifism, neighbor, riches, righteousness, and sex, as well as in faith and doubt, hope and despair, charity, love, forgiveness, mercy, compassion, and pride. Chastity, poverty, and obedience also appear with their counterparts of lust, avarice, and envy; pride is opposed to humility. Anger, gluttony, and sloth are vividly depicted, as is idolatry. Then there are a number of other miscellaneous entries like ''Feet'' and ''Fool,'' ''History,'' ''Science,'' ''Wishful Thinking,'' and ''X.''

Since the point of view is that of an apologist or defender of the Christian faith, the unbeliever is always taken into consideration, his objections expressed and taken seriously. Many entries are dialectical. Buechner the apologist defends the biblical viewpoint but also shows once again great compassion for those who object to the faith. God will judge; men have no right to presuppose the salvation or the damnation of others. Buechner expresses this point of view at various times. We know the visible Church, says Buechner, but who knows the composition of the invisible Church? A Christian is just better informed than anybody else and knows whom to thank. In ''Eternal Life,'' Buechner suggests that people who are ''with it'' and are not with God are probably with ''his brother,'' meaning as good as with God. For those who think that God is the Ground of Being, this may be acceptable; others might think that Buechner is too slick here. What is certain, however, is the spirit of compassion that Buechner displays for the agnostic and the atheist; he gives them both consideration. He is harder on the atheist, however, showing the lack of logic of his position: since any atheist has ultimate concern, he does not take relativism as seriously as he pretends.

Buechner understands the difficulties of religion: ''evil'' concisely expresses the objection to believing in a God, all-good and all-powerful, while watching the suffering in the world. Buechner tends to take the traditional view that the suffering of children is the ultimate form of evil, though in other entries (''Baptism'' and

"Children") he seems unsentimental about them. He reassures the doubter, believing, like Tillich, that doubt is part of faith, that doubt keeps faith from being stereotyped—something he expresses in a flippant way: "doubts are the ants in the pants of faith."[19] In "Bible," he agrees that the Bible is a difficult book to read, and gives advice to those who want to try, confessing that some parts of it are incredibly boring. In "Escapism," he allows for the objection of the fanatics of responsibility, like Sartre, but cleverly plays on the ambiguity of the meaning of the word: escaping from reality is wrong, he says, but escaping from bondage into freedom is right; thus he ties the old existentialist hand and foot.

Buechner's most severe attacks are those that he directs against the Christian fanatics of one kind or another, the reductionists and the fundamentalists who create breaches in the bulwark of faith. In *Wishful Thinking,* few of the denounced are identified; in *Peculiar Treasures,* Buechner calls them by name. Once again Buechner proclaims the metaphorical value of the Bible, claiming that Jesus was not a lamb in the literal sense of the term, and that the historical or geographical inaccuracies of the Bible do not prevent it from being true revelation (*WT*, p. 11).

At this stage of his life, Buechner is equally anti-pietistic. He claims that religion and irreligion are both sinful if they alienate one from one's neighbor, and that the Church is established on earth for our convenience and will be destroyed in heaven.[20] He refuses to reduce religion to morality, since Jesus mixed with the sinners whom he came to save. Buechner dislikes principles and makes them relative to circumstances; he puts the love of God and truth above them. He attacks vices without dramatizing them, using a psychological approach that is very different from legalism. For instance, he says of a glutton that he is "one who raids the ice-box for a cure for spiritual malnutrition" (*WT*, p. 31). He describes the pleasures of anger but concludes that we are wolfing down ourselves. Sloth is as much business as it is idleness, he claims, because our work

---

19. Frederick Buechner, *Wishful Thinking* (New York: Harper and Row, 1973), p. 20. Hereafter this work will be cited parenthetically in the text.
20. See "Sin," p. 89, and "Church," p. 15.

is often an avoidance of life. In this Buechner contradicts the generally accepted Puritan work ethic.

Buechner also launches a crusade against the Neo-Platonists, who divide man into *soma* and *psyche*. They do not take the dogma of the Incarnation with sufficient seriousness, he charges. In "The Annunciation," Buechner portrays Mary crouching down in labor and Jesus coming from the womb with that beefsteak color common to all newborn babies. In "Incarnation," Buechner hammers in the nail of psychosomatic unity even further, and in "Sex" he affirms: "The trouble is that human beings are so hopelessly psychosomatic in composition that whatever happens to the *soma* happens also to the *psyche*, and vice versa" (*WT*, p. 87).

Having rejected pietism, fanaticism, and angelism, Buechner defines religion as the apprehension of some ultimate reality toward which our lives are geared. It is an indescribable experience best evoked in metaphorical language. To define it in one term or another is to reduce it to our dimensions and dispel the mystery of life. Buechner uses comic language to attack such reductionists. He praises wine and good cheer. He has little patience with groups such as the Women's Temperance Union, the Ladies' Missionary Society, the hard-shelled Baptists, the Stewardship Committee— even the World Council of Churches. The truly Dionysiac inspires some of his best passages, in which he mixes humor, wit, and the outrageous, a combination which blooms fully in *Peculiar Treasures*.

With *Wishful Thinking* we see the birth of some flippant sayings, devised like the neological comparative "gooder" (*WT*, p. 3), that shock the reader out of his apathy. One reads that God, at the time of the Covenant, decided to "put his money where his mouth is" (*WT*, p. 17), that "playing the market will get you further than playing it safe" (*WT*, p. 20), and that Paul "had the tact of a pneumatic drill" (*WT*, pp. 67-68). Buechner uses word-play when he talks about swallowing the Eucharist and finding the Bible unswallowable.

Buechner also devises memorable sayings. In "Devil," we can remember his declaring, "The total evil in the world is greater than the sum of all its parts" (*WT*, p. 19). And people have often quoted his assertions in "Sex": "Contrary to Mrs. Grundy, sex is not sin. Contrary to Hugh Hefner, it's not salvation either. Like nitroglycerin, it can be used either to blow up bridges or heal hearts'' (*WT*, p. 87).

The book mixes humor and fun with passages of great seriousness and intellectual rigor. One should read, for instance, the various interpretations that Buechner gives of the minister, or the correction he offers to some of the uses of the word ''Reverend,'' or his distinction between a damned fool and a fool for Christ's sake (*WT*, pp. 28, 37). In ''Pride,'' he describes vividly the man who bumps his head and takes it out on the cat. And in ''Healing,'' Buechner congratulates God on having the support of modern medicine, since the link between the body and the mind is no longer considered quackery as it was for decades.

Buechner redefines words and denounces the common misuse of them. In ''Immortality,'' we learn that the soul is not marching on. Humility is not thinking poorly of oneself but thinking of oneself in exactly the same terms that one does of anyone else. Buechner also analyzes all the possible meanings of ''love'' and ''freedom.'' And he re-mythologizes the Bible, comparing it to a window that is out, whereas religious books are transparencies. Eternal life is similar to the view one has on a fast train. The whole book is composed of flashes of light, illuminating the darkness and dispelling the fog.

Buechner also uses rhetoric as he has in his sermons. He revivifies dead metaphors (though less often). For instance, he says that Lucifer is free to ''get the hell out'' of Paradise. But most often his rhetoric is rhythmical and understated. Of Jesus, Buechner says, ''In that sense what was completed was at the very least a hope to live by, a mystery to hide our faces before, a shame to haunt us, a dream of holiness to help make bearable our night'' (*WT*, p. 46).

Another fine example of rhetorical enumeration can be found in Buechner's description of worship, which for him means, among other things, to ''run errands for [God], carry messages for him, fight on his side, feed his lambs, and so on'' (*WT*, p. 98).

Buechner shows his usual culture and his taste for the literary in this work, as well as his knowledge of everyday speech, as when he assures us that there is some emptiness in man which cannot be filled by the Blue Plate Special (*WT*, p. 12). In this potpourri

Buechner refers to the power of love as shown in *Beauty and the Beast, The Wizard of Oz,* and *The Brothers Karamazov.* He gives an ingenious literary example to show why we cannot demonstrate the existence of God: "It is as impossible for man to demonstrate the existence of God as it would be for even Sherlock Holmes to demonstrate the existence of Arthur Conan Doyle" (*WT*, p. 31).

Lastly, one can say that Buechner demonstrates his linguistic ability more in this book than in any other of his works in his effort to clarify the etymology of the Christian language: this is the method he uses particularly in expounding on the Spirit.

In this book we find traces of the old Buechner still appearing: his delight in literature and linguistics, his vivacity and hatred of stodginess, and his capacity for abstract thought always mingled with imagery. One can also recognize the rhetorical methods of the previous meditations. But the sense of fun is greater, and the ease and the flippancy are already announcing the works of the seventies, in which Buechner seems to do away with cultural elitism and recover the lightheartedness that prompted Erasmus to write *Encomium Moriae.* This boisterousness and Rabelaisian spirit is at its peak in *Peculiar Treasures.*

Peculiar Treasures is a *Who's Who* of the Bible. Buechner is more in his element with characters of flesh and blood, creatures that he can order upon the stage to dance their unseemly dance, like the *jongleur de Notre Dame,* for the greater glory of God. "Treasures" is understandable in the title, but isn't "Peculiar" too peculiar? Surely these encounters are extraordinary. But Buechner's message is that God *is* odd in choosing the people he does as his instruments.[21] This is the major theological point that Frederick Buechner wishes to make: the surprise and strangeness of God's choices. Paul also recognized that the treasures of the Gospel come in earthen vessels: the atheist wallows in the clay, and the pietist is so absorb-

---

21. Buechner made this point already in "The Sign by the Highway" in *The Hungering Dark*:

> . . . the vulgarity of a God who created a world full of hybrids like us— half ape, half human—and who keeps breaking back into the muck of this world. . . . The vulgarity of a God who tampers with the lives of crooks, of clowns like me to the point where we come among crooks and clowns like you with white paint and a brush of our own. . . . (p. 67)

ed in celebrating the treasure that he forgets the struggle to mold the clay to make it a humbler container for the treasure. And the clay so often forgets that it had and has a Potter. The biblical authority for the title is Exodus 19:5: ''Ye shall be a peculiar treasure unto me above all people, for all the earth is mine.'' It resonates also in a popular hymn of dedication, Isaac Watts' *Jesus Shall Reign*: ''Let every creature rise and bring/Peculiar honors to our King.''

Buechner directs this new work at the unbelievers, those who have contemplated man in his misery and share the despair of Beckett. It is geared toward those who have faced their shadow and have given up on the possibility of salvation. Buechner shows the sheer wonder of divine mercy and the unparalleled generosity of grace, and depicts the recipient with humor and delight. Take Moses, for instance, who is usually represented in the movies by ''somebody like Charlton Heston with some fake whiskers glued on. The truth of it is he probably looked a lot more like Teyve the milkman after ten rounds with Mohammed Ali.''[22] This leader of the people of God ''had to clear out of Egypt for doing in an Egyptian Jewbaiter'' (*PT*, p. 1). Or take one of the most unpopular characters in Jerusalem, the IRS man who collected taxes from his fellow Jews for the Roman government, Zaccheus, to whose house Jesus invited himself for supper. Buechner takes a snapshot of him for his biblical I.D. card, describing him as a ''sawed off little social disaster with a big bank account and a crooked job'' (*PT*, p. 180). Buechner sees Deborah, Israel's judge, and Barak, the military commander, as equivalents of Golda Meir and Moshe Dayan (*PT*, pp. 24-25).

It is daunting to read about the trials of the pioneers of faith in the chapters of the Epistle to the Hebrews precisely because they did not see the promises of God perfected in the Incarnation. It is cheering for the ordinary to acknowledge that God made them extraordinary, and in a marvelous entry that is headed ''Yahweh and Alpha and Omega,'' Buechner sums up the meaning: ''The basic plot of the whole True Romance of history seems to be just

---

22. Frederick Buechner, *Peculiar Treasures* (New York: Harper and Row, 1979), p. 110. Hereafter this work will be cited parenthetically in the text.

that Love will have us lovely before he's through, or split a gut trying. He will badger us, bulldoze us, clobber and cajole us till in
the end we all make it'' (*PT*, p. 178). The theme is hardly new
for Buechner, since it appeared in *The Magnificent Defeat*; the biblical
authority for it is Ephesians 4:13.

Buechner's dancing style fits the joy that he feels at seeing all
the crooks saved and welcomed aboard the Ark of God. At the end
of *Peculiar Treasures*, he summarizes brilliantly the whole fair and
circus:

> [There's] Aaron whooping it up with the Golden Calf the mo-
> ment his brother's back is turned, and there's Jacob conning
> everybody including his own father. There's Jael driving a tent-
> peg through the head of an overnight guest, and Rahab, the first
> of the red-hot mamas. There's Nebuchadnezzar with his taste
> for roasting the opposition and Paul holding the lynch mob's coats
> as they go to work on Stephen. There's Saul the paranoid, and
> David the stud, and those mealymouthed friends of Job's who
> would probably have succeeded in boring him to death if Yahweh
> hadn't stepped in just in the nick of time. And then there are
> the ones who betrayed the people who loved them best such as
> Absalom and poor old Peter, such as Judas even. (*PT*, p. 180)

"Why are they treasured?" Buechner asks. And he suggests that
they are treasured not for what they are but for who God is, for
he created them as he did; the whole earth and all that dwells on
it is his. God is compared to the poet, the lover, and the drunk,
three images that Buechner uses constantly to show the delirium
of creation and the "overjoy" of the Maker.

In *Peculiar Treasures*, Buechner preaches rather than explains.
Many of the entries are homiletical, with an application or a conclusion. For instance, the one on Ananias finishes with this comparison: "Lying to God is like sawing the branch you are sitting
on. The better you do it, the harder you fall" (*PT*, p. 12). About
Esau he suggests that God prefers to use crooks rather than dummies like Esau to bring about his great plans (*PT*, p. 33). "Onan"
ends with the right way to approach masturbation. Many examples
could be offered here because, like Aesop in his fables, Buechner
in *Peculiar Treasures* seems to favor that kind of ending.

His vocabulary is salty—too salty for many tastes. But the Word
of God gets home to the minds and hearts of many modern readers

precisely because Buechner is not prudish. He derives his diction from western movies, Mafia talk, even hard-boiled Chicago gangster lingo. The novelist's brilliance is also evident in his capacity to find contemporary parallels for the events of the biblical narrative. Katherine Buechner's illustrations illuminate the topicality of her father's treatment. For example, Gomer, the straying wife of Hosea, the eighth-century prophet, is depicted as a floozy with a heart of gold, drowning her sorrows and staggering down Main Street, where she and her boozy companion have knocked over a garbage can. Hosea forgives her and takes her back: "When he finally found her, she was lying passed out in a highly specialized establishment located over an adult bookstore, and he had to pay the management plenty to let her out of her contract" (*PT*, p. 43).

On the western scene, we learn that Moses married the daughter of a well-heeled rancher, that Abraham was cheated by Lot and was left with only "the scrub country around Dead Man's Gulch," and that when Amos spoke, "Everyone ran for cover" (*PT*, pp. 1, 4, 11). Whether inspired by westerns or Al Capone, we are not sure, but the encounter between Elijah with a ten-day growth of beard and Ahab in his Panama hat, and the picture of the Danites "casually fingering their cartridge belts" give a special flavor to the Bible (*PT*, pp. 10, 110). Surely the sanctimonious and those who would see God's Word as the Good Book might have to revise their categories?

One could not be more contemporary than Buechner is when he describes the Queen of Sheba perfuming herself from head to toe with Chanel Number Five before she meets Solomon; when he explains that she was so adorned that she looked like a Mardi Gras parade; when he says that at the burnt offerings given to Yahweh, she thought "they'd wandered into the Chicago stockyards by mistake" (*PT*, pp. 139-140). Nor could one be wittier than Buechner in finding a modern equivalent to Christ's saying, "It is easier for a camel to go through the eye of a needle, than for a rich man to enter the Kingdom of Heaven." Buechner's wry paraphrase is "[It is] easier for Nelson Rockefeller to pass through the night deposit slot of the Chase Manhattan Bank" (*PT*, author's note).

Peculiar Treasures has two qualities which are extremely rare in theological writing and which are Buechner's in full measure. One

is the gift of laughter—from the chuckle of wit and playful fancy
to the side-splitting guffaw. The other is an unprecedented gift for
knowing the hearts and minds of the defeated—the losers of the
Bible who, according to Buechner's universalist theology, will also
be the winners one day. There's Joseph with his "offensive dreams
in which he was Mr. Big and they were all grovelling at his feet
but he recounted them in sickening detail at table the next morning" (*PT*, p. 77). There's Samson brushing his gorgeous hair every
morning in front of the mirror (*PT*, p. 26). There's Goliath who,
when he tried thinking something out, found "it was like struggling through a hip-deep bog" (*PT*, p. 41). And finally there's
Judas—even Judas. According to Buechner, Christ rejoices at seeing him in heaven and kisses him, "and this time it wasn't the kiss
of death that was given" (*PT*, p. 83). All this is typical of Buechner's
deep sense of compassion.

These purposeful modern twists make the Bible up-to-the-minute
in its applications to our condition. Understandably, they have been
quoted from many pulpits, though some of the wilder statements
have occasionally been toned down and bowdlerized because the
pious in some congregations have seemed too conservative for "the
real thing."

Buechner's "peculiar treasure" is his own imagination, which
he uses to expound the greater Treasure of the Good News, and
which helps him flesh out what is unrecorded in the Bible. The
meeting of Jesus and Judas in Paradise is one of many examples.
We also learn that God, "half tipsy with compassion," saved Hagar
from death, that his "wry sense of humour" is obvious in the inci-
dent of Jonah and the whale (*PT*, pp. 46, 75). We visualize Christ
as the lamb who "has long since gone on to greener pastures where
he's kicking up his heels in the sunshine and calling to others to
come join the dance" (*PT*, p. 80). According to Buechner, God
caused the rebels to be swallowed alive down in Sheol so that later
"he could let them out again quietly through the back door" (*PT*,
p. 89). Buechner hopes that God will clean Lady Macbeth's damned
spot. He assumes that the Witch of Endor was probably so frightened by having to read the future for Saul that presumably she never
held another seance (*PT*, pp. 138, 175). Obviously, Buechner loves

to fill in what is missing in the biblical narrative, and this makes him most original.

Peculiar Treasures, then, is the work of an unsystematic theologian who deals in brilliant *aperçus*, illuminating insights, and fateful and faithful encounters. Hardly any of the biblical characters are taken very seriously, except for the four evangelists, Paul, and Jesus himself. For Jesus, Buechner has the most tender words, and he deserves to be quoted, aware as he is of the weariness of our Lord when he fell asleep in the disciples' boat:

> Lamb of God, Rose of Sharon, Prince of Peace—none of these things people have found to call him has ever managed to say it quite right. . . . you can see why it is you might have given your immortal soul, if you thought you had one to give, to have been the one to raise that head a little from the hard deck and slip a pillow under it. (*PT,* p. 64)

There is a sense of the vertical God who descends in grace to break our neat syllogistic arguments by speaking in action-laden paradoxes. He transcends our categories, manifests mystery, and proclaims the death of Death in the rising again of the man who was God in the flesh.

The Bible for Buechner is therefore God's story: history is His story, full of decisive encounters. It is a tale with 104 major characters and 15 minor or subordinate characters on the cosmic stage. They include Yahweh and Jesus, the fallen angel Lucifer and the obedient angels Raphael and Gabriel, the four evangelists, and two animals: Balaam's ass and Jonah's whale. Of that total of 120 characters, some 30 appear in the New Testament, and with the exception of Judith and Susannah in the Apocrypha, the rest are from the Old Testament.

The beliefs that Buechner disregards or is uncertain about are several. He is leery of predestination that stresses omnipotence rather than grace and denies to humanity the dignity of freedom. He re-interprets the Virgin Birth and deliberately stresses the fact that Matthew traces the heredity of Jesus through Joseph, Mary's husband (*PT*, p. 80). He dislikes the substitutionary theory of the Atonement and the literal and plenary inspiration of the Bible (*PT,* pp. 79-80, 141).

One can marvel at Buechner's lack of social snobbery, evident in his finding something good to say about unpromising people; in this he imitates his master, Christ. One detects, however, a certain impatience for the half-alive and the half-witted. He dislikes the dimwitted Abel and Esau and the slow-thinking jocks Samson and Goliath. Sometimes his great gift of humor, while illuminating, carries the corresponding danger of going overboard and seeming irreverent, as when he speaks of Christ being "cross-eyed with pain" or of the possibility of Mark being the person who "streaked out of Gethsemane" (*PT*, pp. 100, 99). Since nakedness in this case was not deliberate, "streaking" seems inappropriate here. But most of the time Buechner's humor is to the point, witty, apt, and reverent, as it is when he speaks of John the Evangelist's portrayal of Jesus as the Word of God as "*le mot juste* of God" (*PT*, p. 73). There is no question that Buechner has made the Bible and its characters come alive, just as he has brought to life the characters in his novels.

Despite its title and references to the alphabet, *The Alphabet of Grace* is not the work of a lexicographer, as some of its predecessors are. It is the depiction of one day in Buechner's life. Life for Buechner is like watching television with the sound turned off, like the hearing of "Yahweh" to the uninitiated. It is chaos without the right pair of glasses to interpret it. But for one who has been taught the missing letters and can restore the "Adonai," everyday life is full of miracles. They appear in filigree in any day of a man's life—take Buechner's life, for instance. The wonder and the mystery of God-given life is therefore the subject of *The Alphabet of Grace*, as it is the topic of *Telling the Truth*; Buechner himself links the two works together in the first part of his autobiography.[23]

The Alphabet of Grace is a difficult book, as it most reflects the doubts and anxieties of Buechner, who describes himself as "part novelist, part Christian, part pig" in his epistle to the reader. It

---

23. Frederick Buechner, *The Sacred Journey* (New York: Harper and Row, 1982). In *Peculiar Treasures*, written nine years after *The Alphabet of Grace*, Buechner still holds to this romantic view of life: "maybe any one day of a life, even at the most humdrum, has in it something of the mystery of that life as a whole" (p. 62).

is to date the most romantic of Buechner's writings, a sort of confession in which confessions are blurred or suggestions might be misinterpreted. It is written in chiaroscuro, and the weaving technique is very powerful. Yet though "the face becomes the map of the world, becomes the world itself seen from a great height,"[24] one cannot help feeling that Buechner should have used brighter colors and bolder designs to help us perceive the landscape. Even so, we are given some precious biographical information, the ambiguous reasons for Buechner's conversion, and four poems which translate the dominant experiences of his past.

One recognizes most of the Buechnerian themes. Religion is mystical and emotional, a subjective experience though it has objective reality. But Buechner seems less and less sure of his paradigms. He has come to accept the value of almost anything like that of magic in ritual. All human motives are ambiguous because man, created in the image of God, has been separated from him by sin. Therefore God can be recovered only in the broken and misty signs of everyday life. Buechner presses the urgency of living one's life to the fullest, and yet that all is vanity. In this book he summarizes all the contradiction of his own middle-aged soul. This work is thus comparable in spirit, though not in theme and technique, to Camus' *The Fall*.

Buechner repeats his belief that men are unable to grasp God, but his formulas are more vague: " . . . whoever he was, whoever they were. Whoever we are" (*AG*, p. 8). This contrasts with the assurance of faith he gives in the meditations and the amusing passages of *Peculiar Treasures*. He stresses that man's impulses toward life and toward death are inextricably intertwined. This is best exemplified by Buechner's ambiguous attitude toward his own work. He wonders whether his writing is the product of an artful dodger of life, a death-wisher, or whether he has actually been commissioned by God to go and tell it on the mountain, to bring the Good News and affirm life.[25] Buechner's message is clear: who can judge

---

24. Frederick Buechner, *The Alphabet of Grace* (New York: Seabury Press, 1970), p. 112. Hereafter, where appropriate, this work will be cited parenthetically in the text.

25. This is a recurring theme in *The Alphabet of Grace*, appearing on pp. 39-40, 53, 63, 88, 100, 102.

the actions of a human being without showing bad faith or being simplistic? Only God can do so.

Buechner still believes that life has a plot, but any attempt to decipher it is vain. He affirms that introspection is folly, while at other times he stresses the importance of descending into oneself to face one's shadow and raise it all to God.[26] Doubt is part of faith just as sin is a stop en route to salvation; the preacher's love for the limelight is his ascension as well as his downfall. In the encounter group as well as in the pulpit, Buechner both desires and fears to be known (*AG*, pp. 42-43, 57, 107). The limelight enables him to see his own sins, which would be hidden by the dark. So evil and good are but two sides of the same coin. Salvation comes by grace alone, since there is no way out of Charybdis or Scylla but in the saving and sustaining arms of God.

To this picture of all in all in man's psyche Buechner adds a new interpretation of eternity, one which he develops in the novel *Godric*. Man sees in himself all the plots of his family re-enacted, all the people he has been and is becoming, beyond the sequence of time (*AG*, pp. 41, 16, 62). This is eternity. Universality consists in knowing that we all have the same basic needs, that we are all meant to be Christs, that we all have a face that hides our true face. On the other hand, Buechner affirms the preciousness of individuals: he cherishes the idiosyncrasies of his grandmother, his uncle, and his nanny, with their different callings.[27] Buechner sneers at the desire of blacks and whites to be and act the same, and rejoices in the variety of human beings.

The best example of universality is probably that of the child who takes a photo of a woman looking at an album of photographs. Suddenly the woman in the present has also become the past (*AG*, p. 62). This concept is also striking in Buechner's evocation of various men who have been Christ-figures or angels of God to him (*AG*, pp. 104-107). Unity is the final word, unity despite diversity: unity of people, unity of religions or unity within religions. The

---

26. The vanity of introspection is referred to on pp. 24-25, 35, 54. The importance of reflection and introspection is alluded to on pp. 10-11, 15.

27. References to his grandmother appear particularly on pp. 9, 15, 38, 51, and 59.

final message is to let go of oneself; God is about to create us anew as he first created us, if we will let him. Buechner uses his own fiction—*The Final Beast* at the beginning of the book, and later *The Entrance to Porlock*—to explain the creation and the difficulties the Creator encounters with the independence of his characters, who sometimes lead him onto unforeseen paths.

The strength of this book is Buechner's attempt to re-mythologize the Bible and to redefine terms as an observer of life. Creation is thus redefined as waking up, writing a novel, or waking up one's children. Grace is the sharing of breakfast with one's family as a community of love, or the gift of sleep, which erases the sins of the day. Expecting the Second Coming is like waiting for a friend in a pub. Sin is selfishness and brokenness, the film over the eyes or the darkness that stops one from touching the hand of God, the limitations of one's face, insensitivity to the needs of others, as well as rebellion against oneself and God. Healing is to be found in trust, love, and acceptance—acceptance both of oneself and of the path designed for us all to follow, Christ's way. The influence of Tillich is stronger here than anywhere else in Buechner's theological writings. God is the Ground of Being and silence; Christ is both the shape and the word of God, and the Holy Spirit is the shaper. Buechner reasserts his belief in miracle and in the creation being God's love-letter. As in previous works, he also trusts that life is meaningful and that history is God's story.

Out of the corpus of Buechner's work, *The Alphabet of Grace* most strongly expresses the overflow of powerful feelings and of emotions recollected in tranquility. For this reason, the end appears to be uncontrived, though it gathers together all the loose threads of the book. Like Antonio at the end of *The Book of Bebb*, Buechner apparently proposes to ignore his muse and just speak the story of his life. The autobiographies of Augustine and Rousseau are among the most famous, but theirs cover an extended period of time, whereas Buechner considers only a day of his life. What he gives the reader is a succession of freeze frames, flashes of frozen action.

Since the images are the most important, they deserve mention at this stage insofar as they are representative of Buechner's imagery in his theological corpus or show some new trend in his thought.

Blindness and sight, images present in all his other works,[28] are now interiorized. Sight no longer involves seeing only the darkness of the world, but the darkness of the self as Buechner contemplates his face in the mirror. It also consists in recognizing the blessings of everyday life as well as the occasions for charity (*AG*, pp. 10, 107). Thus darkness is no longer limited to the times before and after life, but is an essential component of life, a part of every day rather than a feature of times of crisis.[29] Escapism has also pervaded the whole of life: it is no longer just escaping from what one did or failed to do or escaping from the wrong circumstances of life—it is escaping from oneself. This reiterates some of Buechner's previous warnings about business being a way to kill time and avoid the more profound issues of life.[30]

Though faces and feet have always been important for Buechner, conscious as he is of image-making and of pedestrian reality, he gives them particularly strong emphasis here. Buechner seems haunted by the limitations of his face and the desire to be made better than his face, as C. S. Lewis was in *Till We Have Faces.* The face and the real name are connected: our real name is that of Christ, just as our real faces must be made into Christ's face.[31] Man's strongest desire is to see a face in the trees, but God is a name without a face, and one can hear only the clack-clack of the branches.[32]

Hands have suddenly become important in *The Alphabet of Grace.* God is shown as a hand that could be touched, miracle is the shaking of left hands in sudden recognition (*AG*, pp. 49-50), and mar-

---

28. See, for example, *The Magnificent Defeat*, pp. 47, 79-80, 131; *The Hungering Dark*, p. 28; and *Wishful Thinking*, p. 1.

29. For a study of the evolution of this image, see *The Magnificent Defeat*, pp. 25, 41, 102-103; and *The Alphabet of Grace*, p. 102.

30. See *The Magnificent Defeat*, pp. 85, 93, 129; *The Hungering Dark*, pp. 26, 35; and *The Alphabet of Grace*, pp. 63, 88. See also "Sloth" in *Wishful Thinking* and *Peculiar Treasures*, pp. 35, 64.

31. On this theme, see *The Magnificent Defeat*, pp. 53, 134; *The Hungering Dark*, pp. 13, 27, 39, 47, 64; *The Alphabet of Grace*, pp. 26-27, 58; and *Telling the Truth*, pp. 80-81.

32. This also appears in *Peculiar Treasures*, pp. 55, 112, as well as in Buechner's fiction—*The Seasons' Difference, The Entrance to Porlock,* and *Godric.*

riage is the clasping of left hands (*AG*, pp. 60, 62). To my knowledge, this image does not recur in the rest of his work, whereas the images of swift feet and broken legs are frequently reiterated.[33]

Suddenly there is a need for nakedness, for putting away all disguises, an idea Buechner develops in *Telling the Truth*. In *The Alphabet of Grace*, he is consciously showing us the sinews of his heart—his loves, his fears, and his mystical experiences. He takes a more systematic approach to his life in the two volumes of his autobiography.

Unlike most of his other recent works, *The Alphabet of Grace* has little Dionysiac spirit; the only reference to something approaching it is Buechner's description of the novel as a love letter (*AG*, p. 87). Like the early novels, the work is mainly suffused with images of rain and stormy seas and pools of water into which man should jump to cleanse himself. The spirit hovers over the waters of the lake;[34] God sustains us over stormy oceans. These elemental images are not new. They appear in each one of Buechner's works and are developed particularly in his later creations. He contrasts the rough seas of life with the placid lake of cleansing waters, provided by the downpour of beneficial rains. In his autobiography Buechner describes how as a child he loved to be under a tarpaulin in the rain, so the biblical image is particularly vivid to him.

Buechner insists on the dynamics of life, whether he uses the Buddhist depiction of man as monkey or the more accepted image of the pilgrimage, a favorite of his. Religion is a summons to pilgrimage, the price one has to pay to become a human being. The same road is traveled by all, since all have sinned. In his earlier works, the theme of the pilgrimage was usually succeeded by the theme of home. But the hard road itself is the preoccupation of *The Alphabet of Grace*, which offers glimmers of homely joys as one goes along.

No other work except *The Book of Bebb* takes as many images from daily life. Buechner introduces the themes of bodily processes and

---

33. For the latter, see *The Alphabet of Grace*, pp. 88, 98-99, and *The Entrance to Porlock* (New York: Atheneum, 1970).

34. See pp. 36-37, 96, among others.

kitchen functions: the body tells us of the necessity of absorption and rejection, and the kitchen is a location of constant messing up and cleaning up. Life talks to us through children waking up and going to school as well as husband and wife bickering. All is metaphor. Buechner is more sensitive to detail, as he is to the more discreet noises of the creation: the fluttering of wings announcing the presence of the Holy Spirit and the clack-clack of branches, as well as the arias of people manifesting life in all its melody. The sound of silence is the sound of God, one of the most powerful images in all of Buechner's works. He analyzes sound, language, and music in their various forms, and meanings in their ambivalent values.[35]

The most typical image is probably that derived from the world of photography, movies, and television. In his collections of sermons, Buechner uses film techniques—close-ups, amplification, and panning—but he employs the symbolic value of the silent home movie only from the time of *The Alphabet of Grace* onward. Its magic and its realism both appeal to Buechner. It represents the perfect continuity of life as it is, unfalsified by commentaries; it is similar to T.V. news with the sound turned off. Like the religious book, which is a transparency that reveals heaven, the movie or the news holds life up to us, thus revealing the presence of God. Those who think that this is a commonplace device used by most modern writers should know that there are few old movies that Buechner has not seen. His knowledge of cinematography is almost as inclusive as his knowledge of literature, both of which he refers to in his theo-

---

35. References to the flutter of wings can be found in *The Magnificent Defeat*, p. 72; *The Alphabet of Grace*, p. 5; and *Telling the Truth*, p. 13. The meanings of silence are suggested in *The Magnificent Defeat*, pp. 66, 73, 125, 138; *The Hungering Dark*, p. 14; and *The Alphabet of Grace*, pp. 9, 99. The various connotations of language appear in *The Magnificent Defeat*, p. 139; *The Hungering Dark*, pp. 47, 96-103; *The Alphabet of Grace*, p. 9; and *Telling the Truth*, pp. 17, 21-22, 30, 71-73. The image of God as silence is found in *The Magnificent Defeat*, p. 73; *The Alphabet of Grace*, pp. 5, 43, 68, 70 ff.; *Wishful Thinking*, p. 22; *Telling the Truth*, pp. 14, 16, 19, 23, 43, 53, 98; and *Peculiar Treasures*, p. 30. Music as entertainment appears in *The Alphabet of Grace*, pp. 55, 99; *Telling the Truth*, p. 21; and *Peculiar Treasures*, p. 28; and as the language of passions in *Telling the Truth*, p. 21.

logical works. This is no contrived imagery, then, but an integral part of the author's make-up.

The Alphabet of Grace is different from Buechner's other works and full of personal references. The best part is Buechner's evocation of his own ghosts in four very personal poems, delicately suggestive of his loves and anxieties:[36] two relate to his maternal grandmother, to good times he had by the ocean in North and South Carolina, and to the dawn of girl-watching in his adolescence. Another recalls the difficulties of the relationship between his maternal grandfather and his uncle, his uncle's suicide, and finally the gap and longing left by the absence of his own father, who one day took his own life out of his children's lives. Both good times and bad times are evoked with delicacy and sensitivity. These tragedies shed light on Buechner's works of fiction as well as his vision of sin as waste and broken relationships. Thus *The Alphabet of Grace* has some of the best of Buechner in it, and yet, perhaps because of the overprofusion of life it presents, it does not quite come off; perhaps it would have been successful as a lyrical work, but Buechner's attempt at mixing lyricism and theology rather confuses us.

If Buechner in *The Alphabet of Grace*, like Shakespeare in *King Lear*, "is less concerned with matters of form and clarity and good taste than he is simply with telling the truth,"[37] in *Telling the Truth* he combines truth-telling with perfect clarity and artistry. It is the best of Buechner's theological works in that it is perfect in its genre. It won extended—and well-deserved—standing ovations when Buechner delivered it as the Lyman Beecher Lectures at Yale Divinity School.

Telling the Truth is Buechner's reflections on the task of the preacher. It is divided into four parts: an introduction followed by the exemplification of the Gospel as tragedy, comedy, and fairy tale. In the introduction, both preacher and audience are represented as fallen: Buechner recalls Beecher wondering about his commission of adultery, and each person in his congregation seeming gro-

---

36. These poems have been reprinted and expanded in "Family Scenes" in *The Quarterly Review of Literture* (Princeton), ed. R. and T. Weiss, XIX, 1974.

37. Buechner, *Telling the Truth*, p. 5.

tesque. Thus all are sinners together, preacher and preached at alike. Buechner then proceeds to give us a compassionate account of Pontius Pilate, the precursor of modern disengaged man. Harassed by his busy life, he had little time for the fundamental question that he longed to ask—"What is the truth?"—a symbol of man's yearning for the ultimate. So the preacher must listen to the silence of the Gospel and the longing of men. His business is to reveal life rather than provide answers or particular truths, a theme that recurs in Buechner's theological works. The task of the preacher is to show people's starvation, their hungering darkness, God's nature and their need meeting in the Gospel.

In his introduction to the book, Buechner takes a straight existential line. Man, he points out, does not possess reality by naming it; reality exists, independent of our will, which may want to recover it for our own uses. Therefore, throughout the lectures, Buechner recalls the objective reality of preaching, preacher, and audience. We follow the preacher ascending the stairs, turning on the pulpit light, licking his parched lips before he begins . . . and we feel his awareness of the congregation.

In the second part of the book, Buechner presents the picture of life, of silent truth, which the preacher frames with words. The main points of the introduction are recalled and tragedy is announced. For the literateur the perfect representation of tragedy can be found in Shakespeare's *King Lear*. Christ can come only to men stripped of their pretensions, as they struggle, heavy-laden, throughout the storm. Christ himself knew all about tragedy as he wept tears of sadness and impotency over the death of Lazarus. He anxiously anticipated his own death on the way to Calvary. The preacher must therefore preach his own experience of hell: the absence of God in the world is unbearable, as most good literature, from *The Brothers Karamazov* to *Moby Dick*, has recorded. Modern literature has taught us to weep, and presenting the tragedy of life is the second duty of the preacher.

But the preacher must not stop at tragedy. He must present the unexpectedness of laughter rippling through our lives. Jesus wept, but Sarah laughed, and Buechner analyzes the various stages and the significance of these two facts. He derives examples of tragedy from literature and examples of comedy from the biblical saga and cinematography. As in *Peculiar Treasures*, which appeared two years after these meditations, Buechner insists on the comedy of the election by God. He also stresses the paradox of Christ the beggar-king and Christ the man with a sense of humor about himself and about life, which is evident in the parables: risk is rewarded, all is left to save one sheep, and the prodigal son is given unconditional pardon. All this defies common sense and worldly wisdom. Grace is free, and the Pelagians miss the incredible beauty of life, its givenness and wonder.

Lastly, Buechner presents the Gospel as fairy tale, as a synthesis of tragedy and comedy in which comedy has the upper hand. Man has always written fairy tales, which are part of his subjective unconscious. He analyzes their contents: the closeness of fairyland and the difficulty of entering it; the presence of the extraordinary in the ordinary; the danger and deceit of the world of fairies; the finding of truth through transformation. At last a new name is given to us on a white stone as we leave fairyland. The world of the fairy tale denies ultimate defeat, and all become the best they can be after the battle between good and evil has been won and the powers of darkness have been defeated. Buechner points to the final triumph of joy in old masters like Rembrandt and Shakespeare, assuring us that there is laughter beyond the tears. The beauty of creation appears in the stones that Beecher carries everywhere. Life calls us out of darkness; disguise is part of life, and the beggar comes out a prince.

Finally, Buechner rejects the myth of the wizard of Oz, which he admired. Like the psychoanalysts, Frank Baum showed us that the capacity of coping with the world lies within each of us, but he neglected the possibility of transformation. For Buechner, transformation, mysterious as it is, is central to the Christian story. The preacher must restore the magic and the mystery essential to faith and preach to us as if we were children. Why should religion exclude the unexpected, since even science tells us of discoveries which were once undreamed of? The book ends with a marvelous summary of the duties of the preacher.

I have summarized the book rather than pointing out its themes to show the wonderful way in which Buechner can manipulate logic. A master mind lies beneath the seemingly easy flow of rhetoric, and the text is subdivided with marvelous logical orientation. Nothing is left unfinished. As in a symphony, initial melodies or themes are repeated, summarized, developed, or contrasted. At each point the emotional tension of preacher versus audience is recalled. Each section contains one story: the story of Pilate, *King Lear* (as expounded by Buechner in *Open Heart*), the story of Sarah, and *The Wizard of Oz*. Each point adds to the previous one. One recognizes some of Buechner's dialectical themes: silence and speech, wisdom and folly, temporal sadness and eternal joy, tears and laughter.

Buechner emphasizes psycho-physical unity in the description of the preaching preacher, in ugly tears and side-splitting laughter. He cites snow as an example of unexpected earthly joy. The love of the creation and the universalism of Buechner's thought suffuse the book with warmth and compassion, but the analysis of its structure shows that a very rigorous mind has mastered the brilliance of the imagination and the radiance of the heart.

If we had examined Buechner's books in chronological order rather than by genre, we would have been struck by the maturation in both the thought and the technique of the writer. *The Magnificent Defeat*, however good it is, still seems a little contrived: the effects are sometimes developed for effects' sake. By contrast, *Telling the Truth* offers a perfect, satisfying blend of thought, structure, and imagery. All of Buechner's works have this richness of life, this great sophistication, and some of his later writings show his capacity for amusement, which was typical of Renaissance men of letters like Erasmus, More, and Montaigne. Unlike Donne, who tended to show off in front of the court, Buechner underplays his cultural sophistication. The effects are polished and simple; he adapts his speech to his audience but he speaks in undertones. It is only in *Peculiar Treasures*, as in *The Book of Bebb*, that Buechner lets his fancy loose and explores all the nooks and crannies of his marvelous Rabelaisian imagination.

Thus, if Buechner is romantic in his inspiration and insofar as he finds the supernatural within the natural, he is also a classicist who believes in restraint. For this reason I would include him among the artists who, like the composers Fauré, Saint-Saens, and Frank, have given us the best of their channeled romanticism, preferring most of the time the more delicate effects of strings and voice to the earthshaking power of percussion and brass.

PART II
Mr. Buechner
the Novelist

III

Fictionalizing the
Theological Themes

Hearken unto a Verser, who may by chance
Rhyme thee to good, and make a bait of pleasure:
A verse may find him who a sermon flies,
And turn delight into a sacrifice.

George Herbert, *The Temple*

When asked to describe himself, Buechner once said that he was
"part novelist, part Christian, part pig."[1] The pig might interest a
journalist from *Time* or *Newsweek*, but the critic is interested in the
dichotomy that Buechner sometimes expressed as a novelist before he
became a Christian. *A Long Day's Dying*, his first novel, was a best-
seller, and was followed by two other novels: *The Seasons' Difference*,
which explored how difficult it is for any human being to communicate
a deep personal experience to others, and *The Return of Ansel Gibbs*, the
study of a politician's pangs of conscience.

The first of Buechner's religious novels is *The Final Beast*. It is
because of its critics that Buechner has experienced difficulties in being both a novelist and a Christian apologist. The story is that of a
young minister, Theodore Nicolet, who leaves home to fetch back one
of his parishioners who has suddenly left her husband—Rooney Vail,
a barren young woman who feels guilty because she committed
adultery. In this novel Buechner explores the enormous and unfore-

---

1. Frederick Buechner, *The Alphabet of Grace* (New York: Seabury Press,
1970), p. viii.

seeable consequences of sin in the effect of adultery on three characters and in the destruction of the personality of Irma Reinwasser, the governess of Nicolet's children, who was once tortured in a Nazi prison camp. The book concentrates on the importance of showing love and forgiveness so that life might be restored. Though *The Final Beast* is definitely better in technique and presents more vivid scenes than the previous three novels, critics resented the fact that it was overtly Christian and ruled Buechner out as a novelist, thus creating a schism in his personality as novelist and Christian.

The result was that the Christian hid behind the novelist in the next work, *The Entrance to Porlock*, which combined myth, elemental symbolism, and Frank Baum's *Wizard of Oz* story to point at a reality that would transcend the world of appearance. Buechner tried to recover the technique that he used in his early novels and transmit some veiled religious message. Interesting as the novel may be, it is a Gothic piece of art. Four principal male characters start on a journey at the instigation of the dreamy, airy, eighty-year-old Peter Ringkoping, who wants to give his land away to Strasser, the "wizard," who takes care of retarded children and has psychological gifts. As the men travel along, each reveals himself for what he is and has to face self-discovery. The two women who are left at home set out on a pilgrimage of their own, and they too develop self-awareness. All return home enriched by the process, but none is really changed.

Buechner regained the courage to be himself as both Christian and artist in his next four books, which form the tetralogy *The Book of Bebb*. His technique changed considerably: his writing became more vivid and contemporary, his tone varied rather than unified. The message is undiluted Christianity, though other religions are also considered. The narrator is Antonio Parr, an average twentieth-century man. In his restlessness and his need for causes and fights, he goes to Florida to investigate Leo Bebb, a con man who runs a diploma mill for the ministry.

In *Lion Country*, the first novel in the tetralogy, Antonio discovers that he himself is exposed in the process of exposing Bebb. He gains compassion and marries Bebb's adopted daughter, Sharon, who is as chthonic as he is airy.

Open Heart, the second and most sophisticated of the four novels, deals with the problem of death. Buechner insists on the superiority of Indian wisdom, expressed in its death ritual, over the wisdom of the white man, who in his fear often avoids the issue. Death for Buechner is not an event but a process. Elements of death lurk in each character: in the hypochondriac Charlie, for instance, Antonio's brother-in-law, who sleeps his life away; in Lucille, Bebb's wife, who hides behind sunglasses and drinks spiked Tropicanas until, one day, she commits suicide; and in Antonio himself, an escape artist.

Love Feast, the third novel, explores a low time for Antonio, whose marriage has broken up for a while, and for Bebb, who has neither wife nor church to take care of and who is at loose ends for lack of a task; but things improve for him when he finds a new group of young people to evangelize in Princeton. He becomes joyful again when he is able to give the best of himself in Love Feasts, but he has to fight the powers that be, and his last defiant act is literally the end of him: while flying a plane advertising Christianity over the Princeton Parade, the annual get-together of alumni in procession, the plane bursts into flames, and Bebb disappears in a cloud of smoke and fire.

No one knows what became of Bebb because his body is never found. In *Treasure Hunt*, the last novel of the Bebb series, his disciples—Antonio and Sharon, the octogenarian Theosophist Gertrude Conover, and Bebb's assistant, the ever-smiling Brownie—feel let down, leading an existence as lifeless as a collapsed balloon. But they are united in obedience to Bebb's testament: they are to search Bebb's house, which he has left to Sharon and Antonio with the instruction that they somehow use it for Jesus. There religion, science, and agnosticism meet as Antonio faces Babe, Bebb's twin brother. Sharon discovers who her mother is, and that Bert, Babe's wife, and Bebb were once adulterous lovers, which Babe could neither forget nor forgive. All is false-seeming and destructive in the Babe household; topsy-turviness reigns. Sentimentality replaces sentiment, belief in UFO's replaces religion, and the appearance of clarity and openness disguises resentment and darkness. As much as Bebb's house was attempting to be the house of life, Babe's house is the house of death, its atmosphere punctuated by the rhythmical swatting of flies (reminiscent of Graham Greene's novels). Finally, Bebb's desire is realized: Babe is pushed out of the house, which is given permanently to the parents of a poor blind child, Jimmy Bob Luby.

Though the four novels are not equal in achievement, all display a marvelous capacity for variety in language and characterization. All are boisterous in tone, mixing the sacred with the most profane. And all have a marvelous sense of *joie de vivre* and Rabelaisian humor. Like *Peculiar Treasures*, *The Book of Bebb* reveals the preposterousness of life and the amazing grace of the God who sustains it.

Such is also the theme of what is Buechner's most recent novel at this writing: *Godric*. This is the story of the gradual conversion of a pirate into a holy hermit. The journeys of the saint and the era in which he lived, the eleventh century, enable Buechner to explore different times and territories, such as medieval Rome, Jerusalem, and Northumberland. Buechner seems most at ease in recreating medieval life and spirituality, writing this time with a lyrical Anglo-Saxon cadence that does not shock the modern ear. Godric is dictating the story of his life to Reginald, the monk who tends to sugar-coat reality in his desire for consistency in human beings. Godric, who knows what a wretch he has been, resents this twisting of the reality of his life. This plot enables Buechner to poke fun at medieval hagiography and to assert his own Protestant outlook. Unlike *The Book of Bebb*, in which the Christian artist still uses the evangelist's techniques, *Godric*, one feels, is the perfect expression of both the artist's and the religious man's deepest desires. It is Buechner at his best—delicate, humorous, and reverent. In this novel the dichotomy between writer and Christian has disappeared.

Buechner himself is well aware of the progression of his novels. In an interview in the summer of 1981, he recalled at length the author's progress as well as the pilgrim's progress. *A Long Day's Dying*, he said, sprang from the young man's disgust at the emptiness of the lives of most of those he had met in the society of the rich. *The Seasons' Difference* was looking for a way out of despair; although Buechner himself had had no experience of Christ at the time, still he portrayed a man's vision of Christ. He showed some reconciliation to the world of the wealthy in *The Return of Ansel Gibbs*. Gibbs was an urbane hero and a good man, while Kuykendall was the depiction of a real priest. Buechner wrote this book at a time when, having gone to theological seminary, he had begun facing his true self and becoming more of an introvert. In Ansel Gibbs, he said, he also projected his own weaknesses.

Buechner's new duties as husband, father, and minister at Phillips

Exeter Academy did not allow him much time for writing, which accounts for the lapse of time between this and his next novel, *The Final Beast*. In it, Buechner records his experience with Agnes Sanford, the lay-healer, and his new understanding of the power of prayer and the possibility of healing through the laying-on of hands. In Nicolet's praying to God to forgive him for any face that he cannot look upon with love, Buechner recognizes the adumbration of what is central to the next volumes of *The Book of Bebb*.

Another gap occurred in Buechner's literary creation at the time that he left Exeter, which was also about the time that John Kennedy and Martin Luther King were assassinated. Buechner then sank into despair and questioned the value of his own existence, wondering what, as a Christian, he was doing to alleviate the pain of the world. *The Final Beast* had been rejected as Christian and simplistic; so Buechner sat down to write his most ''desperate book,'' *The Entrance to Porlock*.

Relief came when he was invited to Harvard to give a series of lectures. Buechner recalled the sudden surge of inspiration that came to him as he perused the letter that asked him to deal with Religion and Letters, ''Letters'' meaning, of course, literature. But Buechner decided to use the word ''letters'' in its primary sense and write about his life in terms of the alphabet. This, he confessed, took a lot of courage, but he gained a new sense of liberation and of self-forgiveness. According to him it was smooth sailing, literarily speaking, from then on. He wrote *The Book of Bebb* with tremendous joy and boisterousness, and in *Godric*, a more sober book, he showed his increasing spiritual depth, ''the distillation of everything.''[2]

In this marvelous analysis of the genesis of his works, Buechner explains his spiritual evolution, his turning from a negative reaction to the world to a search for values to live by, and his finding such values in Christianity and realizing his own shortcomings. The young minister gradually gained deeper religious insights as he recognized the value of prayer, the importance of compassion and forgiveness, and the beauty and joy of the creation. *Godric* is almost a hymn of praise

---

2. Personal interview with Frederick Buechner on August 14, 1981, at 3 Hawk Mountain, Pittsfield, Vermont.

to the glory of God. The journey is not uniquely his, nor would Buechner claim it to be. It portrays the stops and turns and blossomings of all those who, somehow or other, are seekers of the way. Buechner affirms that *the way* is the way of Christ, open to all. Therefore, in any life one should be able to read the pilgrimage in progress.

This conviction gave Buechner a new start after his low point and encouraged him to be open about his own life in *The Alphabet of Grace* rather than roll bandages to try to alleviate the pain of the world. Though they considered the objections of the atheist and the agnostic, his theological books were primarily geared toward believers—believers of little faith, perhaps, but church-goers all the same. What the novels could do was take care of the unbeliever, the skeptic who might be trapped into perceiving the Christian view of life as at least an option, if not *the* way.

Buechner's own experience of agnosticism and despair makes him particularly sensitive to those who search for truth, those whom the way of the world does not satisfy. It is this particular audience that he addresses in his novels, which show sinners driving themselves into impasses until they are miraculously saved by grace. These characters are opposed by those who trust in the beneficent flow of life and bounce back despite its tribulations.

Buechner addresses a twentieth-century audience who, in a middle-aged civilization, have faced the failure of their ideals and themselves, and wonder where to turn next for comfort. He clobbers the chirpy optimist and the simplistic person as well as the arrogant cynic, the materialist, and the angelist. Yet despite his attempt to include middle- and lower-class Americans in his fiction, he remains a writer of the sophisticated. Who will keep up with the endless ratiocinations of Antonio, the narrator of *The Book of Bebb*, but those who are familiar with the schizophrenic anti-heroes of Camus, Beckett, or Robertson Davies? For all the compassion he shows toward the common folk—and in this way he is like Cheever, Pynchon, and Updike—Buechner remains a writer of the elite.

In addressing such an audience, Buechner has to pay a price. Most of the sophisticated are not much interested in religion and dislike his direct appeal for Christianity. The average reader misses the overt use of sex, violence, and monstrous happenings or beings common to much of today's literature. The prudish reader resents the presence of down-to-earth language and offbeat characters. In fact, Buechner avoids the use of sensationalism and incredibility in the psychology of his characters: he includes neither the unbelievably good nor the irredeemably bad and distorted. Some readers do not see the point of this sort of fiction. For other readers it hits too close to home. Fiction is great as an escape or as a satire of characters from whom one can disengage oneself, but who wants to read about characters that seem too much like oneself? Buechner has, in short, crossed the line of good taste or good behavior.[3] He might entertain, but his main desire is to be a surgeon of souls. No wonder that his novels, unlike his theological writings, are read and appreciated by only a happy few.

Although most of the themes of Buechner's theological works are found in his novels, I decided, to avoid repetition, to explore these four: the presence of evil in the world and in each of us, the need for grace, the definition of man as *homo religiosus*, and the task of the minister. They will be studied in turn as they are developed in the plots and characters of the various novels.

The Presence of Evil in the World

When asked whether he thought that evil was, in Augustinian terms, *amissio boni*, the absence of goodness, Buechner replied:

> Evil is like an atomic bomb, like a mushroom. It starts with a thin stem and then enlarges. Both in the historical and the human sense, there is a reality in being possessed by demons. Evil is not only the shadow cast by light. It is vast and hideous.[4]

---

3. See Horton Davies, ''Frederick Buechner and the Strange Work of Grace,'' *Theology Today*, July 1979, pp. 186-187.

4. Personal interview with Frederick Buechner on August 14, 1981. For an historical appraisal of the place of evil in the world and Buechner's own position, see chapter I and Theodore Plantinga, *Learning to Live with Evil* (Grand Rapids, Mich.: Eerdmans, 1982). The Manichean view sees evil as co-eternal with goodness and in perpetual struggle with it. Nineteenth-century philosophers modify this position in stressing that evil is the necessary antithesis to goodness without which it could not exist. The Platonists deny evil any ultimate reality; it is a mere deprivation of goodness. Calvin sees it as the result of the corrupt will which has turned away from God in waywardness. Obedience to God is therefore the best way to combat all evils.

Here Buechner introduces the Tillichian difference between evil as absence of God or imperfection of the creature and evil as disobedience to his commandments. Buechner, however, never phrases it precisely in those terms; to the unbeliever, disobedience to a God he does not believe in would make no sense. Buechner tends to show evil as alienation from oneself and from others, or sin as waste of life.

Like fallout from an atomic bomb, evil spreads. Since sex is one of the modern gods, Buechner uses it in many novels to show that, misused, it can have drastic consequences.[5] In *The Final Beast*, Rooney, a married woman who is both rich and bored, is keeping shop when a journalist enters: Willy Poteat, a bachelor. She decides to close the shop early and seduces him on a pile of green rubber ponchos, an action with unforeseen consequences for both of them. Rooney suffers from guilt, cannot bear children, and turns to the Church in desperation. The consequences are even more terrible for Poteat, who suddenly glimpsed the opening of a new door in his life. He worshiped Rooney's very shadow, but in her shame she does not even acknowledge his presence when she sees him on the street. With the door slammed in his face, Poteat is damaged. He becomes introverted, furtively watches Rooney's movements, and resents any joy in other people's lives. He is no longer interested in gossip as it comes, but only in digging up dirt in other people's lives. He hates the beneficial impact of Nicolet, the minister, and hints that Nicolet's relationship with Rooney is more than platonic. When Rooney runs away from home and Nicolet goes after her, Poteat presses his charges with more vigor and torments Irma, the keeper of Nicolet's house and children. Finally all are drawn into the horror of evil.

The main plot is interwoven with a subplot which explains the life and personality of Irma Reinwasser. All comes together at the end in a vortex of flames. The deformed Irma holds the philosophy that whatever man does turns out for the worst. To explain her negative attitude toward life, Buechner explores her past and brings in collective sin. Once a prisoner in a Nazi camp, Irma survived thanks to an officer, Heinz Taffel, who liked her spirit, her voice, and her hen-like

---

5. The theme is not new in Western literature. See Denis de Rougemont, *Love in the Western World* (New York: Harcourt Brace, 1940).

appearance. He therefore employed her and protected her, but this proved to be a mixed blessing. This sentimental German officer, capable of the worst cruelty whenever drunk, one day endeavored to make her look more like a chicken by tearing off some of her toes, urged on by some of the other soldiers. Irma's savior had thus become her tormentor. For the rest of her life Irma is marked by diffidence toward men, a feeling which includes Nicolet, whom she judges by her earlier lesson. By deforming her body, Heinz Taffel has also crippled her mind. But Irma still attempts to make a life of her own and enjoys the love of Nicolet's children.

Evil gets the better of her during Poteat's visit. The digger of dirt points at possible evil within Irma herself, accusing her of jealousy in revealing Nicolet's and Rooney's whereabouts. In the total panic of her turmoil, she decides to sacrifice herself for him whom she thinks she has wronged. She confesses her presumed sin in front of the whole congregation of Nicolet's church in order to save his reputation. Two youngsters who don't listen to Nicolet's defense of her and misinterpret her action as a ploy to get attention set out to punish this Jewish woman whom they spontaneously dislike. They set fire to a bag containing excrement and place it on the front stairs of the house where she is hiding in shame. Asleep and unaware of this, Irma is burnt alive.

The story deserves to be retold to show how Buechner dramatizes historical as well as personal evil until it forms a vast cloud of destructive smoke. In this instance adultery and cruelty perpetrate evil like tossed pebbles make rings in a pool. But Buechner goes further. To begin with, Poteat and Irma did not sin but were sinned against. The experience of sin has engendered in both a mistrust which has stopped the flow of life in them. Henceforth their universe has become closed, and they contribute to the chain of destruction rather than to the flow of life. The compulsion to become destructive can be broken only by love or sacrifice. Both resist love by hiding from Nicolet, who could bring them forgiveness and peace. But finally, in a supreme act of love, Irma breaks the chain of evil with her Christ-like sacrifice.

Buechner develops many of his other evil characters along these lines. In *Love Feast*, Roebuck, the father of a crippled child and assistant professor at Princeton University, dresses like a Nazi, in tight pants and boots, resentful of any fun others might have. Babe,

Bebb's twin brother in *Treasure Hunt*, keeps himself and his wife Bert from really living their lives for fear that she might betray him in adultery again. Though Buechner portrays the enormous consequences of evil, he always describes his evil characters with compassion. Evil was not meant to be a normal part of life, and evil characters are the product of circumstances, though Buechner would agree with Sartre that man's responsibility lies in his reaction to circumstances.

Evil can be resisted, provided it is eradicated in the early stages. The character Chris in *Lion Country* makes this point when he retells the story of Abbott and Costello. Any character that accepts the contemplation and lure of evil will soon be sucked up and devoured by the monster.[6]

Evil as adultery or sexual offense pervades almost all of Buechner's books. In the Bebb stories, as in *The Final Beast*, Buechner also uses the psycho-analytical method of probing human beings. In *Lion Country*, we learn that Sharon is Bebb's adopted daughter, that Lucille, Bebb's wife, has a drinking problem, and that Bebb suffers from some sexual deviation. In *Open Heart*, Lucille leaves a cryptic message saying that no man can completely reveal what is in his heart and that Bebb will never say what happened with Bert on the Hill. The question is left pending in *Love Feast* and is resolved in *Treasure Hunt*: Bebb made love to his twin brother's wife, which caused Babe's madness, Bert's misery (since she never could live a full life as a woman), Sharon's deprivation of her real mother, Lucille's trauma during her pregnancy, and Bebb's need for sexual exposure.

Buechner takes up the theme of adultery again in the relationship between Antonio, his wife Sharon, and his nephew Tony. A young married couple, Antonio and Sharon have hardly had time to get acquainted when they take in Antonio's two nephews, Chris and Tony, whose mother has died. Sharon and Tony share the same enthusiasm for life, the same need to express joy and sorrow, and the same passion for drama and physical exertion, whereas Antonio,

---

6. Saint-Exupéry makes a similar point in *The Little Prince*: volcanoes must be cleaned up and baobabs uprooted or the planet will disintegrate.

the absentee husband and teacher, is too busy to pay attention to his wife's needs. One afternoon, Sharon and Tony catch each other by surprise and make love. Antonio is so blind that he doesn't realize what has happened until Tony, unable to contain his remorse any longer, tells him about it. From then on, Antonio is filled with jealousy, and communicates even less with his wife; their relationship is thus reduced to empty sex, and the two separate.

In this instance, Buechner explores the causes of adultery. The sin is no longer simply Sharon's and Tony's, but has been brought upon Antonio's head by his refusal to communicate with his wife. Anita Steen, who loves Sharon, tries to tell Antonio he has failed in his responsibility as a husband because he has not tried to understand and accommodate the needs of the woman he has married and brought out of her world into his. In this case sin is caused as much by Antonio's omission as by the two foolish adulterers' action.

The last example of sexual misdemeanor is the incestuous relationship of Godric and his sister. The two are strongly attracted to one another, and for a long time they resist temptation, but Burcwen pines away for love of her brother. Godric, tempted by the pleasure of the flesh when he sees her bathe in the river Wear, avoids her. But eventually, seized by compassion, like Scobie in Graham Greene's *The Heart of the Matter*, Godric abandons his principles. When the two consummate their love, their world collapses. Evil piles upon evil. Godric lies to his anxious brother, telling him he does not know Burcwen's whereabouts; Burcwen also lies and sends him to an accidental death. Ridden with guilt, Burcwen and Godric stay forever apart. To repair the evil of her life, Burcwen joins an order of nuns in Durham.

In answer to the modern Freudian craze, Buechner shows the evil consequences of unruly love. Man trespasses against the laws of God at his own risk. The penalty is separation or death.

Traditionally evil has been divided into three categories: natural, moral, and demonic. Most often, as we have seen, Buechner tends to link all three. Natural evil, however, might be blown out of proportion by man's lack of vision. Buechner's thoughts on death vacillate. In *The Final Beast* one feels that the termination of a full life is not sad, except perhaps momentarily so for the onlookers. After

Franny dies her children are taken care of and her husband finds another helper in Irma and another romantic attraction in Rooney.

Buechner also refuses to dramatize the sick and the crippled of this world, and attributes our fear in their presence to shortsightedness and hypochondria. The true Christian can face both, because he knows that the ways of God are different from the norms of man. In *The Entrance to Porlock* and *The Book of Bebb*, Strasser and Bebb treat the crippled as full human beings. Strasser argues the superiority of mongoloids over ordinary men, because they are able to trust and have no fear of death.

Whereas the man of God has a sacramental view of the universe, the atheist, unable to bear the presence of evil, has an excremental view of the world which can arrest his growth. In *The Final Beast*, Poteat has become a killer of reputations, as has Virgil Roebuck, the father of a crippled son in *Love Feast*. In a confrontation between Bebb and Roebuck, the arguments of the atheist and of the believer are presented. Both agree to recognize the great fecal indictment—the amount of stink, corruption, and waste in the world—but Bebb also recognizes the power that supports life, whereas Roebuck is arrested by it and cannot go beyond the tragedy. The consequence is that Roebuck, like Poteat, perpetrates evil in the world, whereas Bebb tries to turn everything into good. Buechner expresses the same philosophy in *Godric*. Elric the anchorite is haunted by demons, and can never recognize beauty and joy; therefore he leads a miserable life. Godric, on the other hand, dies singing God's praises, despite his awareness of evil and his own frailty. For Buechner, trust is the basis of life, trust despite setbacks. For him the "shit of the world" is productive: "if you don't pile it too thick in one place, it makes the seed grow."[7]

The world being what it is and human nature being distorted, the question arises: shall I be a destroyer or a nourisher? Instinct will cause the man who has been hurt to hurt the world back, but the exercise of will only can answer evil by good, thus destroying the infernal circle. Since men are given the power to choose be-

---

7. From *Love Feast* in Frederick Buechner, *The Book of Bebb* (New York: Atheneum, 1979), p. 352.

tween good and evil, choosing to surrender to the forces of evil is sin. In the modern world, sin appears most often as separation from one's brother and sister, and in waste.

Sin as separation comes from the excessive importance given to self-realization. Avoidance of sin is self-abnegation. This is particularly the case in the instances of adultery that Buechner presents. The desire for self-fulfillment pushes Rooney to use Poteat as a mere object, whereas the thought of the sadness others would feel if they should commit adultery and elope stops Nicolet and Rooney from doing so. The desire for self-fulfillment pushes Godric to rape and plunder on the high seas, despite his better judgment.

Possessiveness of people or of things is also a sign that people cannot go beyond the self, though Buechner does not object to wealth. Rooney in *The Final Beast* is rich and puts her money to use, and so does Herman Redpath in *Lion Country*, but he objects to accumulation. In *The Entrance to Porlock*, Peter Ringkoping hides behind a vast amount of acquired books, and his daughter-in-law Alice clutters her house with furniture. Bebb, on the other hand, always travels light, with one suitcase and a T.V. When Godric decides to become a hermit, he gives away his riches to the poor, whereas Flambard, the rich bishop, uses both people and money for his own advancement. Separation from others comes from granting the self too much importance, setting one's own greed, one's own needs and desires above those of others.

Self-absorption produces alienation. We are alienated from others because we take our achievements or our needs as the stick by which the world is to be measured. Hence we hate anything that does not conform to it. This is the reason for the separation between "normal" people and the deformed, between the healthy and the sick, between the morally righteous and the so-called scum of society. Christianity consists in being open to all. Nicolet affirms that we should be the friends of drinkers, and Bebb puts this into practice in *Love Feast*. And yet this friendliness to sinners does not mean that the man of God is going to be included among them. Bebb will serve alcoholic drinks to his congregation if that is their choice, but will not drink himself. The holy Godric separates himself from all worldly comfort and friends in order to be alone with God. The opposite of alienation is not absorption but openness to all, the believer trusting that God will sustain and preserve him from the perils of temptation. Man has first and foremost to be true to his own vocation, which is obedience to the voice of God.

Obedience to God implies that one fulfills one's role as a human being as best one can. Disobedience means self-alienation. The example of Rooney and Poteat in *The Final Beast* could serve again, but let us take instead that of Lucille and Babe in *The Book of Bebb*. Lucille, tired of her screaming baby, kills it during a drunken fit. Unable to forgive herself, she starts drinking on a regular basis, and cuts herself off from all except Brownie, her husband's helper, who brings her spiked Tropicanas at regular intervals; she spends her days in front of the T.V. and wears sunglasses inside the house. She has stopped functioning as a wife and mother, although she has been given a second chance with Sharon, the daughter she and Bebb adopt. She has not conceived again. She is alienated from herself, from her husband, and from the rest of the world.

Babe is different. His apparent friendliness deceives people, but in fact no one can approach him or his household. After the traumatic experience of discovering that his wife Bert and his brother were lovers, he has taken refuge in conning people into believing that UFO's will be the salvation of the world. At times he has almost succeeded in convincing himself of this fiction, but he is an alienated man. A jealous husband, he denies his wife the joys and pains of growing up, and denies himself the supportive companionship of a true wife. Unable to accept the risk of pain, he deprives himself of true life.

All these examples are also related to waste. Sin is waste, is leaving truckloads of perfectly good peaches to rot at the side of the road in order to maintain high prices. Or it is the waste of human beings who are too scared to live their lives to the fullest and trust in God's mercy. Babe played his life safe: he never left home and resented it, never left his wife and resented her—he wasted his life, curling up in his hole like a spider. Waste is women not fulfilling their roles as mothers, like Rooney in *The Final Beast*, Sharon in *The Book of Bebb*, or even Burcwen, the tomboy of *Godric*. Sin is hypochondria, the result of fearing life: Roy Nicolet, the minister's father in *The Final Beast*, looks white as a sheet and is always about to die. The Metzgers, who appear in both *The Final Beast* and *The Book of Bebb*, are similar characters: they make sure that they will get the necessary help if they suffer heart attacks. Charlie Blaine, Antonio's brother-in-law, sleeps his life away and keeps catching colds. Buechner portrays all of these characters as airy, not earthy like Bebb or Godric. The most airy of all is Peter Ringkoping in *The Entrance to Porlock*, who sees Shakespeare's ghost and lives among dusty books. He is so far removed from the world of mortals that his family wonders whether he exists at all. The last and most striking example of waste is, for Buechner, homosexuality. Brownie, Bebb's homosexual assistant, realizes that he is only half-alive. He lacks guts and shuns the struggles of life. He is a man who does not put his hand sufficiently to the plow, who fulfills roles that are traditionally feminine, such as cooking and cleaning the church. He illustrates Buechner's belief that sin is to be an onlooker rather than a participant in life. The narrator Antonio, endless talker and observer of life's comedy, is also guilty of this particular sin.

The characters' deficiencies point to Buechner's idea of wholeness. Women were made to care for children. Men were created to fight against the world, to apply themselves to their work, and to love and defend their family. All are meant to be life-loving and creative in the area to which they were called. And all are interdependent rather than independent. This traditional view of life could be attacked by the protagonists of the gay or women's liberation movements, but Buechner's work does not invite such attacks. Wise women appear in his novels to set men straight: in *The Final Beast* Nicolet is enlightened by Lillian Flagg, the faith-healer, as Buechner was himself enlightened by Agnes Sanford; and in *The Book of Bebb*, Bebb is saved from depression by the insights of the Theosophist Gertrude Conover. Brownie, Bebb's assistant, and Reginald, the monk of *Godric*, lack initiative and aggressiveness, but they are kinder than most, while the lesbian Anita Steen in *Love Feast* knows more about marital commitments than Antonio and Sharon do.

Buechner's message is summed up in *Peculiar Treasures:* however shady some aspect of our lives may be, there is loveliness in us all. Through sin most of us would have sunk, but we have been sustained and redeemed through love. Buechner attacks the particular deviations of our age, but leaves room for transformation and redemption through God's mercy and grace.

The Need for Grace

Since all are sinners, all need to be redeemed. Buechner expresses his trust in life in the preface to *The Book of Bebb*:

> Apart from who the characters are and the places they go and the things they do, there is the sense of what the old hymn quaveringly addresses as "O love that will not let me go," the sense of an ultimate depth of things that is not finally indifferent as to whether people sink or swim but endlessly if always hiddenly refuses to abandon them.[8]

Grace presupposes confidence and trust in a loving God, encouraging life rather than halting it. The presence of such a God is affirmed in all of Buechner's religious novels. Belief in grace also implies that all in nature is not random, that life has a plot. Buechner himself affirms that this is the essential subject of all his novels.

This general idea is usually translated into the theme of pilgrimage common to all the novels. In *The Final Beast*, Nicolet and Rooney leave their hometown in order to recover purpose and peace in their lives. All the characters in *The Entrance to Porlock* set out to visit Strasser. Antonio, Bebb, Brownie, and Sharon, the main characters of *The Book of Bebb*, keep moving around, and Godric sails many seas before he can find the haven that is his in Finchale. Restlessness and pilgrimage is the price human beings pay for their disobedience to God, for their selfish waywardness. But pilgrimage is also God's gift to us, encouraging us to find the right path of obedience. Rest is the prize that awaits him who has found God, but to rest en route, before reaching the goal, is a form of death in life. Buechner's hypochondriacs and the half-alive like Antonio, Lucille, and Brownie refuse to tread the whole stretch of road. The truly alive, either in life or in death, wrestle on the way with their Creator in order to be made into new men and women, eventually to be perfected in their resemblance to Christ, the true man.

---

8. Buechner, preface to *The Book of Bebb*, p. ix.

Grace is therefore the active and beneficial disposition of God toward man. Life has a plot, and death is part of it. From *The Final Beast* to *Godric*, Buechner shows a growing acceptance of the necessity of death. In *The Final Beast*, he portrays death as unimportant compared to the length and strength of life. In *Lion Country*, Miriam sees death as part of the life process. She sees it as the birth of herself, but wonders what life on the other side will be like. Antonio, in his dramatic and literary way, reassures her with the presence of Christ as the great lover. In *Open Heart* and *Love Feast*, the afterlife is envisioned as a pilgrim's progress in which each individual is equipped with the necessary implements to reach the happy hunting ground, an Indian version of Paradise. In *Godric*, Buechner no longer elaborates on the afterlife, except to offer words of reassurance. Godric seems to attain vision as he dies, and his last words are trusting ones: " 'All is lost. All is found.' " Thus death as much as life is the product of God's grace, something to relieve those who, like Lucille, are weary and cannot make it through life, or those who have worked long in the vineyard and are aspiring to rest in peace.

Common grace is available to all. It is the free gift of the creation. But man tends to forget that all is grace in his petitions for particular graces. Nicolet, praying in his father's field, hopes that Christ will give him the final word that will shatter all his doubts, but what he experiences is an incredible and inexplicable joy at hearing the sound of silence: the clack-clack of the branches of a tree. Bebb would like to receive security and wealth in order to be able to do something big for Jesus. But God's interference is to keep him moving and alert until he finally recalls Bebb to himself. Peter Ringkoping in *The Entrance to Porlock* wants to be rid of his land, but finally his land is restored to him, painted with the colors of gold. The earth is given back to him to be cherished and shared with his family. In all his novels, Buechner shows the particular care of God for his people.

The Christian also believes in imputed grace. Through the gift of his son, God has appeased his wrath toward mankind. Forgiveness for all sins is given to those who seek it. In the death of Christ on the Cross and in the Resurrection, evil and death have been overcome, and God has made a new covenant with his people. Yet in his respect for man's freedom, God has given him the choice to accept or refuse the gift of pardon. He is free, according to Buechner, to be meek, to be pardoned and receive eternal life, or to be closed in on himself, to cling to his egoism and self-righteousness and at the time of crisis to experience despair and death.

The stages that punctuate the receiving of grace, like those that mark the granting of forgiveness, are well outlined in most of Buechner's novels. The first stage is man's awareness of his emptiness, caused by either external circumstances or inner turmoil. In *The Final Beast*, Rooney runs away to Muscadine because she is longing to have a child; Nicolet is weary of his work as a preacher; Roy, Nicolet's father, realizes he has not been a good father. All feel empty and discouraged, and all are so close to being at the end of their tether that they swallow their pride and seek help. In *The Book of Bebb*, the young couple Antonio and Sharon must develop self-awareness before they can appreciate each other and their union as an indissoluble couple. Throughout his pilgrimage in life, Antonio learns simplicity, that intellect, culture, and middle-class values are not necessarily the yardstick by which life is measured. He also learns that he has a lot to learn—from Bebb, from his students, and also from his wife Sharon. Sharon, on the other hand, faces her dissatisfaction with life, her sexual voracity and self-disgust. After a separation from Antonio (which occurs in *Love Feast*), during which both realize how empty their lives have become, Antonio is able to pardon Sharon for her infidelities, and she is able to put all grievances away. Emptiness is also at the root of Godric's conversion, triggered by his realization that plunder and accumulated riches have not filled his life. The longing caused by the glimpse of heaven he saw on the island of Farne starts haunting him again.

For man to be open to grace, he should have gone through the dark night of the soul. He is then ready to fall into "the everlasting arms" of God, and to be set free to follow his true path and destiny.

Forgiveness is one of the central themes of Buechner's fiction, the seeking and receiving of God's inherent grace. Neurotic guilt might be helped by consulting a psychologist, but real guilt can be effaced only through the atonement of Christ. No one is ever able to absolve himself from guilt. Rooney, the adulteress, needs Nicolet, as minister, to assure her of God's pardon. He in turn needs for-giveness for failing as pastor and son. Bebb cannot forgive himself for his illicit love for Bert, and throws himself on God's mercy; Bert accepts her husband's unjust treatment of her as retribution for her sin. Lucille keeps punishing herself for killing her baby; Roebuck has stopped all life within himself because he feels guilty for having fathered a crippled child. As Shakespeare once said, "Conscience does make cowards of us all." Those who have faith recover joy at being pardoned, whereas those who have not keep on living a death-in-life existence, in bondage.

The power of inherent grace in forgiveness is to transform the individual from a self-destructive to a constructive individual. Rooney in *The Final Beast* is such a person: once pardoned by God, she returns and confesses her sin to her husband and tries to bring some solace to Poteat, her one-time lover. Nancy Oglethorpe, the Mary Magdalene of *The Book of Bebb*, is completely regenerated. Picked up at random on the street and brought to one of Bebb's Love Feasts, she confesses to being promiscuous, and recognizes Jesus Christ as Lord and Savior.

Inner transformation means abjuring one's evil ways and set-ting forth on the path that Christ has prescribed. The effect of grace is the restoration of life in a given individual. But the individual's response to grace is to become a good person, life-giving and law-abiding.

God's grace is manifested in the turning of a purposeless life into a purposeful one. The pardoned individual is given a new task, as Buechner's characters show. Rooney takes care of poor children; Nancy becomes Bebb's efficient secretary. Lucille is encouraged to arrange flowers in the church, Godric nurses Elric, and the repen-tant Burcwen enters a convent to nurse the sick. God sustains life, forgives sin, and gives each individual a new chance by giving him a suitable new vocation.

God often uses man to manifest his grace, a point clearly made in *Love Feast*. During the feasts, each participant confesses to the person he can best face, the one that most resembles himself, as each has become a priest to the other. Nancy Oglethorpe confesses that she feels inferior when she hears her own name, and Antonio confesses that he is at a loss without his family. The sacramental value of mutual forgiveness is then sanctioned by the sharing of the bread and wine—in this case the biscuits and Tropicanas that each feeds the other—and by the kiss of peace. According to *Love Feast*, the sacraments are the efficacious signs and seeds of God's grace, and whatever form they take is a matter of personal preference.

Unlike Sartre, then, Buechner will not affirm that hell is other people; he affirms instead that grace is gracious other people. In *The Final Beast*, Rooney's crisis enables Nicolet to reconsider the whole business of his ministry. His chance meeting with the boy who gives him a lift forces him to recall why he went into the ministry. And Lillian Flagg instructs him about new ways to make his ministry relevant. All these encounters are blessed ones for him, even if the maturation process is painful.

Though the people in *The Entrance to Porlock* have sometimes painful interactions with each other, their growth in self-knowledge and in humility is a healthy process. The father, Peter Ringkoping, realizes that some of the defects he hates in his sons are, in fact, inherited from him: the cruelty of Nels, hidden behind self-justification, and that of Tommy, paraded as buffoonery. Nels projects his fear of cowardice onto his students, and Tommy has passed on his own sense of insecurity to his son Tim. The two women also act as foils to each other: Sarah, who has let go of everything, still resists the manipulative Alice, who is at heart longing to let go. As in the previous novel, *The Final Beast,* the Holy Spirit hovers over them all, as bird and as fire. The crow, shot by trigger-happy Tommy, comes to die at his feet. To Peter, Strasser's chest looks like the chest of a bird. In the forest, at the moment of transformation, the bodies of Nels and Tommy seem consumed by fire and the windows of the church-like house are aflame. In *The Book of Bebb*, Golden, God's messenger and Bebb's protector, is an angel of fire. Thus the spirit of God broods over the water, but the grace of God often "stamps" people as if with a cattle brand.

Despite man's resistance, God's grace is irresistible, efficacious, and victorious. Through his characters, Buechner works out this optimistic view of life. The best example in the novels is Antonio Parr, the narrator of *The Book of Bebb,* the epitome of twentieth-century man. At the beginning of *Lion Country,* life for him is ambiguous, ironical, and meaningless. His own progress is symbolized by the evolution of his style and of his artistic creation. A man whose life is made up of starts and stops, who cannot go past the first thirty pages of any novel, he manages to get married, hold on to a job, father a child, and be a loyal if not zealous supporter of his father-in-law and even, eventually, of his wife. Finally, he starts seeing some kind of pattern in his own life, and he hopes that the Christian truth might be true, as attested in his dreams. He manages to write four novels accounting for his life, each written in an increasingly simple style, and his artwork changes, too: the sharp, rickety contraption that he builds in *Lion Country* becomes a wooden mobile in *Open Heart*, one that he puts out in the open to be weather-beaten in *Love Feast*, not minding so much the toll of breakage and the unseemly aspect of his nephews' repairs to it in *Treasure Hunt*. Thus Antonio, having begun with an aesthetic view of life, has developed some dim vision of the possibility of a religious view of life. The grace of God has moved him, cloddish though he was, and however reluctant he was to be moved.

Last comes special grace, that which is the direct influence of God on some of his chosen people. Bebb is obviously the recipient of such uncommon grace. In *The Book of Bebb,* Buechner plainly states his belief in angels. God's emissaries can be recognized only by the men of God. One such emissary is Golden, Bebb's companion during his prison years, who paints his life on the prison walls in *Open Heart*, and turns up at all the important moments of Bebb's life. His messages can be cryptic, such as the note to Bebb which reads, "Good luck, sweetheart," sent as Bebb rejoices over Herman Redpath's inheritance. Is this encouragement or a threat? Buechner leaves us in doubt, but the operation Bebb builds with this inheritance, Open Heart, is not successful. Eventually we learn in *Love Feast* that Golden burned down the barn-church. We also learn later that Golden is responsible for an anonymous letter sent to the insurance company which charged Bebb's custodian—himself—with the possible crime of arson, and that should Gertrude try to shelter him, he (Golden) would make sure that the police would know how to find him. Golden stays with Bebb in the underground until Bebb is ready to make his last appearance for Jesus—in the sky in a plane that is consumed by flames. Golden is the angel of fire, watching over Bebb and getting him ready to meet his Creator.

The device of Golden and other "silvers" or "goldens" in *The Book of Bebb* might be a little far-fetched, as is Lucille's often-repeated belief that Bebb might be a denizen from outer space. The intervention of the supernatural in *Godric*—the apparition of St. Cuthbert on the island of Farne and of Gillian, the interpreter of dreams, on the journey from Rome—seems much more credible. Is this because we are able to relate more easily to this sort of experience in a medieval context? Possibly. But other interventions in Buechner's "modern" contexts are more convincing: Lillian Flagg's providential intervention for Nicolet in *The Final Beast* seems more relevant, as does Bebb's intervention for Antonio in *The Book of Bebb*. The character of Golden might be easier to accept if we remember that *The Book of Bebb* is a grotesque carnival like James Ensor's *Entrance of Christ into Brussels*. It is up to us to discern the serious idea of providence behind the farce.

Providence eventually leads all Buechner's surviving characters to walk in the Lord's path, in obedience to his design. But all do not live in bliss. The saint Bebb or Godric who welcomes God's transforming grace endures tribulations in obedience and joy, whereas the rebellious man, like Antonio, still gets bogged down on the way until he recovers the vision of the irresistible and loving care of his Maker.

Man as Homo Religiosus

It is Buechner's intimate conviction that basically all men were created from the same mold, creatures of the earth and the air, ambiguous creatures driven by body and spirit. All men are religious in the Tillichian sense; all need some ultimate concern to justify their lives. The man of experience who has tasted the fruit of the tree of knowledge can no longer take the world for granted. He needs to explain it. Buechner offers a biblical answer to man's quest for his origins and his destiny. For him the Bible is still the finest way to express the mysteries of life, Christianity still the most adequate metaphor for life at the very least, and at the most—as he believes—the unforeseeable and preposterous truth.

Man is religious insofar as he needs faith to survive. Children have faith because they know that they cannot know everything and do not attempt to pierce the secrets of the totality of the world. The dominical injunction expressed in the Gospel of Matthew—''Unless you . . . become like little children, you shall not enter the kingdom of heaven''—is illustrated in many of Buechner's novels, but particularly in *The Final Beast*. The minister's two daughters first lose their mother to death, and then their father leaves them for a time. Despite their previous experience of bereavement, they still trust their father's promise that he will come back, and that he has left Irma the housekeeper to take care of them. Thus their father's absence is not traumatic for them: they go on with their fun and games, their physical need for nourishment and elimination without serious questionings. Their perceptions of people are unadulterated: they play doctor with their hypochondriacal grandfather; they tell Poteat the slanderer that he has a black tongue; they call Rooney, who feels at a loss about her life, Raggedy Ann. This is the state of innocence embodied in *The Book of Bebb* by Antonio's students and his child, by Perkin in *Godric*, and regained by Bebb and Godric in their old age.

For Buechner, innocence does not mean being perfect. Children, like adults, are touched by original sin, but they are able to repent, to trust in the pardon and the grace which heals old wounds and enables man to live again, unburdened by his past. On the other hand, the man of experience has difficulty with the world as it is: he cannot square his own desire for rationality with the irrationality of life, and so enters a period of doubt. This desire to explain the world is another proof that man is basically religious. Religion proclaims man's inability to accept either materialism or naturalism as sufficient answers to the problem of his own destruction. According to Buechner, this question is so important to man that unless he resolves it, he becomes unable to enjoy the creation with gladness, but sinks into melancholy and self-doubt or into anger and aggressiveness. The former attitude characterizes the agnostic, the latter the atheist.

Many of these characters are portrayed in the novels: in *The Final Beast*, Irma Reinwasser oscillates between doubt about God's existence and anger at God for what he requires of his people; Poteat, the atheist, spreads evil and destruction. In *The Entrance to Porlock*, all of the characters are basically doubters, except perhaps Nels, the repressed and aggressive dean, who speaks of justice but comes to realize the evil forces at work within himself only at the time of the group pilgrimage to the land of Strasser. *The Book of Bebb* shows the dismay of both Antonio and Sharon when the dance of life suddenly stops for them and they are obliged to face the evil within themselves, and death; the atheist is portrayed in the character of Virgil Roebuck, who dresses and behaves like a Nazi. *Godric* presents a different set of characters, since agnosticism was not a leading characteristic of the eleventh century. But Bishop Flambard acts like an atheist. He tries to make the best of the world by exercising his religious authority and exploiting people's credulity and fears. He is finally brought to other beliefs as he faces death and encounters sanctity.

According to Buechner, man is so religious that he can find no rest until he has put his trust and love in God. This is expressed in the novels through the themes of man's pilgrimage and his true home. In *The Final Beast*, Nicolet, Rooney, and Irma (in her dreams) travel endless roads until they find rest and peace. Rooney is forgiven and returns to her husband to be a fruitful wife; Nicolet is given better knowledge of Christianity and finds new ways to address his congregation; Irma finds that the road covered with barbed wire which haunted her dreams suddenly becomes a hedge of red roses which bloom for her as she walks by. All of them find rest, though Irma finds eternal rest. All the characters of *The Entrance to Porlock* set out on a journey, at the end of which Strasser gives them some kind of rest and illumination. In *The Book of Bebb*, Antonio is perpetually on the move; at the end of the tetralogy, he has gotten only a glimpse of peace. His father-in-law, Bebb, has reached a relative sort of peace, since the errands he runs are focused on the Lord that he serves. At least he has found a still center in the raging storm. In *Godric*, rest has come to mean precisely that. Godric is able to give up his senseless ocean travels and settles down in a true home, alone with the God whom he worships and loves.

Home for Buechner is therefore not a place but a relationship with the only being who deserves all our disinterested love: God. Until he has found this home, man is condemned to the angst that comes from his perception of transience. This is expressed at the end of *Treasure Hunt* in the sign that Antonio's son displays to welcome his parents back: it is spelled HONE rather than HOME, for man's physical home—the one that children leave and adults depart by death—is not true home. None of the adult characters of Buechner's novels find peace until they have found some religious solution to the problems of the world. But all solutions are not equally good in providing peace to the disturbed soul.

This is where—after having established that all characters are religiously oriented—Buechner distinguishes between true religion and false idols: the true way to account for life and to live one's life, he says, is Christianity; Buddhism is his second choice. All other ideologies fail miserably because most are idolatries, serving the creature rather than the Creator, or the part for the whole.

These other ideologies are mainly tackled in *The Book of Bebb*. Some characters, like Tony, the jock, and Sharon, Antonio's loose-limbed wife, make the body their god; but they soon realize that their strength is ebbing, or even begin to wonder why they are keeping themselves fit. Health-worshippers like Sharon and Anita Steen are equally disappointed; they run a health-food store, but soon discover that vitamins and health food are no answer to the more basic and intricate problems of man. Moral causes are the ultimate concern of others. Antonio and his platonic friend Ellie give blood together, go on marches together, and swear to skin the crook Bebb alive, but soon Antonio comes to wonder, as Pilate did, "What is the truth?" Moral commitments do not fill the whole of man's longings. Still others try to manufacture other forms of religion, but sex proves to be disappointing when divorced from love, as does romantic love when severed from religious perspective. In addition, transcendental meditation, yoga, and belief in the salvation of humanity by interstellar scientific discoveries all fail to bring peace to the searching man.

Treasure Hunt speaks with particular eloquence on the false lure of magic. In this novel Buechner tries to underline the differences between religion and magic by comparing and contrasting Bebb's and Babe's ideals. Both believe in supernatural beings, Bebb in the Trinity and in angels, and Babe in men from outer space. Both also distinguish between the sacred and the profane and have convictions about man's relationship with the powers of the universe. But magic acts through coercion and compulsion: Babe imposes the force of his life-rays on Brownie and Antonio, forces his own dream on their minds. Religion, on the other hand, presupposes dependence and humility. Bebb never forces any of his own thoughts upon his followers; he prays to God for them, knowing that he may be only a channel of grace. Babe imposes his own self-serving will on Antonio and Brownie, whereas Bebb's desire is always for the good of others. While Babe manipulates, Bebb lets people be.

Having thus destroyed the common idols of America today, Buechner proceeds to load the dice for Christianity. All these idols point to man as *homo religiosus*, but none except Christianity can feed his hunger or quench his thirst. The heavy-laden must come to recognize it as the way, the truth, and the life, or be condemned to err, like the restless souls of Greek mythology. At the end of *Treasure Hunt*, Antonio is still one of these errant men, but he has acquired, almost despite himself, the theological virtues of charity and hope. Godric errs upon the seas until, having thrown off all but the love of God, he is given a home at Finchale. Buechner is clear in his message: man can love his neighbor, he comes to realize in *The Book of Bebb*, and even more clearly in *Godric*, only after he loves God. Sentimental love can be destructive, as witnessed by the guilty love of Bebb for Bert and that of Godric for Burcwen, and the ensuing tragedies.

For Buechner, Buddhism is a second-best option. In original Buddhism, Buechner likes the revolt against formalism, the vision of the stages of man's life, the importance placed on escaping from *karma*, and the dissolution of the self. But to these values he opposes the values of Christianity: Christ did not think of saving himself but of saving the world; Christianity believes in faith and in individual existence, whereas Buddha's ideal gives primacy to knowledge and the annihilation of the individual. But Buechner does recognize the value of detachment in his latest novel, *Godric*.

An offshoot of Buddhism also appears in disguise in the last two novels of *The Book of Bebb* in the character of Gertrude Conover, the octogenarian Theosophist. Mrs. Conover, a wealthy widow, lives in Princeton in a rich house, but is singularly detached from her possessions and her social status, so much so that she befriends

Bebb, a widower of much poorer extraction. The Christian apologist and the Theosophist share the idea that matter and spirit are both of God. They both believe that some unknown forces govern the behavior of man, and that man is destined to strive toward a more perfect manifestation of the divine characteristics latent in him. Yet whereas Gertrude would believe in the greater perfection of the mental body that thinks over the astral body that feels and desires, Bebb would override the distinction between feelings and intellect and put greater emphasis on trust in God.

Both believe that man must be freed from the law of cause and effect—*karma* for Gertrude—which can gradually be shed in the various reincarnations of a given soul as it needs a new body in which to act. Thus Gertrude believes that her gardener Callaway is the reincarnation of the Pharaoh, and she explains at the end of *Open Heart* that she herself was Uttah, the ward of the Pharaoh who fell in love with the priest of Ptah, reincarnated in Bebb. In *Treasure Hunt*, her finer perceptions tell her that Jimmy Bob Luby, the poor blind child, is another reincarnation of Bebb; she bases this belief on Callaway's nosebleeds, which occurred each time Bebb was around and reoccur at the approach of the child. Thus the soul is perfected from one reincarnation to another.

For the Christian Bebb, the liberation from the law of cause and effect is achieved in the process of transformation by grace, especially at the time of confession. This process is best exemplified in the transformation of Nancy Oglethorpe. Thus, instead of destroying the individual, Christianity affirms his value. He is best perfected in his obedience to God's laws.

Finally, Theosophy appeals to Buechner because it has annexed the notion of sacrifice, alien to original Buddhism but developed in popular Buddhism's idea of the Bodhisattva. In *Treasure Hunt*, Gertrude Conover explains that some of the perfected beings have given up the privilege of entering into Nirvana in order to come and help their brothers in distress. All selfish thought has been banished from their hearts. Earlier, in *Love Feast*, she shows Bebb the path to love. She turns his feelings away from anxiety and depression about home and personal happiness to compassion for the lonely students at Princeton who have no place to go for Thanksgiving dinner. In the selfless act of organizing the dinner,

Bebb is given his life again. Theosophy therefore seems to Buechner nearer the truth than original Buddhism, which was not based on belief in God and which taught the preservation of the self through total personal detachment. Christianity's emphasis on ontological reality, the sacredness of the individual and the importance of life, remains truer to reality.

Buechner addresses himself to the sophisticated and rational individual. Having asserted that all men are religious, that Christianity is their best existing option, he faces a third question: why, then, are there so many doubters—why are the majority of twentieth-century men doubters? The answer comes in *Lion Country*. Bebb's assistant, Brownie, whom Bebb supposedly raised from the dead, is Buechner's expositor. Brownie argues that he had been electrocuted and given up for dead, but that Bebb resuscitated him by praying in the room where he was laid out in Knoxville. Nevertheless, Bebb never became famous, never had a shrine erected in his honor. People, Brownie adds, do not want real miracles, which would shatter their self-confidence, their self-reliance, and their credal habits. Rather than give up their selves in trust to the loving God and confess their ignorance in the face of the complexity of the world, they suppress the religious in themselves and consequently are maimed.

Thus miracles are explained away. The agnostic's point of view is expressed by Antonio, who assumes that the whole thing was a mistake and that Brownie was not actually dead. People's unwillingness to believe in miracles reoccurs in two subsequent books. In *Love Feast*, Virgil Roebuck's crippled son does take a few steps at Bebb's command during a Love Feast, but the police barge in and the experiment is inconclusive. In *Treasure Hunt*, Callaway's nosebleeds, according to Gertrude Conover, are not the product of circumstances but of his meeting with the divine; but they never restore Brownie to his faith, nor do they instill faith in any of the other characters. As in *The Seasons' Difference*, Buechner concludes with the impossibility of communicating a religious experience. Man is free, at his own peril, to stifle his religious nature.

This theme is developed in *Godric*, where the point of view of the modern, rational agnostic or atheist does not exist. Buechner shows the strength of man's resistance to God's will. Godric has several visions of Saint Cuthbert or his hare on the island of Farne, and he recalls these visions several times, in his heart longing for the purer life. Still, he resists it with all his might; he becomes a pirate, a murderer, and a lecher until, by some uncommon grace, he is turned into Godric the ascetic and the saint. The grace of God works despite man, who cannot accept his double nature: earthly and divine. This is explained by Strasser in *The Entrance to Porlock*, as he teaches man to walk with "tree-foot" and "bird-foot." This theme of man's double nature pervades all of Buechner's novels, and also affects his style, which is too earthy for the holier-than-thou and too religious for the secular. But this style, especially in *The Book of Bebb* and *Godric*, is perfectly in keeping with Buechner's belief in the Incarnation. Christ for him is man as God meant him to be: "tree-foot," enjoying the creation, and "bird-foot," obeying the divine laws.

The Task of the Minister

The minister's role as a man of God is to remind his congregation of their divine creation and purpose, and to present to them the life of Christ and the dogmas of Christianity as he found they applied to his own life. His task is to show with stories derived from biblical and existentialist sources the development of God's Plot in each of our lives. The minister is not to be revered in himself, because he is himself growing on the path to God; but he is to be respected as one who points to a reality beyond himself which he tries to grasp in order to impart it to his charges. The primary duty of the minister, therefore, is to keep in contact with the revelation of the Word of God, both through the Gospel and through mystical union with the Creator. In his novels Buechner presents a whole range of ministers and men of God.

The minister is hardly a new figure in the world of literature. Goldsmith's eighteenth-century, unworldly vicar in *The Vicar of Wakefield* always comes to mind, but he has also been a familiar character in the modern novel. Horton Davies has shown the variety of such portraits:[9] preachers, evangelists, priests, ministers in crisis,

---

9. Horton Davies, *A Mirror of the Ministry in Modern Novels* (New York: Oxford University Press, 1959).

missionaries, and community leaders have been portrayed from the outside or from the inside, depending on the writer's sympathies and personal knowledge of the ministry. To Sinclair Lewis's bitter satire in *Elmer Gantry*, which he tried to soften in *The God-Seeker*, one can oppose, for instance, the inside view of the former Baptist minister, James Stewart, in *The Gauntlet*. Divines therefore appear in the work of writers as diverse as J. G. Cozzens, Mrs. Humphrey Ward, and Somerset Maugham, and recently in the work of Joyce Carol Oates, Iris Murdock, and Alan Paton. Peter De Vries, another contemporary writer, produced a wonderfully hilarious satire on the life of the modernists in the ministry in *The Mackerel Plaza*. The minister also appears in various forms in the work of such authors as Flannery O'Connor and John Updike. But on the whole, more has been done for the Catholic priest than for his Protestant counterpart, considering Graham Greene's *The Power and the Glory*, *The Heart of the Matter,* and *Monsignor Quixote*, and O'Connor's priest figures. Thus Buechner makes a unique contribution in his novels: he shows us Protestant ministers who are neither simplistic nor reduced to their own earthiness.

In all of his portrayals of men of God, both on the Protestant and on the Catholic scene, Buechner insists on their frailties. He does not attribute glory to any man of the cloth, because then he would be the hero, not God. Fools for Christ's sake or their own run across the screen. In *The Final Beast*, Nicolet is willing but immature; in *The Book of Bebb,* Antonio is shilly-shallying, Brownie, the homosexual, emasculates the Gospel, Bebb is an exposeur often tempted by greed, and Herman Redpath is a sex maniac; *Godric* presents a variety of such characters, from Bishop Flambard, who lusts for power and aggrandizement in the Church, and Godric, the former pirate, lecher, and murderer, to sweet Reginald, who probably joined the monastery because he had to edit a reality that frightened him.

Buechner resents congregations who make moral judgments about their pastors. His contention is that the grace of God can operate through the most unlikely vessels. In *The Book of Bebb* he opposes the narrator Antonio to the evangelist Bebb. The former is a chronic doubter, but a very nice man, morally sound, if one is to judge him by his exterior; the latter is an exposeur who has done time, tends to want to cheat the Internal Revenue Service, and runs a doubtful diploma mill for ministers. And yet, Buechner contends, Antonio's seeming morality is due to his shilly-shallying, to his lack of guts, whereas Bebb's slips come from an overflow of energy in a life that is made to be used for the glory of God and the love of his fellowmen. Buechner thus denies anyone the privilege of judging a man on the failings of his life.

The minister's duty is to try to obey the laws of God and to downplay himself, as Bebb does. Bebb wears a black gown when preaching, never speaks or thinks much about himself, but goes about God's service. Buechner's sympathies are with the extroverts like him.

However, one can trace through the novels an evolution in Buechner's thought: in his understanding of the second commandment, love for one's neighbor, he is increasingly influenced by the Buddhist notion of detachment. There is a great difference between the young Nicolet, who leaves his flock and his household to search for the lost sheep, and the hermit Godric, who would rather pray and love God. He no longer goes out to seek and anchor the lost soul, but waits for the lost souls to come to him. His effectiveness in the world no longer depends on activism but on the spiritual strength of meditation and prayer. As a young Christian, Buechner believed that the minister should be totally engaged in the world and the life of the congregation; as he has grown older he has come to appreciate the medieval unity of the ascetic and the mystical in the life of grace. Bebb is midway between these two extremes: he is still an entrepreneur, and quite an activist, but he is listening to heaven; to operate his retreat he occupies the basement of a New York building, away from the bustle of the streets. Godric, like Father Zossima in *The Brothers Karamazov,* has disengaged himself from such enterprises. For him the purgative, the illuminative, and the unitive stages of the ascetic life lead to greater purity in one's relationship to God. The soul is therefore freer to be fashioned by the Holy Spirit, who in turn will elevate it to a purer and truer union with God. In *Godric* one finds that Buechner has subtly come to understand the primacy of the first commandment, to love God, over the second commandment, to love one's neighbor. One could say that Buechner, once a Christian humanist, has become a deeper Christian.

The danger the minister encounters is becoming too absorbed in the affairs of the world and losing perspective. This is Nicolet's problem in *The Final Beast*; he has watched too many people dying of cancer. Unlike him, Bebb and Godric come to view the problems of the world with a certain amount of indifference, trusting that God tests with trials those whom he loves best. When Antonio is dying to talk to Bebb about his marital problems, Bebb does not let him explain his difficulties and abstains from counseling him. But he does check on Antonio from time to time, offering him care and a task to take his mind off his worries.

Another danger awaiting the minister is wanting the love of his congregation. Nicolet is still at this stage; he is especially fragile because he has just lost his wife in a terrible car accident. For this reason he is rather concerned about the slanders that Poteat spreads when he joins Rooney in Muscadine, and feels he has to explain his need to get away. In contrast, Bebb never apologizes and never explains. Symbolically, he goes about his task alone. His wife does not understand him, nor does his assistant Brownie. His strength comes only from God, and he does what he has to do without seeking approval. Godric operates in a similar fashion.

Another false lure of the ministry is wanting worldly goods for one's church or denomination. Nicolet is fairly free of this sin, but it attacks Bebb occasionally and plagues Bishop Flambard constantly. The paucity of people attending his congregation never really bothers Bebb, as it does other ministers, but when Herman Redpath dies Bebb is lured by visions of wielding power and having crowds attend his church. Greed for power and influence dictate the life of Flambard, who has an entrepreneur's eye and always wants to build bigger and better.

The treasures of the minister, says Buechner, are not in the world but in heaven, in the conversion of a sinner like Nancy Oglethorpe, in bringing a strayed sheep back home. A minister's treasure is the knowledge that God grants him of the world and of humanity, which he can then share with his congregation. To receive this the minister must always stay tuned to God's frequency. Such an image is used in *Love Feast* in *The Book of Bebb*: Golden, God's messenger, and

Bebb, when working in the basement of the building in New York City, keep their radios tuned to hear the messages God has to give them. These messages usually concern people in distress whom they must help.

Pride is usually another of the minister's pitfalls, because the congregation often looks up to him for advice and treats him as a demigod. Humility, the willingness to learn from others, saves a minister from disaster. In *The Final Beast* and *The Book of Bebb*, the heroes show a particular willingness to learn, especially from the opposite sex. Nicolet is reminded of the power of prayer by Lillian Flagg; Bebb recovers his altruism through Gertrude Conover, and learns about psychological devices to be used in the service from Nancy Oglethorpe. At all times in his career, the minister must remember the earthen, flawed, and fallible vessel that he is.

The minister's duties are usually threefold: he must counsel his parishioners, conduct the regular services, and preach the Word, as well as administer the two sacraments and other special ordinances such as ordination, marriage, and burial. Buechner emphasizes the preaching of the Word.

In *The Final Beast* and *The Entrance to Porlock*, both Nicolet and Strasser try to counsel adults; but whereas Nicolet uses a direct approach, Strasser uses an approach resembling that of the psychologist in private or group encounters. Bebb in *The Book of Bebb* has given up on counseling; when his daughter and Antonio separate, he merely prays for the two young people. In *Godric*, the only counseling scene is that of the lewd woman who has to be rebuked. Apparently Buechner has gradually de-emphasized the importance of personal counseling; the sermon is enough. In it the minister opens the Sacred Book and that of his own life. Let those who have ears hear and apply the wisdom themselves.

The minister is also required to be present at various stages of man's life and to administer the sacraments of baptism and the Lord's Supper. In *The Final Beast* Nicolet's main occupation is burial. Bebb, too, performs burial services: he presides at Herman Redpath's ceremony, and his assistant Brownie helps him with his wife's funeral. Bebb also performs marriages—one is that of Trionka, the Indian Lady—but his main function is ordaining ministers. At the ordination of Herman Redpath, Bebb calls for the gifts of charity, faith, worldly wisdom, and healing, indicative of Buechner's basic requirements of a minister. Bebb's willingness to ordain anyone who applies shows that Buechner basically believes in the priesthood of all believers. But Bebb limits ordination to men only. Does this reflect Buechner's own belief, or is this part of his satire of the fundamentalists? Buechner avoids discussing the issue.

Conveying God's pardon is one of the essential tasks of the minister, a duty that Nicolet overlooks at first, but that Bebb takes to heart. The twentieth century is overladen with guilt, and joy has often disappeared from it, as witnessed by most of our modern literature. The minister must bring peace to troubled spirits. Nicolet lays his hands on the adulteress Rooney, and she is infused with peace; Bebb welcomes Nancy Oglethorpe, and she is energized. At the time of his death, Godric feels the need to ask forgiveness from Reginald, whom he has bullied and insulted, but strength fails him and he dies, hoping for God's pardon. Clearly penitence plays an important role in Buechner's fiction.

The Lord's Supper appears in many novels, though not in *The Final Beast*. Like any other supper, it is an occasion to reunite people, give thanks for the fruit of the earth, and remember Jesus. In *The Entrance to Porlock*, a family gathers at a birthday meal, but the spirit is not there; all bear grudges toward each other, and the supper is deprived of its sacramental quality. The earth can be enjoyed only by the meek. The flustered Alice, who later comes to some realization of her inner complexity, enjoys at last the piece of bread that Strasser gives her. *Love Feast* best expresses Buechner's views on the Lord's Supper. The feasts Bebb gives are inspired by the Great Banquet rather than by the Last Supper; the latter meal has a graver aspect. Are these feasts also deprived of the supper's sacramental quality? Buechner would argue that they are not. Substituting pretzels and spiked Tropicanas for the bread and wine is just a matter of form; they prove the minister's ability to adapt to the new generation. But the spirit of Jesus is maintained.

Love Feast is as close as Buechner has ever come to showing the minister as conductor of the complete service of Word and sacrament. Each of the Love Feasts is structured in a fashion similar to that of a Protestant service. Bebb first welcomes the students in the name of the Lord and each greets the other. Then he reminds them of God's wonderful gifts and preaches a sermon on the misery of man. Afterwards he exhorts them to repentance; every guest finds a partner, and confession takes place; the kiss of peace is exchanged (during one feast Bebb kisses a black man and Nancy Oglethorpe gives Antonio a chaste kiss on his hand); finally, each gives the other the symbolical elements, and all leave after thanking their host. In his desire for contemporaneity, Buechner strives to make the service relevant to the modern generation.

But for Buechner the culmination of the service is the sermon. This is the time when the minister attempts to translate the Word of God to men. Nicolet in *The Final Beast* shakes at the prospect of the task. The book opens on his discouragement at having to preach about the Holy Spirit, from whom he feels estranged. The whole book in some ways is the preparation for his sermon, which he is ready to deliver when he returns from Muscadine. But the Spirit works in other ways, and Irma Reinwasser steals the show when she interrupts him. With a renewed sense of the Holy Spirit, he resolves to open his own life to his congregation: to expose oneself is to show the measure of God's grace. Bebb proceeds with the same idea in some of his sermons. In *Open Heart*, his wife Lucille leaves the church because she is afraid that he may say too much and get them into trouble. In fact, Bebb is judicious in what he reveals about his life. He tells enough for his congregation to learn from, but does not reveal any intimate detail. Rather, his own life is the pit he plunges into to discover the amount of light that illuminates it and the energy that keeps it going. Bebb's sermons are always samples of the theories that Buechner sets forth in *Telling the Truth*: the misery of man, the surprise of God's grace, and the affirmation of the fairy tale that is true. Even *Treasure Hunt* recalls his sermon notes, the words that he spoke, as they are imprinted on Antonio's mind. Bebb's sermons are always biblical, and his speech itself is full of biblical quotations. Fundamentalist he may be, Buechner affirms, but the ministry is a full-time employment—one can never shed it. And the minister must never lose touch with the Word.

In the service of ordination for Herman Redpath, Bebb prays for one more gift for the minister, the gift of healing. In *The Final Beast* the young Nicolet never thinks much of healing until he is made wise by Lillian Flagg. She teaches him that healing and forgiveness go hand in hand. Spiritual and physical healing play a major role in *The Book of Bebb*. Brownie affirms in *Lion Country* that Bebb actually raised him from the dead through prayer. In *Open Heart*, Bebb attempts to revive his wife Lucille, but the morticians have already worked on her body, and he fails. In *Love Feast*, Bebb again tries to cure Roebuck's crippled son and orders him to walk, but an interruption makes the attempt inconclusive. The gift of healing is also given to Godric, who has, in addition, the gift of vision. Godric can anticipate men's deaths: he sees Perkin killed at war and women and children wrecked at sea. But he does not reveal his knowledge, for it is not good for the unwise to know the future.

Despite his faults and follies, the minister in Buechner's novels is always a positive force. In Bebb particularly, Buechner has answered the criticisms of Sinclair Lewis. Bebb might be tempted by self-aggrandizement, but he does not act upon idle dreams; his house is neglected and his car, a jalopy, has run too many miles. When, in *Open Heart*, he gets a comfortable house up North and a barn for a church, he knows neither happiness nor success. In fact, the rug is pulled out from under him: his wife dies, his daughter's marriage is rocky, and his new church is attended by even fewer people than attended his church in Armadillo. The world gives no dividends to Bebb.

Buechner also answers Lewis's charge in *The God-Seeker* that Christianity is a superstitious religion that even the Indians have rejected. Buechner starts by praising the wisdom of Indians. They have a better sense of ritual than modern man. The joking cousin always turns up at any critical event in the life of man, debunking pomposity and emotionalism by some comic trick. Thus man cannot take himself too seriously and is cut down to size. Indians have a much better sense of ritual at the time of death that enables the living to cope with the fearful moment and the dying to go on their way. In *Open Heart*, the shaking of the rattle accompanies Herman Redpath's death, a noise that imprints itself upon aging Antonio's imagination throughout this novel and also throughout *Love Feast*. Indians do not leave their dead unprovided for, but gird them for the journey they are to undertake. Thanks to the wisdom of ritual, Herman Redpath makes it to the happy hunting ground. In their wisdom, Indians allow for the ebb and flow of life; unlike the white stoic, they do not expect consistent behavior.

Ritual, Buechner affirms, might look superstitious, but in fact it translates some deep ingrained wisdom, inherited from years of experience. Indians are not fools but wise men, and they have, in fact, adopted Christianity, which they feel has superior wisdom. Bebb's church flourishes among them.

Sinclair Lewis had also taxed Christianity with sentimentalism. Buechner recognizes that some men of God, the Brownies and Reginalds of this world, give their faith a bad name. Neither of them can face the hard truth about the world. In *The Book of Bebb*, Buechner laughs at some modern exegetes who emasculate the Bible. They represent life as seen through rose-colored glasses— and Brownie is one of them. He translates "dog" as "poochie" in the story of the Syrophoenician woman, and resorts to historical criticism to "interpret" the Apostle Paul when he urges the Romans to heap coals of fire upon their enemy's head. For Brownie, this is a sign that God loves the enemy and wants to give him a feeling of warmth, because at the time of the instruction, people carried hot coals from the baker's on their heads, bringing them into the house to light a fire. Buechner laughs at the bland minister who will thus take the sting out of the Gospel. In *Godric*, Reginald is criticized along the same lines. Reginald betrays both Godric and God by editing and whitewashing the old pirate's life. He does so, he thinks, for the sake of the greater truth of God's saving and blessing some of his chosen. Nonsense, says Buechner: this just exalts the human spirit, not the Holy Spirit. Both Brownie and Reginald are discarded as heretics.

Buechner's favorite figures in the ministry are those of the parish priest, the evangelist, and the mystic, as exemplified respectively by Nicolet, Tom Ball (in *Godric*), and Bebb and Godric. These people keep the world in focus, tending their charges and trusting in the gifts that God has bestowed on them. As Buechner matures in faith, his desire to be united with God in the creation has increased. The young Nicolet is still irrationally involved in people's problems and hopes for a sign from God independent of the creation. Bebb and Godric to an even greater degree realize that God is to be revered through the creation. Vision is the supreme reward of the man of God, a vision that will help him to contend with the prob-

lems of evil, recognize the presence of God's grace, restore the err-
ing to the God-given path, and proclaim the joy of the Kingdom
to come. This is itself a "transcript" of the beatitude of eternity
experienced in time.

IV

The Influence of Secular Philosophy

. . . as the heathen man sayeth . . .
L. A. Sasek, *The Literary Temper of the English Puritans*

The unity of Buechner's work as Christian and as artist is stressed in many of his interviews and written works. In a 1971 issue of *Publishers Weekly*, he affirmed:

> Writing is a kind of ministry. I do not feel that I am doing much different in my preaching and in my writing. Both are designed to illuminate what life is all about, to get people to stop and listen a little to the mystery of their own lives. The process of telling a story is something like religion if only in the sense of having a plot leading to a conclusion that makes some kind of sense.[1]

In *Telling the Truth*, he claims that truth can only be translated by the language of metaphor, image, and symbol,[2] and that poets, playwrights, and novelists are the most powerful preachers of our times because they speak of the absence of God in our time and the helplessness of man.[3] And yet preachers, poets, playwrights, and novelists can only point to the truth, for they can speak only from their experience of it, from the corner of the world in which they are placed. They may speak of the truth and nothing but the truth, but they can never utter

---

1. Interview with Frederick Buechner in *Publishers Weekly*, March 29, 1971, pp. 11-12.

2. Frederick Buechner, *Telling the Truth* (New York: Harper & Row, 1977), p. 25.

3. Buechner, *Telling the Truth*, p. 44. Most existentialists like Sartre, Simone de Beauvoir, and Merleau-Ponty have stressed the closeness of literature and philosophy. See Edith Kern, *Existential Thought and Fictional Technique: Kierkegaard, Sartre, Beckett* (New Haven, Conn.: Yale University Press, 1970), p. 85.

the whole truth, for, Buechner asserts, ''at its heart, most theology, like most fiction, is essentially autobiography.''[4]

Buechner thinks that those who really believe that Jesus was both lamb and tiger, sun and rose of Sharon are but dunces; for him the Bible is both truth and metaphor. For this reason, in his theological works he does not hesitate to call upon literature to illuminate the text on which he preaches or the ideas that he expounds. *The Alphabet of Grace* contains references to Saint-Exupéry, G. K. Chesterton, and Mark Twain. *Wishful Thinking* alludes to Gertrude Stein and *Beauty and the Beast*. *Telling the Truth* offers us a rainbow of allusions to and citations from Shakespeare, Stephen Crane, Camus, Sartre, Gerard Manley Hopkins, Dostoevski, Tolstoi, Kierkegaard, C. S. Lewis, George MacDonald, Tolkien, Lewis Carroll, Frank Baum, and others. Nor is Buechner bashful about quoting from his own works. In *The Alphabet of Grace*, he refers to *The Final Beast* and *The Entrance to Porlock* to show the unpredictability of God's grace and the independence of the creation. In *Telling the Truth*, he describes students' sudden awareness of the wretchedness of man as they read *King Lear,* using his own rendering of the experience in *The Book of Bebb.*

One can therefore conclude that Buechner, who graduated from the English department of Princeton and was a writer before he ever was a Christian, is at least as much influenced by the world of literature as he is by theological thinkers. Predictably, for a man who refuses to be classified either as a theologian or as a thinker, the strong influence in his life is the existentialist philosophy developed by both Sartre and Camus.

Existentialism seems to have been born of the modesty acquired by twentieth-century man in his inability to find solutions for the world's problems, to trust in the all-powerful and loving God of Christianity, and even to know himself. Since the sixteenth century, man has offered a succession of possible solutions to the problems of the world— man as a whole being, reason, passion, and science—but these answers have all failed. Man, made modest, turned to the contemplation of his own existence as the only certainty he could grasp, and from observation tried to deduce some principles by which to live. Like

---

4. Frederick Buechner, *The Alphabet of Grace* (New York: Seabury Press, 1970), p. 3.

science, philosophy had shifted its primary principles once more from induction to deduction, from essence to existence. The post-existentialist school sank into complete pessimism. After Mauthner, they proclaimed the failure of language, communication, and absolutes, and the dissolution of the self. It is against this background that we must place Buechner, who has absorbed some of their philosophical concepts and rejected others.

The existentialist school affirms that since God is dead, or never existed, or at least is absent from the world, nothing can save us from death and destruction. In contemplating his death, man experiences anguish, an anguish that can lead him to suppress life itself in suicide. Kierkegaard, Heidegger, Jaspers, and Husserl, Danish and German philosophers, were all haunted by the concept of anguish.

All existentialists, however, stress that value is found in life itself. Sartre, the French theoretician of existentialism, affirmed that man is in the process of being formed, in the making. Man has freedom, a mixed blessing, since in any given situation he must choose his own destiny. In this concept appear both freedom and contingency, which Sartre has to unite as contraries; hence his assertion that man is condemned to be free. Since man is totally free to make choices that in turn shape his life, he is also fully and totally responsible for his own actions. Therefore he is the author of his own self. But he often prefers to behave like a stone or a vegetable in order to escape from the weight of his responsibility and to be alienated from his own future. Sartre's philosophy is clearly contradictory: he begins with the existence of man and concludes that his essence is an essential condition of his existence. Man totally free and totally responsible for his own actions cannot escape from the consequences of his doings and cannot rearrange his life according to imagined concepts to which he would be bound. Such bondage is religion, which presupposes looking toward the future instead of dealing with the present, and also gives man a preconceived idea of himself to which he must conform. Yet Sartre judges the characters in his novels and plays according to a norm. They appear as good or evil according to what they have done with their lives. This presupposes judgment and an essential view of life. Garcin in *No Exit* is a coward by Sartre's standards just as much as by the standards of what he would call the ''bourgeois mentality.''

Adverse as he was to oppression as he saw it in the bourgeois mentality, in fascism and capitalism, how could Sartre adhere to communism as he did? Communism, he thought, was a lesser evil. Eventually it would lead the world to be a freer and better place. Therefore one could sacrifice the present for future happiness and freedom, an idea that he had at first totally repudiated in the character of Electra in *The Flies*. For a time communism became Sartre's religion. Later, he rejected it: it had become as stilted as the concept he had of religion. But he stuck to the idea of violence as inevitable: from the total freedom of men sprang the necessity of collision between their varied self-interests. He found it impossible to reconcile individual freedom and mass solidarity.

Camus became divorced from Sartre when the latter became a communist. He believed that the present is to be enjoyed. He also believed that fate has a role to play in the existence of man, who is not completely responsible for all his actions. Life is to be encouraged at all costs. No present sacrifice will ensure a better future. Camus' philosophy evolved from an early realization of the absurdity of life to a later reaffirmation of almost Christian values, but without Christ.

In *The Myth of Sisyphus*, Camus insists on the absurd in life. Life for most men is a succession of habits. Camus believed that there is no profound reason for living and that life is but endless and aimless agitation until man finds a reason to polarize his activities. When man starts wondering about life's meaning, he is at a total loss for an answer. He realizes the strangeness of nature and the basic hostility of the world. His only certainty is the certainty of death; the contemplation of suicide reveals the true meaning of life. Intelligence tells him that the world is absurd, that is, irrational.

For Camus the absurd is the confrontation of the irrationality of the world and the rationality of man. Human drama is composed of the irrational of the creation, the nostalgia for the rational in man, and the feeling of absurdity.

Like Sartre, Camus refuses any temptation to succumb to escapism. Suicide is the suppression of man's consciousness; religion is looking to another world for compensations one does not find in this one; existentialist theologians like Kierkegaard, Jaspers, and Chestov try to create a god of the irrational. Camus insists that we must live with what we know. A healthy reaction to the world is to revolt, affirm our liberty, and live our lives passionately. Like Pascal, whose books he kept at his bedside, Camus affirms that the grandeur of man lies in the fact that he alone can face this truth. We must live confronting the absurd and ready to re-interpret the world. To avoid partisanship and narrow-mindedness, we must enlarge our experience of life, and be consumed in the process. We alone of all the creatures can defy death by living our lives to the fullest with complete lucidity.

Camus stressed the freedom of man, but disagreed with Sartre, who claimed that man is absolutely free. This, argued Camus, would imply some ontological existence of freedom. At least we can free ourselves from our bourgeois ideals and ideas. For we are in the world of absurdity. Lucidity frees us from the common rules, and we learn to live without appealing like cowards for forgiveness or mercy. Lucidity can be gained only through the multiplicity of existential experiences, designed to free us from inherited and now outmoded notions. Conversely, our capacity to enlarge the realm of our experience will depend on our degree of lucidity.

The logical result of this philosophy should be the praising of a world like that in Anthony Burges's *A Clockwork Orange*, in which even murder should be one of the enlarging experiences of the free man. But the heart is against it for reasons unknown to reason itself, and Camus, like Sartre, rejects amoralism. He advocates yea-saying, morality, and the fostering of life, and will not condone Ivan Karamazov's ''all is allowed.'' Man is an aim in himself to himself, and humanity must be served. Sisyphus knows that he will die, but his joy consists in pushing his rock as high as he can and in helping others in the process. Stoicism and human love are enough to fill the heart of man; therefore all is well.

This philosophy is exemplified in *The Plague*, in which Doctor Rieux finds an aim for his existence in succoring the plague-ridden population and relieving the suffering around him. The expression of this philosophy falls short in Camus' last novel, *The Fall*. There the world is no longer divided into yea-sayers and nay-sayers but is made up of creatures of varied grays. Clamence feels the need for confession but can never be redeemed; he has lost the innocence of the first stages of life. Unable to choose between different philosophies, Clamence views life from the balcony, which eventually leads to the destruction of the individuals he preys on. Unfortunately, *The Fall* was Camus' last novel; he was killed in a car accident a few years after he finished it.

Buechner is not the only modern writer to have profited from the philosophy of Sartre and Camus. Aimlessness and restlessness have been fully exploited in the plays and novels of Samuel Beckett, in the plays of Eugene O'Neill and Tennessee Williams, and in the novels of John Updike, Robertson Davies, and others. But Buechner acknowledges the influence of these men on his own work, whether he accepts their ideas or refutes them, and it is appropriate to see what part they have played in his writing from 1970 to 1980.

Like Camus and Sartre, Buechner agrees that full appreciation of life comes to the adult only after he has confronted his own finitude and come to terms with it. The preciousness of life can be fathomed only by the middle-aged person who has experienced the tragedy of death. In *The Brothers Karamazov*, Alyosha kisses the earth only after the shock of finding that his beloved Zossima's body is decomposing like any other body. In *The Final Beast*, Nicolet becomes weary and run-down a year after his wife's death; suddenly his ministry seems empty and senseless. And yet the forces of life are reasserting themselves in him as he feels increasingly attracted to Rooney Vail, and as he finds new ways of exercising his ministry. In *The Entrance to Porlock*, Peter Ringkoping and his family come to value their land at the time when they are ready to give it away. In *The Book of Bebb,* the restless Antonio learns the value of life from his sister Miriam, who is dying in agony, and Bebb finds a new surge of energy after the low of mourning his wife's death. Godric's first realization of the preciousness of life occurs when he nearly drowns in the river's mouth, carving a great fish for his family; yet he answers the voice of selfish grasping until, like Macbeth, he has waded in blood and perpetrated death to surfeit. Full appreciation of life comes to him later.

Thus the mature man develops a love for life out of his horror for death. The process, nevertheless, is painful. Faced with their death, people experience anguish. The healthy seize their lives, which they live more fully and positively after a time of crisis. But all are not survivors; some cannot make the adjustment and live in hell. In *The Final Beast*, Irma, the tortured Jew, has become a misanthropist and curses God, despite the change for the better in the circumstances of her life. Lucille Bebb in *The Book of Bebb* is another character unable to reach contentment; unable to accept forgiveness, she lives a life of shame, retreating behind dark glasses and drinking herself into a stupor, until one day she summons up enough strength to do away with herself.

The temptation of physical or mental suicide pervades Buechner's novels; it is a way of alleviating the anguish we feel once we are confronted with our own limitations, finitude, and destructiveness. Physical ailments and mental sickness are interrelated. Unable to live like "the lilies of the field" or like children, we stop life within ourselves and others. In *The Entrance to Porlock*, the schoolchild Mullavey is driven to suicide by "squares" who deny the genuineness of his mystical experience. In *The Book of Bebb*, trigger-happy Roebuck shoots at anything living in sight. Sometimes Buechner explains why his characters are warped; at other times he only describes the effects. Hypochondriacs are strewn like fading flowers in his creations, while those who have some guts can look back, face themselves, accept pardon, and live anew. In *The Final Beast*, Metzger and Irma are contrasted with Rooney, Nicolet's father, and Poteat, who in various degrees are given a second chance and accept it. In *The Book of Bebb*, hypochondria, homosexuality, and promiscuity are all classified under the label of psycho-physical illnesses of maladjusted individuals. In *Godric*, the character Elric suffers from raving dementia. Death is the price of evil; death-in-life is in those cases the effect of evil on characters.

For Sartre there is no such thing as partial suicide, and each character is fully responsible for the way he reacts to circumstances. Buechner maintains the tension between contingency and absolute freedom. Sartre's position supposes equal intelligence and lucidity in all human beings, a position that Buechner cannot accept. Influenced as he is by modern psychology, he looks into men's past for reasons for their misdoings. An unhappy love affair, a childhood spent in an orphanage, cruelty, a birth defect, or a single instance of foolishness can warp the individual; contempt and hatred are failures of the imagination. In *The Book of Bebb*, after his violent encounter with his enemy Virgil Roebuck, Bebb suddenly notices the lines on Virgil's face, his compulsive cigarette smoking, and his failure to live up to his given name. His anger is suddenly transformed into compassion, and he says: " ' . . . we are far from home, all of us are. Who's going to judge which of us has got the farthest way to go through the shit and the dark?' "[5]

---

5. Frederick Buechner, *The Book of Bebb* (New York: Atheneum, 1979), p. 353.

Without discarding the notion of responsibility, Buechner adheres to Camus' hatred of judges and judges-penitent. A second argument against such an absolute notion of responsibility is man's difficulty in perceiving the truth, which we shall explore later. A third argument is the unforeseeability of the consequences of our actions: *Godric* affirms that many a bad deed has been done for love, and, conversely, that some bad deeds have produced the fruits of beauty and strength. Here Buechner introduces the notion of mystery and grace against the Pelagianism of such philosophies. We are responsible for our actions insofar as we can perceive the difference between good and evil and obey the commands of God. But we cannot control the world.

It is Buechner's intimate conviction that people are always given a second chance if they wait long enough, and that they have no cause for despair. Characters in his novels are often paired according to their response to life's opportunities. Either they let them slip by, or they grab at a new lease on life. In *The Final Beast*, both Rooney and Poteat are adulterers, but she looks for something positive to do, whereas he has to face the result of his own destructiveness, Irma's death, to accept the hand extended to him. The same opposition occurs in *The Book of Bebb* between Bebb and Babe, but the antithesis is subtler here than in *The Final Beast*. Buechner affirms that forgiveness springs from the realization that no heart is pure. Bebb's capacity to forgive Lucille for the murder of their son comes from his own awareness of guilt as an adulterer. Babe, Bebb's twin brother, is incapable of such generosity, because he wallows in resentment and self-righteousness.[6]

For Buechner as for Sartre, action is what shapes the life of man. ''Do good'' is Cuthbert's injunction to Godric; whatever you feel, do good. Like the existentialist philosophers, Buechner insists on the importance of the will. In *The Final Beast*, Irma, who is a pessimist, and Nicolet, who is more of an optimist, both do good despite temptations to do otherwise. In *The Book of Bebb*, the de-

---

6. Buechner insists on the possibility of choice. In *Love Feast*, Antonio oscillates between the two solutions. When he discovers that his wife and his nephew Tony have had sexual intercourse, he is devoured by jealousy. Yet when the two of them have been apart for a while, and Antonio learns that Sharon might be expecting Tony's child, he is able to forgive her and raises the child as if she was his own.

pressed Bebb regains his composure and his *joie de vivre* when (in *Love Feast*) he organizes a Thanksgiving party for the lonely students of Princeton University. Nancy Oglethorpe, the reformed nymphomaniac, becomes a superb church secretary. In his wisdom, Bebb knows that Antonio, who is going through a marital crisis, and his own wife, who is a manic depressive, need tasks to perform. Even old man Godric, locked in his cell, is given a task: many come and seek him out, and he has to open the book of his life to be recorded for posterity. Action makes the man good as the good man acts righteously.

Yet unlike Camus and Sartre, Buechner does not think that salvation lies solely in the hands of man. He believes that God holds the reins of man's destiny. The unaided are bound to slip, like the austere monk who suddenly succumbs to lechery.[7] Bebb's efforts at the end of *Love Feast* all prove failures. On the other hand, those who are guarded and prudent in life, who take no risks, end up far worse than those who struggle and err. Like Antonio and Brownie, they lack courage; they are the pussy footers of the world.

Buechner has no time for those who refuse to soil their hands, who prefer to abstain from the messy business of life. But, like Sartre, he also distrusts the busybodies who meddle in other people's lives. We have seen how he came to dismiss the importance of direct counseling. In *The Book of Bebb*, Bebb has no time for Antonio's confidences. It is up to Antonio to face himself and sort out his marital problems, and time will heal his wounds.[8] Similarly,

---

7. From *The Book of Bebb*, p. 26: "As long as they are on their guard, they are safe. . . . But take them by surprise, let the temptress leap out unexpectedly from behind a piece of temple statuary, and in case after case the game is lost. All the vast quantities of psychic energy that they have accumulated at such enormous cost through life after life of total abstinence are released in an instant to be squandered in one great orgy that may go on for centuries. It is a tale with both its comic and its tragic dimensions."

8. When Antonio is trying to pray to Miriam, his dead sister, to ask her for advice, she answers him when he is half-awake:

"What do I do for Christ's sake? Do I tell her I know or pretend I don't? Do I send him back to Charlie? Do I ask for a divorce? Do I wait till I catch them in the act and take care of them both with one bullet? Do I play it like wop opera or like Noel Coward or don't I play it at all?"

"You're the boss," she said, moving on as if I was after a dime for a cup of coffee. (*The Book of Bebb*, p. 189)

Godric's function is to heal. He foresees the future, but is wise enough not to reveal it to the unwise. It is not for another individual to try to shape a man in the making. Babe, who tries to manipulate Antonio and Brownie, is a fake and a magician, one of the death-wishers of the world.

Unlike Sartre, who was ready to sacrifice the here and now for the hope of a better society based on communism at the price of violence, Buechner will sacrifice neither the present nor any individual. The Kingdom of God can be reached now through the community of loving Christians, who care for each other in humility, forgive each other, and accept each other's diversity with the knowledge that basically they all have the same need for food, for love, and for a task to perform. Camus reached basically the same conclusion in *The Plague*. Yet Camus' point of view changed, and so has Buechner's. In *The Plague*, Dr. Rieux and Tarrou are good humane characters, univocal, like Nicolet in *The Final Beast* or even Strasser in *The Entrance to Porlock*. But Camus' *The Fall*, like *The Book of Bebb* and *Godric,* shows new awareness: good actions do not necessarily come from pure hearts.

Buechner also adds that the road to hell is paved with good intentions. This becomes more obvious in his last two books, *Treasure Hunt* (in *The Book of Bebb*) and *Godric*. Brownie, Bebb's assistant, dies of a heart attack, not only because of the positive evil caused by Babe the impersonator, but also because Antonio, his well-wisher, who has discovered Babe's masquerade, is unable to act to warn Brownie or protect him. In *Godric*, the final separation of Godric and his sister occurs as their love leads to incest. Lack of control mars the saint, like Graham Greene's whiskey priest. Sartre would quote all of these instances as examples of *mauvaise foi*, bad faith; Buechner is kinder, though he deplores the human predicament.

But Buechner and Sartre would share a view of our lives as dynamic, as changing from birth to death. Man in the making is the subject of all of Buechner's novels. In *The Final Beast*, Nicolet learns to be a minister while his father learns to be a grandfather and Rooney learns to be a better wife. Other examples can be given, but this theme joins the theme of transformation which we have studied before.

Like Camus, Buechner believes that life becomes absurd when it is mechanical and when it has lost its significance. In *The Final Beast*, Nicolet needs to get away from the ministry, if only for a weekend, because his work has become meaningless. In *The Entrance to Porlock*, family relationships have become predictable: at the birthday party the old boy will dwell on his coming death and will tell his usual story about the ghost; Tommy will play some goofy trick; Alice will manage to lose some object in order to look for it and escape the boredom of the whole affair and of her own marriage; Nels will sit through the festivities, wondering when he can get back to his school. All assume that they know what to expect of the event and of one another; the birthday party is as stale as some of Ionesco's dialogues. Such life is doomed to be absurd. The staler characters remain blocked until some event shatters them, while the more alive, like Nicolet in *The Final Beast*, the adolescent Tip in *The Entrance to Porlock*, and Sharon in *The Book of Bebb*, try to ask the ultimate question about life and its meaning.

Like Camus, Buechner notes the failure of man's intelligence to account for life, but, unlike Camus, he does not oppose the irrationality of the world to the rationality of man. For Buechner man is a creature possessed by irrational forces that he cannot account for. Bebb, despite himself, is an exposeur; Godric to the end of his life will insult Reginald, though he regrets his impatience.

For Buechner the tragedy of life lies in the impossibility of man's accepting the world or himself and his inability to surrender to mystery. Camus wants man to revolt, whereas Buechner urges acceptance of the laws of the creation, trusting that they are for the best. Rebellion leads to sin and estrangement. Of the kinds of rebellion man wages, adultery and bitterness are Buechner's main targets. The bitter, like Poteat in *The Final Beast* and the IRS man and Virgil Roebuck in *The Book of Bebb*, hate the creation out of their deep anger against God or themselves. In Buechner's world, freedom is conditional. The choice is an existential one: man is free to choose for life or for death, for heaven or for hell. Man is free, but only to obey the laws of life and growth or to deny them at his own risk. Thus the prisoner who follows the laws of God, like Bebb, is freer than the compulsive and unattached Antonio. The path of life is not easy: we fumble along the road, hindered by our own blindness and waywardness.

Camus urges us to live our lives passionately, that is, to multiply experiences. Buechner is of two minds on this matter. He prefers the passionate, like Godric or Nancy Oglethorpe in *The Book of Bebb*, to the prudent, who have never tested the way of the world and tasted its disappointment. On the other hand, this testing and tasting are but a waste of time, the way of waywardness. In *The Book of Bebb*, Sharon tries sex, motherhood, yoga, health food, the guitar, and speed-reading for self-fulfillment, but never finds contentment and peace. Buechner's point is that we should give up prying into the mystery of things and concentrate instead on what has been revealed to us and the task set in front of us.

Buechner's insistence upon obedience to the revealed Word springs from his fundamental distrust of human judgment. This basic skepticism is in keeping with the modern trend of thought, from Mauthner to the present. Our knowledge is only subjective, memory is but the rearrangement of the past to suit the present, and language is treacherous. Sartre insists on the presence of opposites which are locked in continual warfare, but he leaps from nihilism to faith by an arbitrary choice for life and progress. Camus, having affirmed that the world is absurd, still advocates stoicism and love. Buechner, convinced of man's inability to find the truth without revelation, goes to the Bible for inspiration.

Like Camus, Buechner starts from the principle that absolute truth kills. In the name of truth, human beings judge, label, and libel each other and deny each other the possibility of change and growth. Families are particularly prone to boxing each other in this way. In *The Entrance to Porlock*, the flow of communication between family members has stopped. All regress to their given roles. The doors are closed in their lives, and they are closing doors on others, so the novel presents us with an almost Kafka-like world.

The subjectivism of this so-called "absolute truth" that each of us erroneously claims to have is expounded in *The Book of Bebb*.[9]

---

9. In *The Entrance to Porlock* (New York: Atheneum, 1970), Tip expresses this in so many words: "When it came to other people, you could never be sure what was true about them and what was your own invention"

Ellie, Antonio's platonic friend, shows Antonio a newspaper cutting about Bebb exposing himself to children. The dynamics of their reaction to this piece of news is typical of man's subjectivism. Ellie is at first morally indignant. But Antonio, whose sister is dying and whose cat is sick, reacts with even greater violence; this is for him the occasion to voice his anger against the world and against suffering. He resolves to expose Bebb and skin him alive. Ellie, meanwhile, who has found appeasement for her own aggressive feelings in Antonio's anger, expresses compassion for the man. He should be pitied, she says, because he must be sick. Later, when Antonio has found some satisfaction in life, in sexual union with Bebb's daughter, Sharon, his desire to expose Bebb subsides. He then wants to rearrange the truth, to deny that Bebb ever exposed himself and assume that all was a misunderstanding. Thus man's apprehension of the truth often depends on the circumstances of his life.[10]

The world is full of conflicting truths, the many voices that assault a young man like Godric. In Buechner's novels opposite views of life are often expressed through opposing characters: Nicolet and Poteat, respectively the bearers of good and bad news in *The Final Beast*; Penrose and Nels, representing mercy and judgment in *The Entrance to Porlock*; Bebb and Babe or Virgil Roebuck in *The Book of Bebb* and Godric and Elric in *Godric*. In each case the first character tends to take a lenient and affirming view of life, whereas the second is more rigid and condemnatory. Buechner prefers the former to the latter, the planters and growers of seeds in God's garden to the weeders and pruners.

(p. 56). The idea is developed in chapter 7, when Nels sees the ferryman as either his nephew Tip or as Mullavey, the young student he knew who committed suicide.

Furthermore, the old Peter Ringkoping confesses that he never saw people for what they were, but only as shadows. Of his sons he thinks: "It had never been the boys themselves who had interested him particularly except as they were clues to the mystery of himself" (p. 130).

10. See particularly *The Book of Bebb*, pp. 14-15, 19, 29, 82, 119, and 165 among others. Subjectivism is also the basis of the feud between Penrose and Nels in *The Entrance to Porlock*: Nels believes that he is just in punishing the boys, but he is often repressing some hidden anger and taking it out on them. The other teacher resembles the priest of Mauriac's *A Woman of the Pharisees*; he cajoles the boys because he wishes he had a son of his own.

In *Siddhartha*, Hermann Hesse asserts that no truth can be affirmed without realizing that the opposite is equally true. Buechner would agree that this applies to particular truths, but that *The* Truth is to be found in Christ, the life-affirmer. Antonio is the picture of modern man, shilly-shallying between particular truths and lacking vision, though he is gradually brought to Bebb's position of affirming life. For Buechner the solutions given by Sartre and Camus to the problem of existence are still particular truths. Sartre's emphasis upon freedom denies the fact that we are all meant to follow the same path in life. Buechner believes in pre-existing order and harmony. Camus had stressed the importance of lucidity; Buechner is less elitist. Obedience is enough. Camus had underlined the value of stoicism and love and the triumph of the human spirit. Through the character of Bebb, Buechner shows that in dejection the human spirit is broken and past mending unless a healer infuses it with strength. The human spirit cannot resurrect itself.

Solutions like those of Camus and Sartre still suppose a linear view of life as opposed to a dialectical one. Sartre, however, had rightly affirmed the simultaneity of opposites in the world and in man's life. For Buechner, Christianity accounts fully for the double nature of man as both good and evil; but the destiny of man is perfectly fulfilled in the unity of divine and human in the personality of Christ. The mature man must take a stand for Christ or perish, though vision does not come to all at the same time. In *The Book of Bebb*, Antonio first holds a linear view of life, then bogs down into holding two views simultaneously without being able to reconcile them, and is finally brought, willy-nilly, to take a stand for life.

Symbolically, Antonio has the same problems with language that he has in grasping the basic truth. Sartre had explained his distrust of language in *Words*. Wittgenstein and Mauthner had increased suspicion about the possibility of verbal communication. But none of them, of course, could refrain from writing. The same is true of Antonio, who, unlike Grand in *The Plague*, can get past the first sentence, but who can't read beyond page thirty of a book at the beginning of *The Book of Bebb*. Antonio, the chronic doubter, is never sure whether he sees or hears right. Did Bebb say "see me" or "semen" when he was exposing himself? Is "A" for *alleluia* or *amen*?

Does Herman Redpath speak of "butt" or "button" at the end of his life? Antonio stresses the difficulty of communication between people, and suggests other, equally eloquent forms of communication. Lucille's language is similar to cartoons—her words frame silences—and Callaway the black servant is totally incomprehensible to him. Sometimes circumstances interrupt the speech of revelation; the listener is then at fault. This occurs many times in *Open Heart*. Antonio often cannot concentrate hard enough to know what Bebb has said. In a passage very similar to some of the scenes in Godard's films, the noise of a passing train blankets an important revelation from Golden, from whom Antonio is trying to extract information about the missing Lucille.

Language, Buechner affirms in his maturity, does fail. The simpler it is, the better it is. But the truth can still be grasped despite silences, lies, and dressing up. It comes out of actions or dreams, not out of words. It also comes out of the convergence of testimonies. In *Treasure Hunt*, Buechner sensed that he might have driven himself into an impasse by agreeing to the subjective philosophy of today. If words fail, if memory reinterprets the past at will, if images are partial, how then could you defend the veracity of the Gospel? All Bebb's friends, twelve of them, in fact, come together at the end of *Love Feast*, and some of them get together in *Treasure Hunt*; each had a different opinion of Bebb, but all agree that where he was, life was there, too. All sensed that he was sustained by a life-force, and therein lies the truth about him.

Buechner's heroes use words sparingly, whereas doubtful characters are often journalists, writers, or talkers. Most of them are attacked by self-doubt. In *The Final Beast*, Poteat wonders whether he is not a fake, living his life by proxy, while the good Nicolet plunges, like Bebb in *The Book of Bebb*, into the sweaty center of things. Antonio is laughed at, loaded down as he is by the clutter of his literacy. Peter Ringkoping in *The Entrance to Porlock* is another such character, surrounded by books and unable to cope with family relationships. In *Godric*, Reginald, the writer and editor of Godric's life, shuns reality by whitewashing the picture of the man.

Words are deceitful. During their first encounter, Sharon tells Antonio three lies in order to protect her family. In *Open Heart*, as

Bebb rejoices over Herman Redpath's legacy and, like the milkmaid of the fable, dreams of wealth and power, Golden, the mysterious messenger, leaves him a cryptic message: "Good luck, sweetheart"; is it encouragement or a threat?

Action indicates the truth. In *The Book of Bebb*, T.V. is better watched with the sound turned off because apologies or explanations tend to twist the truth. In *The Entrance to Porlock*, Strasser the wise man hardly talks, but he organizes situations in which people break down and are healed. Bebb is perpetually involved in new schemes and plans to help others, whereas Antonio is wordy and ineffectual. Godric, who is reluctantly relating the story of his life, sticks to the facts. Words, Buechner affirms in *Telling the Truth*, are only there to frame the truth, to attract attention to it, not to explain or replace it. After Wittgenstein, Mauthner, and others, Buechner affirms that meaningful language is fact. Chaucer said it many years before: "The word must be cosin to the deed." Still, it is refreshing, after the garrulousness of the Romantics, to see the needle once more turning toward clarity and concision. There is a salutary return to *art engagé*, art involved in the struggles of the world rather than art for art's sake.

Language has anagogical value. The language of metaphor is the best way to recount the truth. Secular and sacred literature, art of good or bad quality—all point to the eternal and universal truth. In *The Book of Bebb*, Gertrude Conover speaks it through *The Oxford Book of Verse*, whereas the fundamentalist Bebb quotes the Bible to answer most human situations.

In a tragicomic episode in *Open Heart*, Antonio phones Brownie to try to find out whether he has found the missing Lucille, Bebb's demented wife, or even heard of her. Brownie, who has sworn to keep silent about her whereabouts, still wants to reassure the distressed family. He uses the biblical text to reveal that Lucille is with him and that they should come quickly. Once more the Bible serves as both disguise for and revelation of the truth.

The Book of Bebb is particularly eloquent about the possibility of using various languages to express the same basic existential truth. Bebb uses biblical language; Antonio employs the drawn-out language of a mediocre introvert, making references to literature and cinematography; Herman Redpath praises life in vivid and chthonic terms; Lucille leaves out the mystery by turning every statement into a question; and Golden both paints the life of Bebb and philosophizes about time and space. All these forms of language are valid, whether sophisticated or crude, pictorial, musical, or literal. The sentimental picture of the boy fishing in the pool in *Treasure Hunt* tells the truth as forcibly as the more sophisticated El Greco; popular songs are as truthful as Mozart. For Buechner, all is one, though he certainly does not go out of his way to write inferior literature, but chisels and refines his prose. All point to the same existential truth.

Thus, for Buechner, the truth can be perceived. Like all other existentialists, Buechner stresses ultimate commitment and lack of wisdom in particular commitments. His Christian philosophy is more empiric than systematic, but he does not share the existentialists' disappointment in rationalism. For Buechner the truth is whole, both rational and emotional. Whereas Camus and Sartre had reasserted first principles in asserting human freedom or stoicism and love, Buechner reasserts supernaturalism, the existence of guiding forces outside human control. Like Camus and unlike Sartre, he reunites the individual and the social through the salvation of all individuals, who are not to be sacrificed to an ideology of futurism. He believes that there is a genuinely existentialist message in the New Testament, capable of overcoming any sense of the tragic and asserting the possibility of an authentic human existence.

Some existentialists have taken into account the discoveries of psychiatry. Jaspers even practiced psychiatry, but he attacked Freud for being over-deterministic. Sartre, with his emphasis on human freedom, was bound to take the same view, but his sense of the reification of the person by others has been taken up by many modern philosophers and psychologists. Buber in *I and Thou*, which has inspired so many theologians of today, stresses the importance of interpersonal relationships in a world where machines (and now computers) put heavy emphasis on output and outcome. Buechner echoes such concerns in *The Entrance to Porlock*, *The Book of Bebb*, and *Godric*. In *The Entrance to Porlock*, Nels and Alice have a quantitative approach to life. Nels condemns Mullavey because his sensitivity does not conform to the ideal pattern set for the majority of students. Alice does not understand the sentimental value of the Ringkoping land, but sees only the possibility of income from its sale. Tip, the young adolescent in search of himself, is still flexible. He is still capable of projecting himself into the minds of others, whereas the adults have classified each other, boxing each other in until grace liberates them.

In *The Book of Bebb*, Nancy Oglethorpe has also been reified: the students she sleeps with have used her as a commodity, a sex object with no soul of her own. When she renounces her previous life, she becomes a person again. The same is true in *Godric* of the wife of the Lord de Granville; married at the age of twelve, she is both an object to be displayed by her husband and a means of getting children. Since she has not succeeded in conceiving, she is treated brutally by the one who should love and encourage her.

As we have seen, Buechner owes much to Freud in his depiction of evil characters, people who are death-wishers because they themselves have been maimed. But he is mainly influenced by the philosophy of Jung, from whom he derives the importance of the oneiric as revelatory of truth unbounded by space and time. In *Memories, Dreams and Reflections*, which Buechner particularly appreciates, Jung insists on the importance of inner rather than outer experiences as meaningful parts of his life. Life seems to him a process of the self-realization of the unconscious toward wholeness, what Jung calls the process of individuation. Man cannot control this psychic process any more than he can know the contents of his own psyche. The first part of life is devoted to the assertion of the ego, the conscious part of a man's personality, and consists largely of assertions of sex and power. But in the second part of life man finds that he has to search for life's meaning, that he can no longer conform only to his persona, the role that society has conferred upon him. He has to face his shadow, the darker side of himself that has not been developed previously but that still exists in his unconscious. If he does not, he is bound to experience neurosis or psychosis, which is an attempt to compensate for a one-sided attitude toward life.

Through this process called individuation men and women become aware of the masculine or the feminine side of themselves.

Instead of looking for complementarity in marriage, a woman will integrate her *animus* into her personality, and a man will integrate his *anima*. At the same time they will also relate to the image of the great mother or the wise old man, archetypal images. Individuals who have reached the stage of individuation will feel a sense of unity with all living things, although they will maintain their uniqueness.

Such a process is helped by the study of dreams. What happens in dreams should be paid as much attention as what occurs in waking life. Man is haunted by both personal and collective dreams. Personal dreams are usually easier to decipher than collective dreams, which reveal the presence of archetypal concepts. Jung gives examples of his own dreams, which correspond to his personal worries, hint at solutions, reveal him as preoccupied by religion, warn him about the death of his friends, and link him with the dead. They are most important translators of the unconscious, personal or collective, into consciousness.

Jung's relationship to religion is para-Christian, although he takes Eastern religions very seriously. The natural in man is not to be denied. Dreams show that many an agnostic is really a believer at heart, and also that many believers are pagans at heart. The completely individuated man will find that he puts God at the center of the mandala, the symbol formed of a circle and the cross which indicates the wholeness of the self. The mandala is Formation, Transformation, and the Eternal Mind's eternal Recreation, which is the self in all its complexities. It resembles a child and is of God because God is equally composed of contraries. Here Jung deviates from the idea of an all-good and all-powerful God, but implies that God too has his shadow, his darker side. Christ is the supreme example of the self, and therefore each man is called to live in neurosis or to become Christ-like, perfectly himself and submitting in awe and love to the power of God.

One can see where Jung deviates from orthodox Christianity. On the one hand, his resolution of the problem of evil ends in the assertion that God is not entirely good or bad. On the other hand, he affirms the necessity of understanding and reflecting on Christian concepts, whereas most Christian denominations make an appeal for faith and humility of the intellect.

It is easy to see how much the religion of Tillich and Buechner

owes to the psychological outlook of Jung. Our concern here, however, is with the literary. Buechner is not original in the use of
psychology in his works. Actually, our contemporaries, in their
delight over the use of this "new science," forget that even in the
sixteenth and seventeenth centuries, treatises of psychology great-
ly influenced the writers of the time. There is no doubt that Ben
Jonson used the psychology of his day in the characterization of
Every Man in His Humour, and that Robert Burton's *Anatomy of Melancholy* influenced Caroline preachers. The awareness of polarities and
the force of the unconscious permeate the writings of our contemporaries, but Buechner may be unique in combining religion,
psychology, and literary creation.[11]

Although Buechner probes the unconscious in all his novels, he
uses psychological material more directly and systematically in *The
Entrance to Porlock*. In this story three generations of a family are
portrayed. The youngest character, Tip, is moving toward individuation through daydreaming. He writes an endless letter to Libba
Vann, a girl he loves but dares not approach. Since he is relatively
unspoiled, he is able to size up the other characters quite accurately,
though because of his youth he cannot probe into the causes underlying their actions. He has intuition into the mystery of things and
into a reality which goes beyond the obvious, but he is afraid to
act. When his Uncle Nels takes off his glasses, Tip is unable to deal
with him because this reality is different from the one he knows.
His imagination shows either his fear of life—he imagines that a
figure approaching him is the devil: part bird, part serpent, part
cloven-foot—or his repressed sexuality, as when he imagines he has
enclosed himself in a glass bell.[12] He enters the woods a virgin, but
leaves them having tried masturbation, which releases in him new
strength and a new appetite for life.

For the other characters, dreams and the individuation process
are not so strongly connected with sexuality. In the character of

---

11. Walker Percy makes the same attempt, but in his books the propor-
tionate emphasis on religion and psycho-analysis favors the latter. However
brilliant his books are, his religious message is somewhat elusive.

12. This image may also be derived from the painting of Hieronymus
Bosch, *The Garden of Earthly Delights*.

Tip, Buechner disposes of Dr. Freud. Nels, the Dean, resembles the different Metzgers found in *The Final Beast* and *The Book of Bebb*, and has some traits in common with both Poteat and Roebuck. Nels is a workaholic, a man afraid of both life and death who projects his own cowardice onto his students. Though he prides himself on being a just disciplinarian, his inflexibility actually hides his repressed anger. His public utterances are empty; finding everything "splendid" is a way of dodging any real relationship with people. He deals with reality by being an iconoclast, by smashing things. He has to face his shadow when, after having driven over a cat and fled from the scene, he is overtaken by the cat's owner. Instead of confessing his misdeed, he lies in front of his entire family by telling the owner that he did not know he had killed the cat. Partly because he knows they know his shame and partly because his brother continues to confront him with the truth as a psychiatrist or a sadist would, Nels feels the pangs of guilt. And yet he is able to escape again when his body translates what his consciousness won't admit: his stomach bothers him, a symptom which he takes for a heart attack. Unable to drive anymore, he has to be coddled and nursed by his father and brother until the scare is over. Receiving love gives him hope, but the rigid Nels cannot let go, and thus his agonizing pain recurs. Yet, at the end of the book, having learned of the suicide of Mullavey, a boy he punished, he is able to gather some courage and confess partial responsibility for the boy's death.

Nels thinks about the school and dreams about his own death. The killing of the cat, his concern about the boys of the school, and his vision of himself on his deathbed keep recurring intermingled. In fact, everything is tangled in Nels's existence. He has no sexual life and is frustrated in his desire for fatherhood. On the other hand, he has not come to terms with his own father, against whom he bears a grudge because of his absenteeism. In punishing Mullavey, who dreams of a world in which his hand would be that of Christ or Buddha, Nels is symbolically killing his father, who sees extraterrestrial reality where Nels sees only matter. He thus overreacts to Mullavey because he has no self-knowledge. When he learns of the boy's death and is able to take a stand for himself, he is able to weep and burn the folder in which he carefully recorded every detail of the case for his own protection. In this way he faces his shadow. Nevertheless, his fears return because he has to attend Mullavey's funeral.

Nels's actual dreams show that his subconscious suggests that he should more fully develop the other half of his personality. In his dream about the hospital he longs for his students to visit him and surround him with love, while he would put on a brave front in the face of his own death. He opposes an unconscious resistance to his father's desire to sell the land, and he longs to confess his cowardice, enjoy the beauty of the creation, and be loved. The cold persona asks to be shattered so that the real self may come out. But Nels fights against the other half of his personality, something Buechner dramatizes through Nels's fight with another character, the soft-hearted Penrose. Penrose appeals for mercy each time Nels calls for justice. He is interested in the boys' troubles and tries to bring them out. Yet both men share a frustrated desire for fatherhood; just as Nels's harshness comes from an unresolved conflict with his father, Penrose's sentimentalism comes from the desire to have his pupils' attention and love. Neither of them is as disinterested as he seems to be. It takes Mullavey's death to arouse in them some kind of compassion for each other, to make them reach at least a truce. Symbolically, both of them represent the school at Mullavey's funeral; and the two sides of Nels's personality come together for a moment as he faces the reality of death.

Of all the novel's characters, Nels is the most developed, but the process of individuation also occurs in others. His brother Tommy, for instance, comes to terms with his own cruelty. Unlike Nels, Tommy knows that something is wrong with him, but he tries to hide the fact by compulsive clowning. His problem is not that he lacks heart but that he has too much heart: the world touches him too deeply, and he has to hide the hurt. Like the child who begins to be told "no" by adults, Tommy responds by hurting the world back. From Barnum the clown he has learned to laugh away his tears, but he often clowns at the expense of others by teasing them cruelly: he reminds his father of his absenteeism and his brother Nels of his hitting the cat and running away. The doll-makers at the heart of the forest by whom he would like to be changed remind him that he must rid himself of his cruelty. Bonzo, one of the pilgrims of Strasser's village, enjoins him to be wiser or he will ruin his health. (Bonzo himself lost his hair worrying about things, worrying because he stopped crying.) But it is mainly at Strasser's magic session that Tommy realizes that he is not the only one to be hurt by the darkness of the world; his family is hurt, too. Strasser teaches him compassion.

Peter Ringkoping, the father, escapes from the world into the clouds. His element is air. He gives away anything tangible for dreams of bliss, and is an absentee father and husband. His constant dream is to peer behind the paper to find reality, and he often peers at his own face to try to see beyond the mask. But he forgets that God is to be found through the creation, not despite it. Having claimed that he wants to get rid of his property, his sudden weeping at the beauty of the creation in the forest takes him by surprise, as does the heartache that he feels at giving away his land and at the absence of his wife. He realizes that his own wishes have been egotistic, that he has valued his sons only as clues to the mystery of himself. But only when his magic tricks fail him does he realize his impotence and his need for his family, for something tangible. Only then is his land restored to him. Once more the process of individuation develops from the realization of the importance of the neglected part of the self: in this case Peter needs and finds a heart.

At the other extreme stands his daughter-in-law, Alice. A hoarder of things, she has no time for what lies beyond the material world. Because her own life hasn't moved or changed, she cannot care for her husband and child in ways that would help them grow. She keeps people for the same reason she keeps objects—for reassurance. But her house is the house of death, and she is a manipulator. Her main reason for going to Porlock is to keep an eye on Peter, the foolish old man. Like him, she is selfish, but in a different way. Her criticism of him is typically a projection of herself: he is generous with things but not with himself. In fact, she is generous neither with things nor with herself. He looks beyond reality toward the future, whereas she hangs onto things and to the past.

Alice faces her shadow when she wants to manipulate her mother-in-law, Sarah. She coaxes Sarah into relaxing, but when she suddenly betrays her bitterness toward her father-in-law, Sarah answers back. From her Alice hears that life changes. At Porlock she learns about the ambivalence of human beings whose love for each other is tinged with hatred, and she has to face this within herself. When she arrives, her husband and her son have not yet reached Porlock. Though she fears they may have had an accident, at the same time she has the delightful impression that she might be free to start her life all over again. She is both surprised and shocked at herself for having such feelings. Alice then realizes that after the death of her father, she never let herself live. She dreams that she is again in Avignon, where as a girl she was happy. But this time she is alone, and she is able to pluck a sprig of parsley and walk on toward greener pastures. Thus Alice achieves some degree of wholeness by going back to her childhood, seeing where her life had stopped, and realizing that in fact she has moved on.

Sarah, an old woman and Peter's wife, has given up on her life. She has given up looking at reality for herself; she sees everything through the eyes of her husband, and lets herself be manipulated by her family. But the instinct for life still lurks in her, and she reveals it when she resists her daughter-in-law. And her dreams show her that she can think for herself: she dreams, for example, that someone is burning grandmothers. This fear of death enables her to regain some life. As she enters the woods (after the car has broken down and Alice is seeing to it), she takes some steps on her own. She thinks of Strasser and the wisdom she acquired from him. He told her that man is both tree and bird, symbolism also used by Alan Paton in *Too Late the Phalarope*. He had painted unrealistic landscapes suffused with gold, and had urged her to let the autumn leaves enter the house of her soul, so she would live her age. But she had confined herself to household chores. In the forest, however, she realizes that she is more than her persona. She accepts death as a process necessary before rebirth can occur. Symbolically, she gets drenched in the rain but dries off, unharmed, in front of Strasser's fire.

One way or another, all of these characters come to terms with themselves and with a new vision. The process is painful and makes them fragile, in need of particular care and love. But Buechner is subtle enough to know that behavior patterns do not change from one day to the next, even if an individual's vision has changed.

Entropic tendencies resist the change urged by the spirit. Still, each character is on the way to a better understanding of the world and of himself, and the experience that he has had is indelible.

For Buechner, as for Jung, individuation comes at a time when there is a conjunction of internal readiness for a change and favorable external circumstances. Tip, Tommy, Peter, and Sarah are ready for such changes, for a leap into the unknown, because their unconscious urge has become a conscious one. Nels and Alice are not ready, and suffer the greater shock. Like Jung, however, Buechner thinks that this is an unavoidable process in any healthy human being; the death of the ego is the price human beings pay for the rebirth of the true self. Integration of opposites—death and life, love and hatred, introversion and extraversion—is indispensable if a human being is to become whole. Only after this experience are individuals able to make a lucid choice about the path their life is going to take: they can refuse or slight the growth life offers, and wilt as a consequence, or they can bloom as they are meant to.

Buechner uses both Jungian psychology and Christian wisdom to effect the progress of the characters in *The Book of Bebb*. Once again the younger characters are mainly concerned with their discovery of sex. Their realization of this normal desire leads them to understand that man is more than just a libido. Antonio is as airy and absent as Peter Ringkoping in *The Entrance to Porlock*, but, unlike him, he does not lack a heart. Neither does he lack brains like Tommy, nor courage like Nels. But he does lack solidity and direction, and wanders aimlessly through life, busy at one task or another. What he lacks is the essence of life itself. His dreams express sexual repression and spiritual frustration; what he needs is physical sustenance from a woman and spiritual guidance. He finds both in Bebb and his daughter Sharon.

In both *The Book of Bebb* and *The Entrance to Porlock*, Buechner suggests the difficulties of marriage. People are usually attracted to their opposites. Sarah the earthy one marries airy Peter, as Sharon marries Antonio; each woman is her partner's complement. Tommy, insecure as he is, marries the realist Alice, and Bebb the worker marries the dancing Lucille. Attraction is based on eros, the love that seeks for otherness out of need. But there comes the time of individuation, when human beings need to become complete in themselves and the basis of marriage has to be reconsidered. True love is possible only when both individuals have come to terms with themselves and each sees the other not as the missing part but as a traveling companion on life's road.

The need for this change is what unsettles Sharon and Antonio's marriage. Complacent Antonio does not realize that his marriage is rocky; he corrects his papers and goes on with business as usual, unaware that his wife, in moving from the South to the North, has suffered culture shock. She, on the other hand, feels inadequate in a house where intellect and achievement seem to reign and where she is not sufficiently appreciated as mother and cook. She therefore neglects these duties and takes up speed-reading and other activities in an effort to develop her *animus*. Antonio resents this change, yet he never sees himself as the cause of it, nor does he understand Sharon's need for wholeness. It takes facing adultery and a good telling-off by Sharon's friend Anita to force Antonio to be considerate of Sharon as a human being.

In Jungian terms, Sharon is very much Antonio's *anima*. She appears as both the New Jerusalem and the seductress. She is the other side of him, the living part in him that lies dormant. He is more intellectual; she is more physical and intuitive. Through the process of integration, she becomes more intellectual and he more physical. When he makes love to Laura Fleischman, he realizes that his need for an *anima* is independent of that of a particular person, which is Bebb's intimate conviction. Finally, Antonio and Sharon become newly aware of how precious they are to each other, and establish their relationship on a different basis. He is able to think of her need and let her be the leader; she becomes more self-sufficient and does not try to compete so much with others.

As Buechner shows, mature marriage is based on agape, not on need. Bebb remains faithful to Lucille although she does not fulfill her part as a wife. He has completed the individuation process, whereas she has not. Like Poteat in *The Final Beast*, Alice in *The Entrance to Porlock*, Roebuck in *The Book of Bebb*, and Elric in *Godric*, she halted her life when she discovered evil and tragedy. Thus her eventual death comes as a deliverance to all. Still, Bebb feels deprived when he loses her, because he valued her presence, even after she developed her zombie-like manner. But before her death Lucille does show some sparks of life: in *Open Heart* she needs to put her thoughts and questions to Jesus in a letter, and she asks Bebb some questions about the afterlife. Feeble though it may be, life is still pulsating within her, which suggests that her subconscious may be working through life's pattern but that her consciousness refuses to change, thus forcing her into neurotic behavior.

Buechner would then agree with psychologists that neurotic behavior comes from a conflict between the wise forces of the unconscious that require man to grow according to an archetype and the resistance imposed by the ego. These forces do not always appear clearly to man's consciousness, and he sometimes needs a translator. Such is the function of the elusive Gillian in *Godric, anima* as priestess, revealing to the pirate the contents of his dream: the bear trampling on the figs is Godric wasting away his life, which could be used for good. The dream, therefore, is most often the translation of the unconscious to consciousness.

But a dream can be more: it can be a revelation of the future. Godric's dreams reveal such para-psychological powers. He is able to foresee the drowning of men, although he has no vision of the afterlife. Such visions occur twice in *The Book of Bebb*. At Lucille's request Bebb tries to recreate the path taken by Herman Redpath on his way to the happy hunting ground. The afterlife is a pilgrim's progress of the self without the help of the ego, symbolized by Redpath's stripping himself. But the pilgrim is given new strength, as well as other things, for the road. The journey is undertaken alone, beyond any notion of space and time. First the pilgrim's courage— as well as his intelligence and skill—is tested as he has to fight the dragon. Then he must overcome the life of the senses (Herman has to do without sex and grapes to go on on his journey); next he has to resist materialism and the comforts of the world; after that he struggles with the no-man's-land, where he does not know who he is and doubts reality; and last, he has to answer the final question and give the password before he reaches the happy hunting ground.

In *Love Feast*, Antonio's dream is slightly different. He is pursued by something which bogs him down but that he cannot make out. Finally he realizes that it is his shadow in the shape of the pig that he ate for Christmas. Thus Antonio realizes that he too partakes in the killing that goes on in the world. Antonio sprints away to hide his shame but is washed clean in a stream before he reaches Lion Country. There he finds Lucille (his deceased mother-in-law), his sister Miriam, Herman Redpath, and the pig, unharmed. Herman Redpath then draws signs on his body that will enable him to go through life uncrippled. Having died to his ego, Antonio can go on with his life, because his self is now armed for the life struggle.

The two dreams are slightly different, but both emphasize the necessity for pilgrimage, the cross of man's destiny, and the ultimate triumph. In both *The Final Beast* and *The Entrance to Porlock*, temptation, or the facing of one's shadow, occurs in the shadows of the woods, but in *The Book of Bebb* it occurs in open country. Both journeys end with mandala shapes. In *Open Heart*, Herman can enter the walled city; in *The Entrance to Porlock*, Alice is offered sprigs of parsley, a symbol of hope from such a walled city, the holy city of Avignon. Antonio reaches the pool where all can bathe in safety. In *Treasure Hunt*, the idea of a pool imprints itself more and more strongly on Antonio's mind. In Brownie's room a stock picture of a boy fishing in a pool gives Antonio an unexpected sensation of relief and joy at a time when he and his friends are struggling against the forces of evil. Later he dreams that the child is sleeping next to the pool and is approached by a serpent, while Bebb fishes in safety in the middle. Later still he sees Bebb and Babe in the same boat, which swirls because their oars are striking the water in opposite directions. But at the center of the pool is stillness and peace.

Many dreams accompany Antonio's gradual individuation. He dreams of seagulls and freedom, but two other dreams are worth mentioning: one occurs while he is awake and the other when Babe hypnotizes him. In *Lion Country*, after having read the Apocryphal Gospels (edited by M. R. James), he portrays Christ as Don Giovanni, the great lover, who awaits the dying Miriam beyond the tunnel of death. (Part of Buechner's invention is based on recent experiences of people who had been declared clinically dead but who "came back" a few minutes later and explained what happened.) The second dream expresses Antonio's concern for his nephew Tony. (Antonio has forgiven Tony for committing adultery with his wife Sharon, but he cannot forgive himself.) Antonio sees Tony tied to a railroad track as a train is approaching. He cannot do anything for his nephew, but Christ appears at the last minute, looking like the Lone Ranger, and delivers him. God alone can forgive sin.

All dreams bring the final assurance of peace. Like Jung, Buechner hardly speculates about the nature of the afterlife, but indicates the unconscious need most people have for such reality, which may point to reality itself.

For Buechner, dreams are not only the indications of repression mechanisms derived from the psychology of neuroses. They can open up reality, point to the future, recall the past, heal the present, or evoke the numinous. For him as for Jung, dreams evoke the urges of either the personal unconscious or the collective unconscious. As man becomes individuated, he becomes increasingly aware of the unity and basic simplicity of the great drives common to humanity, for at the center of the mandala stands Christ, man as designed by God, whom we are all to resemble.

Buechner works much like a bee, gathering the pollen of the variegated flowers of Buddhism and Christianity, of existentialism and Jungianism. He is clearly obeying his universalist impulse. The result is Buechner's particular brand of honey, a poetic prose that assimilates the perfumes of them all. Yet each can be recognized in the fictional techniques Buechner uses to express his eclectic metaphysics.

V

The Rhetoric of Fiction
and Truth

*But the novelist, if he have a conscience, must preach his ser-
mons with the same purpose as the clergyman. . . . Truth
let there be—truth of description, truth of character, human
truth as to men and women. If there be such truth, I do not
know that a novel can be too sensational.*

Anthony Trollope, *Autobiography*

Thomas Mann suggested that the duty of the artist is to pay attention to the changes of the world. This cultivation of attentiveness links
the artist, the philosopher, and the religious man, since all seek wisdom. Some authors have looked at history, others at the bustle of
human activity; still others have peered into the self and analyzed its
evolution. Buechner belongs to this last category. In his novels he reflects the modern existentialist trend of thought and the new
discoveries of psychology while affirming that the revelation of the
Bible still holds true. He could have chosen poetry or the theatre as
his medium, and he has tried both. But Buechner prefers the novel as
a form, with its possibilities for inner monologue as well as its display
of action and interaction. Buechner's novels are therefore novels of
the self which do not focus on external events but emphasize the characters' minds and their concentration on inner happenings.

This emphasis on man's psyche gives human beings primary importance. Though Buechner places man in situation in the world that
surrounds him, he does not focus upon outside reality. If we were to
judge his fiction with the eyes of Robbe-Grillet, we could say that he
exploits nature and physical settings. In most of his novels they serve

as foils to human happenings rather than as things important in themselves. *Godric*, Buechner's latest novel, is an exception: in it Buechner renders the medieval world with the accuracy and care of a miniaturist. But most often he paints his landscapes with a surrealistic intention or a symbolical value. Thus his novels are totally centered on man, the king of the creation.

Such an attitude poses the problem of the relationship of fiction to truth. Since Buechner discards the outer world in favor of the inner world, are his novels simply a figment of his mind, a projection of his many possibilities? Is man totally immured within himself and unable to communicate with the outside world? The relationship of the author with his characters, the use of personal pronouns and the point of view, as well as the treatment of paradox, should give us a clue to Buechner's manipulation of truth in fiction.

The Author-Narrator

Most artists have at some stage of their careers attempted to represent themselves; among the most famous self-portraits of painters are those of Dürer, Rembrandt, and Van Gogh. Those authors who have written themselves into their work include Shakespeare, who shows actors at work, and Molière, who put himself in *l'Impromptu de Versaille* (brought up to date by Ionesco). But the artist never occupied the center of the picture until German Romanticism. Ever since then authors have used the author-hero as the central character of their fiction, and philosophized about the relationship of art to life. In *Counterfeiters*, Gide pits Edouard against the phony Count Passavant, whose life is as much of a cheat as his literary production. In *Nausea*, Sartre affirms that wholeness in an individual depends on his capacity for literary creation, and Beckett portrays the deliquescence of man conjointly with his inability to think or to create any further.[1]

Relativism brought about the notion that all truth perceived was subjective and that therefore the author was totally incapable of perceiving anybody other than himself. Thus some novels embody the

1. See Edith Kern's excellent book, *Existential Thought and Fictional Technique: Kierkegaard, Sartre, Beckett* (New Haven, Conn.: Yale University Press, 1970).

many possibilities of the author, those selves or personae which he did or did not actualize in his own life. This creates an ambiguous situation: how much does the author identify with the hero-author and with the other characters in the book?

This ambiguity arises in Buechner's work. He asserts that all writing is at heart autobiography, and he portrays a number of characters as authors in his novels. A common feature of these characters is that they are all pitted against the figure of the minister, whether they are minor characters, as in *The Final Beast* or *The Entrance to Porlock*, or major characters, as in *The Book of Bebb* or *Godric*. We have already seen that Buechner portrays the minister as an anti-hero, a flawed character made into something of a man by the grace of God. Compared with the writer-figures, these earthen vessels are made of pure gold. The difference between the two types expresses Buechner's ambiguous attitude toward his art and his God-given gifts.

In the previous chapter I noted that Buechner praises artists as framers of the truth; thus we would naturally conclude that he takes pride in his art. But we have also seen previously that Buechner has not arrived at this conclusion without a fight. How he portrays this struggle in his novels is what interests us now.

In *The Alphabet of Grace*, Buechner expresses his ambivalent response to artists: "But there is another class of men—at their best they are poets, at their worst artful dodgers—for whom the idea and the experience, the idea and the image, remain inseparable, and it is somewhere in this class that I belong."[2] "Artful dodgers" is the key phrase here. Poteat in *The Final Beast*, Peter Ringkoping in *The Entrance to Porlock*, Antonio in *The Book of Bebb*, and Reginald in *Godric* are all artful dodgers. Are they satirical portraits of the bad writer, like Grand in Camus' *The Plague*? Perhaps. In any case, the fact is that Buechner never portrays the author as a hero; the author is always cast as the anti-hero.

In *The Final Beast*, Poteat, the journalist, is compared to a drone, the bee that does not work but waits on the queen's pleasure. The image is a double one, alluding both to Poteat's brief affair with Rooney

---

2. Frederick Buechner, *The Alphabet of Grace* (New York: Seabury Press, 1970), p. 4.

Vail and to his work. Poteat goes around town gathering information for his newspaper, so in a sense he does not actually work for a living but is a parasite feeding on the lives of other people. Later we learn that as a child he longed to be old, to be safely beyond the heat of combat, the struggle for life. He was longing for death, which is why he stuck to words. His main subject is irony, the irony of life: behind fair faces, he discovers excremental reality. His words have the power to kill; with them he tries to harm Nicolet, the jovial minister, as well as Rooney, and succeeds in driving Irma Reinwasser out of her mind by sowing the seeds of self-doubt in her. In Poteat the writer appears as the dissector of life and therefore the killer.

Poteat is also his own destroyer. He says that words are his undoing: " 'Like a golf ball when you take the cover off—all those miles and miles of rubbery string. I've been reeling words out of my gut for years, I suppose to find out one day what there is at the middle of me.' "[3] The message is clear. Writing is just another form of narcissism, a vain attempt at self-discovery. And readers of books are no better than authors. Metzger, the hypochondriac who is Poteat's friend, thinks of books as "a mirror of his variegated soul, hoarded by Squirrel against the coming of winter."[4] Yet buying books is not enlarging his experience of the world but merely cushioning his shadow-like self.

Both characters are blended into one in Peter Ringkoping in *The Entrance to Porlock*. Peter, detached from earthly realities, is a collector of books as well as an author. His narcissism is evident in his habit of always looking in a mirror in the hope of seeing behind his face, discovering what lies behind his persona. The suggestion is that only air can be found. This insubstantial character who dodges reality has the drama of life shelved in his library stacks and hears only echoes of people's voices. Secondhand reality, as recorded in books, is not so hurtful as life itself. Even the book Peter authors is a protection from the world, because fame enables him to be seen without his ever having to go out of his way to be interested in others. Here is a man who never reads a book to the end; he browses through them as he does

---

3. Frederick Buechner, *The Final Beast* (New York: Atheneum, 1965), p. 185.

4. Buechner, *The Final Beast*, p. 211.

through the faces of people, never attempting to pierce the underlying reality. His own book, *Doorway in the Air*, is as vague as his character, advocating insubstantial religion, pointing out that reality appears different only because of the varying light in which it is seen. In this assertion one can perceive Buechner's comment upon his own book, for he had turned away from overt Christianity to write *The Entrance to Porlock*.

The satire of the author is even more complete in the character of Antonio Parr in *The Book of Bebb*. Antonio is a ghost of a character. Like Beckett's Murphy, he has withdrawn into the life of the mind, which enables him to arrange and rearrange reality at his convenience. In his attempts at writing he never gets past page thirty, and his attempt to create some visual form of art ends in a rickety contraption that he can rearrange at will. His style follows the fad of the day and has little unity.[5] He perceives reality secondhand through the world of poetry or music or painting. Antonio is a shadow of a man. When we meet him he is at the point of disintegration, unsure of anything, the prey of his own versatility. As the narrator of *The Book of Bebb*, he is not omniscient but omnescient. He affirms the impossibility of painting the truth since all truth in the process of description becomes reified, fixed and only partial.

Yet Antonio is Buechner's first attempt at expressing a positive view of the writer. Despite all his problems, he does change through his contact with Bebb, the life-giver. As he gains more life, he is able to complete a book; in fact, the dried-up man gains enough vitality to write four books. His style changes from the self-conscious weaving of a literary fabric to the framing of life as it is, the rendering of firsthand experience. His other artistic impulses also become truer to life: he replaces the jagged mobile with a wooden stabile in the shape of an A, the first letter of his own name. Eventually he summons the courage to put it out-of-doors to be weathered and beaten by the wind and the

---

5. This enables Buechner to provide extremely amusing literary pastiches, since this most easily influenced character always reproduces what he has most recently read or experienced. Thus he depicts Christ to his dying sister in the stylistic manner of Dr. James, writes with cinematic technique when he has been given a camera, and writes like a reporter with a scoop after he has read the newspaper story on the Princeton Love Feast.

rain. Despite his setbacks, Antonio is the embodiment of Sartre's belief in a unified vision of existence and art. At first Antonio's style is, in Nietzschean terms, Apollonian—formal, self-conscious, ruled by the precepts of teachers in creative writing or by one's resistance to them. As Antonio progresses, there is a Dionysian squandering of all rules and a giving away of the self. At this point the novel is no longer written in the third person, but in the autobiographical first person. Pale shadow though he remains compared with his counterpart, the minister Bebb, Antonio has gained some substance. The author-narrator's function is to be a witness of his own life and that of others. He is both teller and told, both "I" and "him."

This more positive vision of art as contribution to the creation recurs in *Godric*, but there is still a gap between the teller, the told, and the actual writer of biography. Godric is both the teller and the told. His life is told according to an angle. What he wants to show is the working of God's grace. The story has to be true to life; he has to be painted warts and all. Although the narrator selects the events of Godric's life in order to suggest its particular flavor, it remains the truth: the truth and nothing but the truth, but not the whole truth—only what is relevant to life as an illustration of God's grace.[6] Thus the poet in opening the book of his life becomes the dirty window that reveals a reality lying beyond it. One might argue that the beauty and clarity of the glass might equally praise its maker, but this is not Buechner's point of view. Nevertheless, he has succeeded in affirming a positive value of art in its relationship to the truth. Art is meant to frame the truth and draw our attention to it. The artist is no longer he who can draw reality as it is not, as wishful thinking, like Strasser does in *The Entrance to Porlock*, but he who, like the Elizabethan miniaturists Hilliard and Oliver, can paint life as it is, with the greatest accuracy and sharpness.

---

6. Godric's discriminating choice of events should be contrasted with Antonio's lack of discrimination. In *Love Feast*, Antonio gives us petty details. For instance, in his attempt at accuracy, he tells us that he missed the heat of the action at Alexander Hall because his bladder was aching and he had to leave to relieve himself. At the end of *Treasure Hunt*, his mobile has become a broken form repaired with toilet paper. Antonio cannot maintain a balance between the Apollonian and the Dionysiac, whereas Godric can. According to Buechner, the man of God, having gained a bird's-eye view of life, sticks to essentials.

And yet Buechner seems to be doubtful about the recorder of events. Reginald, the writer, is an escapist and a dodger of the realities of life, a mouther of piety, a brown-noser, a man who lives by proxy instead of fighting the bloody life-struggle. He is a traitor to both life and art because he edits the truth in order to make it pleasing to the onlooker, and makes it fit the preconceived notion that a saint is a consistently holy man. Withdrawn into a monastery, he lacks the guts of the former bird of prey, Godric, guillemot made dove through the grace of God. In fact, Godric despises and abuses the meek Reginald to the end, though he finally begs his pardon. Thus even at the end of *Godric*, where Buechner asserts the value of art (as he does in *Telling the Truth*), the writer remains a shady character.

As I have previously mentioned, this reflects the tension Buechner feels as a man who is both a Christian and an artist, with the minister opposing the litterateur. None of the ''writers'' in his fiction is to be equated with him, but signs show that, at least partially, Buechner is satirizing himself in Poteat and Antonio, who are self-conscious stylists. If any reader wonders if Buechner is winking at himself in his characters, he should read the preface to *The Book of Bebb*. There Buechner carefully distinguishes himself from Antonio at first, but by the end he has adopted Antonio's aria-like tone, that of the self-conscious writer who has some misgivings about his task:

> Dear Bebb. Dear Brownie. Remember me as I remember you. Forgive me for summoning you up into something like life, for afflicting you with griefs and visiting you with joys, only to kill you off in the end. . . .[7]

Antonio alludes to the monkey-god, uses many different techniques which echo those used by Buechner himself in previous books, and has a passion for playing with the letters of the alphabet. And yet Antonio's writing is so clumsy that one cannot equate it with Buechner's lively prose. The vision is therefore blurred and ambiguity is maintained, although this attempt at self-disparagement shows that Buechner has not yet achieved a complete truce between the minister and the author.

---

7. Frederick Buechner, preface to *The Book of Bebb* (New York: Atheneum, 1979), p. ix. This self-debunking technique in not new. Erasmus used it in *The Praise of Folly*. In his latest novel, *Bech is Back*, Updike also expresses some of these misgivings.

Though Buechner would agree with Camus that art detached from its creator is unthinkable, he would never consider his characters to be mere projections of himself, as Beckett does. Rather, he would proclaim with Plautus that because he is human, nothing human is foreign to him. Like an actor, Buechner is able to enter into the psychic life of others. Lillian Flagg, for instance, is based on the living Agnes Sanford. Such characters as Bebb and Brownie with his china teeth actually existed, and so did Godric, the eleventh-century saint. Furthermore, Buechner's anti-heroic author and the heroic minister or saint are always "en situation." In Buechner's books the self is connected to the world rather than isolated like Watt, Moran, Molloy, Malone, Murphy, and other characters of Beckett's saga. Buechner's novels also move in a direction opposite of those of Beckett. There is a dilation in Buechner's world, whereas Beckett's world is distinguished by general diminution. The former lets his characters bloom and squander away their petals; the latter gradually shrinks them and allows them to wilt away. For Buechner, characters like Lucille, Roebuck, and Elric are sad exceptions; for Beckett, they represent the general law of entropy.

For Buechner, autobiography consists in revealing the universe as well as the "me." The novelist warns us against his point of view; it is fallible and one-sided, only a particular truth. But the poet can reveal himself because, more than other men, he has learned to know himself and the texture of which men are made. His conviction that in all human beings lurks the seed of the figure of Christ, ready to be developed, makes the journey of one man interesting to all. This is affirmed in the epistle to the reader in *The Alphabet of Grace*: "Thus strangers though we are, at a certain level, there is nothing about either of us that can be utterly irrelevant to the other."[8] This statement accounts for Buechner's courage in dropping the third-person narrative and taking up the first person, and his transition to using both in the character of Godric.

The He, the I, and the Point of View

The young man discovers the world, the older person discovers himself, and the wise man sees the unity between the two. This

---

8. Buechner, *The Alphabet of Grace*, p. viii.

is the path Buechner has followed. His first novels are concerned with "them." At the time of his conversion, Buechner needed to tell of his experience but did not dare write direct autobiography, and so used the third person in the character of Nicolet in *The Final Beast*. This device enables Buechner to relate events that have deeply touched his life with a certain objective perspective. Buechner also uses dialogue and interior monologue to reveal his characters' inner thoughts. Division and isolation need not be expressed through the immured ego but can be revealed through different points of view. On the other hand, Buechner shows the ability of his characters to grow and change by the shifting of their points of view. Nicolet, for instance, grows in maturity. He comes to see things through the eyes of Lillian Flagg and to consider his father as a fellow traveler on the *via dolorosa*. Rooney has her memory restored, so she can face the darker parts of her life. Irma Reinwasser is momentarily sucked into Poteat's evil vision of the world, but she breaks away from it. At the end of the novel, Poteat shifts to a more positive viewpoint of his life and that of others. Thus in Buechner's fiction points of view are not fixed, but express human growth. Eventually most characters are drawn toward a greater affirmation of life.

Buechner uses the same technique in *The Entrance to Porlock*. In this book there is not one narrator but apparently several, as in Lawrence Durrell's *Alexandria Quartet*. The novel consists mainly of a series of interior monologues, as each character reacts to objective reality—Peter's desire to give away his land—and to the subjective reality in themselves and others, the "I" and the "thou."

In *The Book of Bebb*, Buechner is able to switch from third-person to first-person narration. This gives him greater leeway for the expression of the inner person. Antonio is a boring philosopher, but average man that he is, he depicts the difficulty that most people have in becoming truly human beings; his quest stresses the vanity of introspection, since the self is infinitely elusive, yet he cannot break away from it. Antonio, the slave of introspection, becomes sadder and sadder until he is drawn out of himself by action. His style then changes, becomes more lively and interesting. Through the contrast between the "I" and the "he" in Antonio and Bebb, Buechner is able to show separation among human beings. Antonio gives us a first-person depiction of his psychic reality that has nothing in common with the third-person perception of him by his student Laura Fleischman. In turn, Antonio sees only the activist in Bebb and ignores the private difficulties of the man. Thus the outer appearance never reveals the inner struggle. Just as the "I" is incapable of ever knowing the "me," so the "I" is unable to account for the "him."

Yet there is a correspondence between internal progression and outward behavior which is apparent only to the enlightened. At the end of *Love Feast*, Antonio is weighed down in his interior monologues. But as he is ready to patch up his marriage and bring up as his own the child of dubious parentage his wife has borne, she recognizes that the seeds of Bebb have bloomed in him and exclaims, "This Bop," which echoes the admiring "This Bip" she used to apply to her father. The progress Antonio does not see in himself she is able to bring to his attention. Thus an appraisal of the objective "me" can enlighten the subjective "I."

This theme is emphasized in Godric, who uses first-person and third-person pronouns in speaking of himself. Though this double use of pronouns has appeared in modern times in Joyce's *Portrait of the Artist as a Young Man* and in Beckett's *Watt*, it is derived from the Old English ballad.[9] The use of these pronouns marks the stylistic quality of *Godric* as well as the presence of an "I" and a "me" within the character. The subjective and suffering "I" is often opposed to the objective "him." In Godric, the "I" laments his father's death and cherishes the fond memory of the enlightening Gillian, whereas the "he" is all rags, an interesting creature in the process of evolution. The particular qualities of the "I" and the "he" are best exemplified in Godric's fear that Ailred will reject him because of his past misdeeds: "Did he [Ailred] but know where

---

9. The medieval derivation I owe to the kindness of Dr. Hallett Smith, Research Associate at the Henry E. Huntington Library in San Marino. Other modern writers who use the mixed personal pronouns are Franz Werfel in *Der Abituriententag* (1928) and *Der veruntreute Himmel* (1940), Aldous Huxley in *Eyeless in Gaza* (1936), and Ernest Hemingway in *To Have and Have Not* (1937). See Bertil Romberg, *Studies in the Narrative Technique of the First-Person Novel* (Stockholm: Almquist, 1962).

Godric's path has led or what sights his light has lit, he'd bushel me back fast enough.''[10]

Another device in *Godric* stresses further dichotomy within the character's psyche: the use of two different names for Godric, which symbolizes the forces of good and evil at war inside him. Godric also answers to the name of Deric. The shortened name Deric is introduced by Mouse, the hero's friend and fellow plunderer on the high seas; he is Godric without God, as God has been excluded in the pirate's life. Deric is Godric, the beast untamed. As Godric's spirituality develops after his encounter with Gillian, the priestess, he hides the shameful name of Deric from his beloved sister Burcwen when he returns home, and dismisses this part of himself in no uncertain terms: '' 'Deric's a lout that gives himself to lust and thievery. The world would be a better place with Deric dead. And so he'll surely be and soon, if Heaven's just.' ''[11] In Jerusalem, Buechner insists, Deric dies and Godric is reborn to lead a life of devotion and righteous action. Godric is thus re-united with himself and God.

In *Godric*, both the personal pronouns and the double names interweave to express the division of the psyche between the subjective and the objective and between opposing moral forces. In all Buechner's novels a character's true name is the key to the mystery of the self. In *The Final Beast*, Poteat dreams that someone writes his true name on the bar counter, and he wishes he could have read it. Antonio sees his secret name written on a dollar bill but cannot make it out. It is so compelling that he affirms that he would follow to the end of the world the one who would call him by his mysterious name. Godric is given back his baptismal name and takes comfort in it. All the seekers in Buechner's novels express the desire to conform to their created selves at the expense of an ego which they can no longer bear. These characters embody Buechner's belief that division of man from himself or from his brothers is the expression of waywardness. All eventually long to conform to the archetype of the human being.

---

10. Frederick Buechner, *Godric* (New York: Atheneum, 1981), p. 171.
11. Buechner, *Godric*, p. 171.

Division implies judgment. Thus the teller judges the told and the I/he/they judges the me/him/them, the objectified. Mercy, on the other hand, takes a more subjective and sympathetic point of view, appraising the difficulty of the beast in becoming a truly human being. Hatred is a failure of the imagination, but there is room for both judgment and mercy to be felt for the progress of man. In *Godric*, Godric's judgment of Deric is negative, whereas that of Godric as "I" on Godric as "he" is life-affirming. These two attitudes give a clue to Buechner's position regarding the dialectical relationship of negation and affirmation, and to his use of irony and humor as a way to resolve the tension of paradoxical life.

The Problems of Negation

Most writers have agreed that negation as such cannot be studied, but can be examined only with dialectical reference to the principle of affirmation. Traditionally, the Western world has affirmed that life and creation are superior to death and barrenness. At the same time Westerners have also held that chaos and darkness are the matrix of life. Thus affirmation and negation have been polarized. Thinkers are further divided into those who believe in being and those who advocate becoming as central to life. For the former, negation is averse to life and has to be eradicated. Revolutionaries, for instance, believe in suppressing negation by negation, by killing the oppressors. Mystics believe in killing the destructive self to be united with the Other, the principle of affirmation and creation. Contrary to these groups, those who believe in becoming have a more organic view of life, and take negation in stride as the necessary way out of one stage of being into the next.[12]

These points of view are alternately acted out in the characters of Buechner's novels. Pascal, the French philosopher of the seventeenth century who was also a mystic, distinguished between those who have "esprit de géométrie" and those who have "esprit de

---

12. For this section, I am largely indebted to Maire Jaanus Kurrick, *Literature and Negation* (New York: Columbia University Press, 1979), who is both very solid and widely read.

finesse.'' Buechner uses the distinction in the character of Irma Reinwasser, who has a geometrical mind. She reduces any human dilemma or problem to geometrical figures. But she is not alone in doing so. Poteat and the boy who drives Nicolet to Muscadine in *The Final Beast*, Nels in *The Entrance to Porlock*, Roebuck and Babe in *The Book of Bebb*—all are simplistic. For them right is right and wrong is wrong, and nothing can link the two. Negation is then an attempt to restore order in an apparently disordered world. Irma has dreams of a road surrounded with barbed wire. She cannot cope with the idea of negation in the world within or without and her statements are thus all-inclusive: whatever man does turns out badly. When she discovers the possibility of evil within her, she naturally desires to suppress herself. She in turn is being negated by the young admirer of Nicolet, who resents her having stolen the show from the clergyman. In his view, Irma is to be punished for not keeping the law of decorum and decency. The negative has to be opposed by negation. In fact, the punishment far surpasses the crime, because Irma is burned to death by mistake.

In *The Book of Bebb*, Babe reasons along the same lines. His meeting with evil in his wife's adultery results in his infinite distrust of the world. He seeks revenge: he destroys her beauty, banishes her child, and pretends that she is mad. Because she feels guilty, she accepts a punishment far beyond what her crime deserved. She negates herself while Babe negates her. Like the ill will of vendettas, Babe's negation also extends to the next generation. When Sharon comes to claim her inheritance, he summons all the forces of evil to fight her: he employs ruse and force ruthlessly. But like Vindice in Tourneur's *The Revenger's Tragedy*, Babe is ultimately defeated, trapped in his own interaction and relieved to be so, because nothing positive has been accomplished by his revenge and his negation of the world. Ultimately the poisoner is relieved to be delivered from his own poisoning, which has also shriveled him.

For Buechner, negation is clearly the product of sin. Men either openly negate themselves or the world, or do so unconsciously. In Buechner's books, all those who, consciously or unconsciously, answer negation with negation, like Poteat, Roebuck, Babe, Lucille, and Elric—and, to a lesser extent, Irma, Rooney, Bebb, Antonio, Godric, and Reginald—become negated or warped themselves. Life can resume only if negation is answered by affirmation.

Buechner thinks that the nay-sayers are just shortsighted. In *Godric,* the affirmation of Elric's existence does not come from within himself but from grace. His life is maintained because Godric has been sent to him. The weak are in fact protected by a circle of love. In *The Book of Bebb*, for example, Lucille is taken care of. And the crippled child is loved by his parents even if they feel guilty for having produced such a child. Grace abounds in the world; life always provides new chances. The nihilist's eyes are closed to this basic cause for joy, whereas the believer sees negation as part of the life process.

The principles of affirmation and negation are found in the young man, as a beast, with equal force. In *The Final Beast*, the Nazi Heinz Taffel is both lover and torturer, life affirmer and killer:

> . . . Heinz Taffel had the smell of life about him in a world of death, and even among the prisoners it won him a measure of wary popularity. He would always let them see him coming: he would leap and wave his arms, roaring like a young bull at their ragged clumsiness, kicking and thumping the laggards, but even his brutality was endurable not because it was any less brutal than the others' but because, though swift and terrible, it had a kind of boy's passion to it and was quickly spent.[13]

He saves Irma from death, but he also molests her and tortures her. Influenced by this memory, Irma also perceives Nicolet as lover and torturer. He gives her a good life in his home and a job taking care of his children—but he denies her the love that she might want as a woman because of his love for his past wife Franny and the growing affection he has for Rooney Vail. Thus she is both affirmed as mother and negated as woman.

The principles of affirmation and negation are also portrayed forcefully in the young Godric, tumbler of maids and pirate at sea. Perkin, the young man who helps Godric in his old age, is also an ambivalent being. Buechner's position is that man eventually moves from innocence into a state of experience; he has to choose, with

---

13. Buechner, *The Final Beast*, p. 120.

eyes open, for one or the other principle. Not to choose is in fact to opt for evil and death.

In Buechner's works negation and evil are not necessarily equated. The power of man for negating springs from the gift of choice allocated to human beings. Following the way means discarding treacherous by-ways. Thus Nicolet in *The Final Beast* says no to the romantic lure of adultery, Bebb refuses atheism in *The Book of Bebb*, and Godric batters his pride. This form of negation is part of the principle of affirmation of the basic rules of human behavior necessary to bring about the kingdom of peace. Thus the "no" has a place in Buechner's world.

Negation holds an important place in Buechner's view of life. Although, as we have seen, he prefers the planters to the weeders of mankind, he affirms that imperfection within man has to be rooted out. The human being must negate the beast within himself—in Bebb's words, keep the tiger within the cage—in order for the garden to bloom, undestroyed by wild forces. This stern puritanical ethic had been rejected by Hawthorne, particularly in his short story "The Birthmark," but Buechner believes that self-discipline is important, and that the battering of life has a positive function in the making of a human being.

The resistance offered by circumstances adverse to man often provides the necessary ferment for the seed of life to grow. This is the root of Bebb's great fecal indictment of the atheist Roebuck in *Love Feast*. In *The Final Beast*, Rooney would have led a superficial life had she not had to deal with barrenness; Nicolet would have been a stale minister had he not had to cope with more than he could tackle, too many deaths and Rooney's flight. We have seen how Tommy in *The Entrance to Porlock* wishes for death in order to be recreated. In *The Book of Bebb*, Brownie dies and is raised again before he can give up his homosexuality. Even Antonio understands that he and Sharon need to experience a crisis in order to achieve greater stability in their marriage. Many times over Godric lives the principle of death in life, and has integrated negation in his life process; his last words—" 'All is well' "—are an affirmation of life as it is, with its negative and affirmative impulses, and echo the final verdict of the medieval English mystic, Julian of Norwich.

Though Buechner can see positive value in negation, he still would not subscribe to the cheerful philosophy of Hegel, who believes that the mind progresses steadily through thesis, antithesis, and synthesis. The negative principle essential to life causes anguish and pain. In the face of pain, there is a retraction of the beast. Even Bebb gets discouraged and stalls when everything he attempts turns out for the worst. Faith that the affirmative principle of life will ultimately be victorious does not diminish the immediate pain. But it sustains Bebb through the rough patches, whereas Antonio gets bogged down in negativity and misses most of the joys of life: the beauty of his wife, of his child, and of himself.[14]

Bebb accepts negation as part of the life process: he insists on the importance of burning one's bridges and moving on. What deprives Antonio of joy is looking back at a past he would like to hold on to; he never reaches the point of trust in the future and acceptance of the ambivalence of life, although he is able to affirm this for his nephew Tony out of love for him.[15] Thus the spirits of affirmation and of negation are always at odds in Antonio, whereas in Bebb they are integrated.

Buechner's view of the importance of negation is portrayed in the character of Golden, the angel of fire. Antonio thinks of him as a hound of heaven. He is present at all the important events in Bebb's life, ready to strike him if he becomes self-willed or complacent. Almost every time he appears, Bebb is frightened: he is there at the ordination of Redpath when Bebb exposes himself; he

---

14. Antonio proceeds by constantly rejecting his past instead of integrating it in a life process. He does so indiscriminately: in the same breath he rejects the superiority of dry martinis and fidelity in friendships. Antonio is never able to get out of himself and consider each age a blessing. In some ways, he echoes Jacques in Shakespeare's *As You Like It*.

15. Tony refers to his guilt at having betrayed Antonio by sleeping with his wife, and feels that whatever he does, it ends up wrong. Antonio encourages Tony and tells him that he is the one that has to deal with the problem now.

> "I can't change it for you, but maybe I can change it for me. In time I think I can make it for myself as if it never happened. At least I can make other things happen around it so it won't louse things up. It might even help somehow."

Tony then asks, " 'What do you call that?' " and Antonio replies, " 'Call it a going-away present' " (*The Book of Bebb*, p. 264).

leaves a cryptic message for Bebb when he is happy about the money Redpath has left him; he is present when Lucille commits suicide; he burns the barn Bebb had used as a church; he discloses Bebb's life to his children; he pilots the plane which bursts into flames. . . . Though Bebb fears him, Golden is a gentle presence who sustains him in adversity and reminds him not to be afraid. He embodies the importance of negation for the shaping of man's life.

In this context, death is considered a necessary step in the making of man. Bebb had gained this wisdom, and it is reaffirmed by Godric. When he is near death, Godric looks back on his life and considers the many previous deaths he has had to undergo—the death of his ego, the death of some of his friends—and he expects new deaths and new births. In Buechner's novels, negation is finally negated by the principle of affirmation; as dead limbs give birth to new shoots, as the dying tree fathers new saplings, so the life process is always victorious.

In the process of letting go of his past, man asserts his faith in a manageable future. Does the renouncing of the past turn Buechner's characters into hollow trunks? No. The past, according to Buechner, needs to be absorbed and digested rather than discarded or repressed. Rooney's mistake in *The Final Beast* is that she has repressed the memory of her adultery because she is ashamed of it. Thus she has become a dead body, an empty shell. Alice in *The Entrance to Porlock* and Lucille in *The Book of Bebb* are unable to digest their past, but hang on to it. To some degree they are like Lot's wife, changed into pillars of salt. Like Bebb, Sharon has tried to sever the links of the past to follow the one she loves; but in a situation foreign to her, away from the South she knows, she is unable to cope and only feels inferior. But life and strength return to her when she searches again for her roots, something Antonio is unable to do because both his parents are dead. Fortified with the knowledge of her ancestry, she is able to return to the North. For Buechner the past cannot be denied or the human being becomes fragile; on the other hand, the pulp of the past must be discarded while the nurturing elements are absorbed. Life moves on.

The wise man remains in touch with his past but also knows how to liberate himself from it. Having reached the stage where only the universal is important, he can move freely in space and time. Thus Bebb is able to move to the North and adapt, whereas his wife, used to the South, cannot. He can rejoice in the company of intellectuals without being one himself. Godric the pirate moves easily through time. Past, present, and future contribute to the making of a man. *Chronos* gives way to *kairos*. The present and the remoter past are told unsequentially, but significant moments, for better or for worse, have all been equally absorbed. The negation of the past is therefore an organic process which leads to the affirmation of growth. Only the wise man can truly let go. Most men are afraid of the unknown and of the process of death involved in life; they shun the dark night of the soul and physical death.

Possible Solutions to the Paradoxical Nature of Life

The modern man's way of coping with the reality of death and the paradoxical nature of reality is to arrest his growth or take refuge in his intellect. Irony and humor are two basic responses made in the attempt to cope with the paradoxes of the world and of the self. Both flourish at those times when the traditional values of society are in decline and man has to deal with competing truths. During the Renaissance, for instance, they flourished, as did paradoxical literature. In the twentieth century, authors like Peter DeVries and John Updike have in their middle age come to assert with Rabelais that laughter is essential to humanity.

There are two sides to irony. One, Socratic irony, is the result of dissembling about one's knowledge in order to advance the truth. The other is merely destructive, emphasizing a discrepancy between words and their meanings or between reality and what it ought to be. In *Love Feast*, Antonio expounds on the idea as he teaches his English classes at Sutton, developing the difference between an ironic statement and an ironic situation.

Bebb occasionally uses the first kind of irony. Most of the time he preaches, but sometimes he encourages Antonio to think for himself. He nudges him by reminding him of his education, which should help him solve the problems of life. This is, of course, Bebb's way of being ironical, his way of unsettling Antonio in his superior stance—just as Golden unsettles Bebb with his ambiguous statement, "Good luck, sweetheart," letting Bebb infer his meaning.

Ironical situations are also used to deflate the pomposity of those who behave ignorantly but should know better. We see the minister who does not know how to pray in *The Final Beast*, the lover of all except his own father. *The Book of Bebb* depicts situation after situation that is ironical. Ellie gives the chaste Antonio a little pussy-cat, but he does not see the pun she intends. He goes down to Amarillo to expose Bebb and ends up being seduced by Bebb's daughter. He criticizes Dr. James's *Apocryphal New Testament* for not being able to maintain a high note and for moralizing until the reader is bored to death, but Antonio is plagued by the same weaknesses in his novels. He rebels against the principle that writers have to bring all loose ends together at the end of a novel, but he does it anyway. He is married to Sharon, but cuckolded by his own nephew because of his lack of involvement in his marriage. He tells Sharon that it is better not to think too much about life and just live it, yet his tetralogy shows that he does the exact opposite of what he preaches.[16] Antonio never acts; he always misses the boat. He knows much about literature, music, movies, paintings, and other academic or artistic subjects, but he overlooks or misinterprets the basic signs that give clues to the understanding of life. A most amusing ironical situation occurs when Sharon and Tony have one of their stormy confrontations: she threatens him with a banana, but Antonio once again misses the sexual symbolism and imputes it to his wife's innocence. Antonio's whole world is topsy-turvy. He blooms in November and dies in the spring. He does not communicate with the living but tries desperately to communicate with the dead. When he is told of his wife's adultery, he is the one who becomes shifty-eyed and consoles the cuckolder. Once again he is seduced by a girl, Laura Fleischman, and once again he sees her as a goddess or a nun; she is the one who is matter-of-fact about the whole affair. Finally Sharon becomes pregnant by Tony and Tony marries Laura and Antonio returns to Sharon; and all returns to order.

---

16. He is the perfect illustration of the Pauline statement in Rom. 7:15-21, particularly "For the good that I would, I do not; but the evil which I would not, that I do."

Though Antonio is the main object of Buechner's satire, there are many more examples of irony in *The Book of Bebb*. It also touches Bebb, the hero who preaches about nakedness but hides the main facts of his life from his own family. Bebb exposes himself sexually, although he always appears dressed in a tight raincoat and believes in suppressing oneself to serve the Lord. Bebb has given up everything for the Lord, yet he is happy when he receives Redpath's legacy. Other ironies include the peace demonstrator who wears a Nazi overcoat in *Love Feast,* and the reversal in *Treasure Hunt:* the horny but guilty Tony is invited to produce pornographic movies while his dreamy brother becomes increasingly business-like. The irony of situations and the irony of life serve precisely to reveal the other side of the human psyche, the side which is hidden from view but which asserts itself despite man's endeavor to suppress it.

It is not always easy to distinguish between irony and humor. Aristotle suggested that humor is laughing at distortions which are not great enough to cause pain. Others have suggested that humor is sympathetic laughter. In Buechner's novels, there is definitely a difference between irony and humor. Most of the time he treats his characters—even Antonio—with gentle humor, but the nay-sayers use irony to shut their doors against the world. Thus humor has an affirming quality that irony lacks. Nicolet is a young fool of a minister in *The Final Beast*, but he is learning. Bebb sometimes lets his Dionysiac nature take over, as when he writes Jesus' name on his IRS form, but he is trying to be God's faithful servant. Godric looks back on his life with the same tone of gentle mockery, but he has made it.

Therefore one can truthfully say that in Buechner's works irony is the tone proper to tragedy, and humor that proper to comedy. The mistakes of one's youth are revalued in old age, and put in the right perspective. They are re-appraised within the flow of life.

It is an autobiographical fact that Buechner's vision of the world has slowly changed from tragic to comic. Like Erasmus, elated by his crossing of the Alps as he returned from Rome, Buechner has moved to "the Praise of Folly." And yet his work, like that of Erasmus, has two sides: folly which can be good can also be un-comfortable and harmful. Wisdom should be tolerant of the first and condemn the second.

In *The Book of Bebb* as well as in *Peculiar Treasures*, Buechner deals with the paradoxes of life in a very Renaissance-like manner. In many ways his treatment of the modern world resembles that of Rabelais. In *Gargantua*, it may be recalled, Rabelais mixes the genres and exercises parody as DeVries does in *The Tents of Wickedness*; Buechner also uses literary parody without admitting it. The parody or imitation may be unconscious, but who cannot recognize some of the style of William Burroughs' *Naked Lunch* in Herman Red-path's unpunctuated rambling about life and sex in *Lion Country*? Isn't Antonio a satirical representation of our modern anti-heroes à la Beckett? There is an echo of Proust's emphasis on memory and subjective reality in *Open Heart* as Laura and Antonio are sipping a drink, and it would hardly be surprising if there were not a little nudge at Robbe-Grillet's *Jalousie* in the depiction of the two possible ways their relationship might turn out.

Thus Antonio mixes the genres, aping the past masters in literature and deriving much of his technique from the world of cinematography, switching from elegiac and romantic arias to the language of introspection and occasionally to epic language, as when he gets caught up in the Love Feasts at Princeton. All of this has a lucid appeal. Like Rabelais, Buechner also uses a variety of languages: he mixes French, German, Italian, and Latin with a variety of English argots.

Buechner speaks these languages through his characters. In Nancy Oglethorpe, for instance, Buechner parodies the language of undigested psychology:

> "I haven't been able to look myself in the eye for seven years. I wanted to sever connections with the past and make a fresh start but psychological factors having to do with long-term patterns of behavior and the unfortunate reputation I have acquired in certain circles plus the fact that my professional work is constantly exposing me to situations that are too much for me to handle, these have all contributed to making it problematical at best that I could ever change. . . . "[17]

Bildabian the dentist has a curt, matter-of-fact way of expressing himself; Billy Kling is as precise as a nurse. Gertrude Conover uses

---

17. Buechner, *The Book of Bebb*, pp. 309-310.

the language of Theosophy, which contrasts with that of the reporter from the *Daily Princetonian* in the most amusing way when the two of them describe the effect of the punch served at a Love Feast. The first of the following paragraphs is Gertrude's description, and the second, more florid one is the reporter's:

> "It was the karmic energy of Jesus Christ at the Cana Wedding that turned water into wine, and I believe it was the karmic energy of Leo Bebb that had a similar effect on the Tropicana punch."

> *Pandemonium! Agape vies with Eros as Gott-und-Ginver-trunken cultists rise in pews embracing with dionysiac abandon. Aisles aswarm with sweating, rainsoaked bodies. Barechested boys and bra-less coeds tangle. Beardless frosh hug hairy legged lettermen. Even atheists amorously aroused as inhibitions wilt in steamy atmosphere of Turkish bath or Methodist massage parlor. . . .* [18]

Here Buechner plays with the alliteration, polysyllabic modifiers, and staccato style of the newspaper "scoop." Throughout his work, literary genres and linguistic modes vie with each other to create a sparkling style. Even silence is carefully imitated, as when the Indian Joking Cousin mimes a ritual at the death of Redpath, or accompanies Antonio on his spiritual journey after he has passed out from smoking a strong peace pipe.

Characters are also juxtaposed, contrasted, and finally united, symbolizing the union of paradoxes in the kingdom of God. The horny Herman Redpath selects as his favorite audience the inhibited Antonio, and tells him about life and sex. Antonio shows a very Renaissance spirit when, ironically, he blames his sex life on the voracity of women. (The voracious woman is one of the favorite topics of Renaissance comedy.) Ellie, the girl on the train, and Laura Fleischman only drop heavy hints, whereas Sharon virtually rapes him. Although Bebb is also a fool and part of the human circus, he, like Pantagruel in Rabelais' work, considers all the relative follies of men with tolerant wisdom. Men have faults but they often pay dearly for them. [19]

---

18. Buechner, *The Book of Bebb*, pp. 372-373.

19. In Shakespeare, there are two sorts of fools: one is the dunce who, unawares, tells the truth; the other, through his wit or learning, makes people self-aware and distracts them at the same time. Antonio and Bebb could be considered as similar counterparts.

It is certainly one of the paradoxes of Buechner's philosophy that he is on the one hand stern and unbending in his will to eradicate sin in people and curb the beast in them, whereas on the other hand he can laugh at their foibles, cry shame on their critics, and assert that they mostly need encouragement. The hammer-and-coax method designed to curb unruly children can turn tigers into lambs. It is another paradox of his that, throughout his novels, the lambs are in fact despised and the tigers praised for their involvement in the affairs of life.

In *The Book of Bebb*, as in *Godric* and *Peculiar Treasures*, comedy provides a picture of the doubleness of life. As artist, Buechner both creates and destroys. He praises the unexpected: Bebb the exposeur, Godric the pirate, Jacob the crook—all have been chosen to be God's representatives. He debunks the proud: Antonio, self-satisfied with his mediocre talents, fortune, and achievements; Flambard, the prince-bishop who has reached his elevated position in the world by stepping on the poor; the monks who think themselves a superior breed but who will not condescend to struggle and dirty their hands in the midst of excremental and suffering humanity. Buechner praises imprisonment and disagreeable conditions: one gives a person time to think; the others help the seed to grow. Sir John Harington praised the water closet, John Donne, the flea, and D. H. Lawrence wrote about the mosquito. Like many Renaissance writers, Buechner praises *doctora ignorantia*, following Saint Paul and other Christian thinkers. Folly teaches worldly wisdom because it points through things to their ideal significance. In this context, the poet and the creator is himself a fool and as worthy of being shattered and destroyed as the gallery of portraits he has created.

But finally laughter prevails, acceptance is victorious, and the many fools that gad about are but the variegated colors of refracted light. Thus the one and the many are reconciled, space and infinity and time and eternity. In *The Book of Bebb*, the train turns all places into one as it passes through so many at great speed; as an old man Godric finds the notion of eternity in the past, the present, and the unknown future of his life. Opposites live on the same planet even if they are on opposite sides of the same fence, like Roebuck and Bebb, or if they are in the same boat on the same pool, like Bebb and Babe. Movement is only appearance, and stillness is at the center of the storm. All truths are united into one, and life is re-affirmed. Buechner has overcome the tragic movement of life to reassert its comic features.

Tragedy, according to Aristotle, was the passing of happiness into misery. Tragedy centered on the actions of men, which constituted the plot, and pity or fear arose in the audience according to the nature of those actions. Shakespeare made tragedy an *exemplum*, showing that misery was the effect of wrongdoing. Hegel showed that tragedy was rooted in those times in life when two rights collide, whereas modern writers like Ionesco and Beckett show that it is rooted in the absurdity of life.

Although tragic figures appear in Buechner's books, he does not write tragic novels. Nicolet in *The Final Beast* and Bebb in *Open Heart* pass from the state of happiness to that of misery because both lose their wives and the purpose of their work. But they are not tragic figures because they accept setbacks, trusting that they are part of a divine and mysterious purpose. Death being part of the life process, its tragedy is overcome. Both Irma Reinwasser and Lucille die, but while they are alive both of them bloom as much as they are able to.

Tragic events occur in Buechner's novels. Like Shakespeare, Buechner tends to make his works *exempla*. The presence of the slanderer Poteat in *The Final Beast* is the cause of Irma's absurd death. Babe in *The Book of Bebb* has halted the progress of his wife's life. Godric is responsible for disaster on the sea. Tragedy is therefore the product of evil.

But it is also the product of ignorance. Fraternal wars are waged because of the one-sidedness of individuals. This is the basis of the quarrel between Antigone and Creon in Anouilh's *Antigone*. Each holds a partial truth but neither is ready to understand the other. Buechner, too, explores such quarrels: Roebuck and Babe see the evil side of man, whereas Bebb affirms his good side. The representatives of the two stances in life are bound to act in ways that clash until in their minds the union of contraries is achieved in a universalist perspective. Thus turmoil is caused, blood is shed.

Finally, tragedy is also life wasted. Antonio has gotten bogged down in the absurd. Unlike Beckett, Buechner has made him a comic character, similar to Robertson Davies' Marchbanks, because his world is incredibly narrow and because he lacks vision. Buechner overcomes tragedy in his later works like *The Book of Bebb* and *Godric* because, despite man's difficulties, despite his tragic falls and flaws, Buechner has come to believe that life has a plot which man can discover if he is attentive and obedient. It is the job of the artist and of the minister to discover the plot of life and proclaim the good news.

Since life is a sustaining force, the writer can no longer write tragedies in good faith, because though tragedy is a part of life it is a *limited* part of life. There are times when activity comes to a halt and man's spirit is broken, but something new always springs up. Sometimes it is an individual's reconsideration and realization that scheming is useless, that feverish activity to the detriment of one's health and that of others is sheer vanity. Thus Alice in *The Entrance to Porlock* finally understands the value of surrendering to the currents of life. And in *The Final Beast*, Poteat begins seeing new life.

Life reasserts itself, but comedy does not spring out of the will of man. As William Lynch has contended, the modern theatre has reversed the law of tragedy in reaffirming the indestructibility of the human spirit. This, Lynch rightly affirms, may be a valid form of art, but it bears no relation to existence as perceived by every one of us.[20] Unlike the actor at the end of the play, a broken man cannot rise to his feet and dance a jig. A broken man is down; he needs a hand to steady him. This is also Buechner's position. The individual who is down and refuses the friendly hand extended to him in Christ's love is doomed to die. In *The Final Beast*, Irma goes to her death because she refuses Nicolet's love. Antonio sinks into despair for a long time because he refuses the care of his father-in-law, Bebb, who wants to involve him in the joy of life. Godric goes his own piratical way and has nothing to show for the first part of his life because he refuses the messages of God. Man does not lift himself up by his own bootstraps, but needs the help of others or of God to get him back on his feet. The sick man needs a physician.

---

20. William F. Lynch, S.J., *Christ and Apollo: The Dimensions of the Literary Imagination* (South Bend, Ind.: University of Notre Dame Press, 1975), pp. 65-81.

Comedy strips man of his pretense. Like Bebb, the writer of comedy never forgets the foul smells that rise from the subterranean avenues—those of the New York subway, for instance—but he tolerates them, accepts them, affirming that "things are really funny—because wonderful realities can come of their lowermost depths."[21] The comic writer deals with man as Lilliputian. The humorist plays with the seven deadly sins and with peccadillos, but affirms that man, monkey or pig that he is, surprisingly manages to survive and even to improve. Nicolet in *The Final Beast* finds new ways to minister to his congregation; so does Bebb in *Love Feast*. All the characters of *The Entrance to Porlock* are sent back home and back to their lives. Men somehow bounce back; few are destroyed until it is their turn to fade away and make room for new generations. Comedy asserts that man may sometimes have had a brush with death, but that he is still alive. He has survived the storm.

Whatever Buechner describes is based on experiential reality, on his perception of the world. Irony is a deadly process because it cuts all communication between the world and man or between man and his fellows. Irony leads the way to tragedy as man cuts himself off from the sources of life. Buechner prefers the humorous mood that re-affirms the beauty of life, and has faith that, despite failings, man will be sustained by a life force which he calls God. Thus comedy is the form proper to the existentialist.

Observation has also taught Buechner that at their core men are really made of the same material. Despite external differences, the study of one is the study of them all. Both *Godric* and *The Book of Bebb* affirm the variety and complexity of human psyches. The wise man has lived many lives and therefore can relate to many undeveloped and one-sided human beings, encouraging them in their exploration of multi-faceted reality. The wise poet can therefore portray the lives of others with insight, through his experience of their psyches and the subjective knowledge he has of his own. Although his world will be limited to what he can comprehend, it will be wider than most because he has transcended the superficiality

21. Lynch, *Christ and Apollo*, p. 91. See also the whole chapter on comedy, particularly pp. 91-110.

of appearance and plunged into the depth of the human material. The novelist of the self is therefore relating to both subjective and objective reality; he is an observer of life as it is, but his acumen enables him to pick and choose what is most relevant to the human predicament. The discerning writer both gives and withholds the real, keeping what is central to the reality he focuses on and eliminating all confusing details.

VI

The Craftsman
Ut Pictura Poesis

> *Who can measure . . . how differently confirmed movie-goers like me would have turned out, both as artists and as human beings, if we hadn't grown up at the time of* Les Enfants du Paradis, Rashomon, The Wizard of Oz, *and* Casablanca?
>
> Frederick Buechner, *Now and Then*

Although it is impossible to dissociate themes and forms, every artist has a particular trademark that distinguishes him from others. Thus the stubbly fields of Van Gogh and the softer meadows of Millet differ in both atmosphere and technique. In the same way the representational horses of Stubbes and the symbolic animals of Marc bear very little resemblance to one another. For this reason, the distinctive technique of every artist deserves separate consideration.

Buechner's craft has been shaped by a threefold influence. We have already seen how Christianity and the modern trends of philosophy and psychology have left a decisive mark on his work. Still to be shown is how Buechner's love for the visual arts has left a definite imprint on him as a writer.

Buechner was well-trained in both literature and the visual arts. In *Now and Then*, he recalls how, as little boys, he and his cousin Tom (now a museum director) used to go to the Metropolitan Museum in New York and draw sketches on the second floor.[1] His friends say that

---

1. *Now and Then* (New York: Harper & Row, 1983), p. 23. This is the second part of Buechner's autobiography.

his favorite pastime at Lawrenceville School and elsewhere was to go out for supper and then go to a movie.[2] This passion for the visual arts is also evident in his choosing a course in architecture as a Princeton undergraduate. It may also have played some part in his attraction to his wife Judy, who used to paint. Thus the visual and the literary are strongly related in Buechner's fiction, as they are in the fiction of Flannery O'Connor and John Updike, who at some point in their lives painted or considered a vocation as painters.

Buechner's literary background is more obvious. At Princeton he majored in English literature. It is particularly interesting that he decided to write his senior thesis on the metaphor. Indeed, Buechner commonly asserts in his writings that the Bible is to be taken as metaphor, that the Christian vocabulary should be re-mythologized, and that the language of truth is poetry, in which contents and imagery are linked. Thus a study of Buechner's works would do him an injustice if it did not insist on the combination of the literary and the visual and how it is worked out in various art forms.

What characterizes Buechner's art is not the great sweep of a Rubens or a Delacroix, but the detailed portraits of a miniaturist. He could be better compared to someone like Oliver, the Elizabethan miniaturist, rather than to Hilliard, his contemporary, because in most of his portraits there is a sense that light is coming from above. Ideally, he would like to resemble the Rembrandt of the later years,[3] although until *Godric* one is reminded more of Franz Hals or even of the earlier work of Brueghel or Bosch, which focused on the agitation of life.

Although *Godric* shows that Buechner has come to appreciate the medieval period, his particular love up until that novel was for the

---

2. Personal interview with Mr. Hlavecek on June 8, 1981. He said that when Buechner and he were colleagues at Lawrenceville, they would often go to Princeton, eat a light meal at Lahière's, and then go to the movies, good or bad. That Buechner's taste for movies has not died is something he confirmed, as did Douglas Snow, interviewed on May 24, 1980, at Exeter, where he is manager of the bookstore. He stressed Buechner's love for movies when he was at Exeter, and said that when he visited Buechner in Pawlet, Vermont, he left just in time for the Buechners to go to see an old movie in Dorset.

3. Personal interview with Frederick Buechner on August 14, 1981.

Renaissance, from which he has derived many art forms. In fact, it was in the seventeenth century that the teaching through images called emblems appeared, although the literary form existed previously. Emblems had the advantage of uniting the visual and the didactic. Like metaphor, they produced a condensing of reality. Daniel Bartoli compared the emblem to a work of inlay that was not designed to look like a contrivance but to suggest that art is barely distinguishable from nature. We have already seen how Buechner's art delights in imitating life, in contrast to that of Robbe-Grillet, and in creating an illusion composed of elements that are all true. In this he is a creator who imitates and reflects the work of the greatest Creator of all, God. We have already seen how carefully *Telling the Truth* was contrived, a work of tapestry rather than inlay. Although pictorial images occur in only a few of Buechner's works—in *Peculiar Treasures* (thanks to the author's daughter, Katherine, the illustrator) and in *The Faces of Jesus*, a commentary on historical images of Christ—the influence of emblems on Buechner's novels is as strong as it is in the metaphysical poets or preachers whom he particularly admires.[4]

In Buechner's fiction, as in seventeenth-century literature, we find a combination of profane and sacred emblems, sometimes static and sometimes animated. The double nature of man is thus rendered in *The Entrance to Porlock* by a vision of an ambiguous creature, bird-footed and tree-footed, whereas in *The Book of Bebb* the congregation is seen as a forest of trees which, when it hears the right words, starts putting out more leaves. Sensual love is traditionally represented as naked— Bebb exposes himself, for example—and Dionysiac: when Bebb and Bert committed adultery on Shaw Hill, they were gathering grapes, and when Bebb exposes himself to the children in Miami, he is holding a bunch of grapes. Sexual love is also linked with fire. In *The Entrance to Porlock*, Tip, who masturbates, feels as if he is on fire, and in *The Book of Bebb*, Chris, whom Bebb apparently masturbated, wakes up as if the

---

4. In an interview in Stonington, Connecticut, on August 31, 1981, the poet James Merrill recalled Buechner's admiration for Thomas Brown and Donne, whom he often read. He also loved the decadent fantasy of writers like Oscar Wilde and Walter Pater, De Reigner, Hérédia, and Baudelaire. All were chiselers of prose and poetry, miniaturists of a kind. In his fiction Buechner has carried on this preoccupation with detail.

house was on fire. In *Treasure Hunt*, Babe's house, the house of death, is a place where flies are constantly being swatted; only black coffee and dark chocolate are served in the kitchen. The kitchen and its goings-on are the emblem representing life, in which so many things are perpetually done and undone: the creative process, the cooking, occurs first, then the eating and sharing takes place, followed by the washing-up of the mess made—endless tasks that have to be performed three times a day.[5]

Buechner occasionally uses devices as well. For instance, in *The Entrance to Porlock*, the most symbolic of Buechner's books, Tommy wears a hat with an arrow through it to symbolize his jocularity and lack of brains. Nels, the repressed, angry man who lacks courage, roars when he talks. Alice, the witch from the cold, lies with her feet under the house and has flaxen hair. In *The Book of Bebb*, Sharon is an ambiguous figure. Sometimes she is Circe, a creature of sunshine and moisture, as when she seduces Antonio in *Lion Country*, making love to him in the broad daylight after she comes out of the shower, a scene suggesting Botticelli's *Birth of Venus*. Sometimes she is a promise of a world to come, as she is when she appears at night at the party given by the Indians at the end of *Lion Country*, a promise of the New Jerusalem. At other times, as in *Treasure Hunt*, she is dressed in moonlight, an Athena ready to fight for her own and protect them from the forces of evil.

As one could expect, Buechner also uses many Christian symbols. The Bible says, ''Our God is a consuming fire.'' Buechner illustrates this metaphor in *The Final Beast*: the Pentecostal atmosphere is rendered by visions of flames, and Irma Reinwasser is burned to death in the house in which she has taken refuge. References to fire appear frequently in *The Book of Bebb*. Bebb keeps talking about burning his bridges and severing his ties to the past. At the beginning of *Love Feast*, we learn that his barn has been burned by an arsonist, and at the end Bebb disappears in flames and clouds of smoke. A phoenix, symbol

---

5. It is also the means Buechner uses to introduce bathos, to reduce man's preoccupation to proper size and transform tragedy into kitchen drama. In *Open Heart*, Sharon's brandishing the banana at Tony, with whom she has committed adultery, reduces the sin to a sordid little slip and a means of laughing at the blind, cuckolded husband.

of the resurrection, Bebb must have risen from the ashes, because his body is not found among the debris of the plane.

We have already mentioned the image of Bebb as a vigilant soldier of Christ who hardly ever sleeps. He is also a bouncing ball, an emblem which was first used by Ledesma in *Epigramas y hieroglificos a la vida de Christo* as a symbol of the conversion of Saint Paul. In *The Final Beast*, the Holy Ghost is perceived as the Hound of Heaven breathing heavily down Nicolet's neck; in *The Book of Bebb*, Golden, the messenger of the Lord, is represented as a swarm of bees, an emblem for loquacity.[6] The adage "where your treasure is, there will your heart be also" is translated in the scene in which Bert shows Sharon her treasure box, where she keeps the proof of her love relationship with Bebb and of Sharon's parentage. Christian love as lion-tamer, an image exemplified by Bebb, originates pictorially in the emblems of De Bry, though the idea goes back to Greek and early Christian history and lore. All these form neat and memorable pictures which disclose ethical or religious truths, like the windows and murals of medieval cathedrals, the embroidery on the dresses of Queen Elizabeth I, or the pageants of King James's Progressers.

Allegorical thought is a component of Buechner's art; he makes full use of the bestiary. Animal imagery is particularly strong in *The Final Beast*. Rooney calls herself a bitch when she is in fact represented as a mare. Nicolet's secretary is compared to a blackbird. Irma is a chicken with broken wings, an image repeated and applied to Bert in *Treasure Hunt*. Eventually Irma will fly on a white horse with a red mane, apocalyptically taking her to her death. Clem is a fish who goes into his underwater hole and is afraid of being hooked. Lillian Flagg is a chipmunk who stores variegated objects in her house, and Poteat is compared sometimes to a drone and sometimes to a cur. Nicolet

---

6. The emblem is also ironical because most of the time Golden is a silent figure who appears and disappears without uttering a word, or leaves short cryptic messages like "Good luck, sweetheart." The only time that he speaks at length is in *Open Heart* when he talks about time and eternity at the station to the all-too-loquacious Antonio. But his silent presence always reminds Bebb of the Word, of the paradox of God's presence in a world where he seems to be absent.

alone escapes the pattern; he is a human being, for better or for worse, a Bluebeard because of his love of women, or a red rose, a Christ-figure, since Christ is often called the Red Rose of Sharon and Nicolet is his disciple.

Allegorical elements persist in *The Entrance to Porlock*, but Buechner makes no particular reference to the bestiary, except in the inner roar of Nels. Buechner simply follows the pattern established by Frank Baum's *Wizard of Oz*. The bestiary recurs metaphorically in *The Book of Bebb*. Bebb is the lion-tamer, and his message is that all human beings should cage their beasts lest they escape and destroy all. Antonio is never directly compared to the cat, but is constantly juxtaposed to him. The cat is utterly independent; he is as distant, aloof, and uninvolved as the narrator himself. Often he is caged, and sometimes he hurts himself against the jagged metal enclosure of his master. In the same way Antonio keeps himself caged, and sometimes gets hurt because of his angularity. Yet when issues become matters of life and death, the cat and Antonio thrash around and make a thorough mess in their effort to survive. The life process is a painful one for both, as it is for all human beings. Buechner also uses the metaphor of the cat to describe other characters: Sharon's smile is like letting the cat out of the bag, and so is Bebb's exposure. From the cat that he was, Antonio is gradually transformed into a half-Christian, half-alive fish. In the last few paragraphs of *Treasure Hunt* we find this description of him: "I can think of Antonio Parr with his glassy El Greco eyes rolled heavenward like a fish on cracked ice in a fishstore window."[7] Antonio is still caged, and more than half-dead, but he is now potentially a fish.

Buechner makes full use of the bestiary again in *Godric*. But in this book several animals represent the different aspects of the fully rounded characters. The basic image for Godric is a bird. His great aquiline nose, noted by his contemporaries, gives him the appearance of a bird. In Buechner's fiction, he is a bird of prey, a rapacious guillemot with hard beak and red feet, a raven, an owl, and even a ravaging bear. As he gets older and his strength weakens, he is likened to a squirrel,

---

7. Frederick Buechner, *The Book of Bebb* (New York: Atheneum, 1979), p. 530. Hereafter, where appropriate, this work will be cited parenthetically in the text.

a lobster on a stone, and a cackling hen. Caught by God, he becomes a fish. Ailred, the abbot, smells of fish, but he is also a raven because, as a Benedictine monk, he wears a black habit; Reginald, with his fish-belly tonsure, is something between a herring and a goose. The other pilgrims on the way to Rome are also characterized through the bestiary. (Only Gillian is a true human being.) Peg is a sparrow who pecks at her husband Richard, a waddling goose. Ralph, with his flat, frayed fingertips, could be a duck. Perkin and Elric are squirrels because they are always trembling. And Mouse the pirate, Godric's friend, dances on the surface of life and drowns, squealing, as his ship shatters on the rocks. The main images for Godric are those of the bird, denizen of two worlds, and of the fish, both Christian symbols.

Although none of Buechner's works is a sustained allegory, he does employ allegory to express his thought. In *Open Heart*, Herman Red-path's traveling to the happy hunting ground is as much an allegory as Bunyan's pilgrim's progress; the device is repeated in *Love Feast* as Antonio comes to terms with death on his way to the heavenly pool. Buechner's attempts at science fiction in *Treasure Hunt* in *The Book of Bebb* work along the same lines. As in Langland or Chaucer, the dream is an analogy destined to express the archetypal longing of humanity. The space man is a messianic symbol.

Other of Buechner's symbolical narratives can hardly be called allegories because his characters are both round and fluid, whereas allegorical figures are mostly flat and static. Still, many allegorical devices appear in these works. The woods in *The Final Beast* and *The Entrance to Porlock* are, as in Tasso or Spencer, places of wandering into the psyche of an individual who is confused and in search of a goal. Rooney first enters the woods as she rakes her memory for what she cannot face in herself; she trips in the mud and avoids the puddles. The road is fairly dark, but the end of the path is flooded with light.[8] She enters the woods again with Nicolet and they sit in a clearing, full of

---

8. Two symbols are connected in Rooney's case: going into the woods and walking through the corridor of a house, opening doors in search of what is hidden. Both devices have been used in "Gothic" literature, which traditionally deals with the divided self. The reaction of characters reflects their fear of the unknown.

green and golden light, where they sort out their feelings for each other in veiled terms and establish the limits of their relationship. As they leave the woods and race along through the countryside, one knows that they have not reached the bottom of the sickness that gnaws at her. Metaphorically this time, rather than allegorically as before, the omniscient narrator affirms that they will have to return to the woods. When they do, it is among the plants of Lillian Flagg's house, where Nicolet can fulfill his role as priest and forgive Rooney in the name of Jesus for her adultery.

The journey and the woods, linked in *The Final Beast*, are even more clearly joined in *The Entrance to Porlock*. All journeys of any kind are a sign of disease, of a confusion of goals. Peter Ringkoping, the instigator, is pursuing the wrong goal in wanting to give away his land and thus deprive his sons of their patrimony. As in Tasso, the woods are neutral grounds, but the shading and the light play on each of the characters. Nels appears mottled, and his self-assurance is toned down; Peter projects his own desire for extra-terrestrial reality, but realizes that he is only a poor old man; Tommy comes to terms with his own cruelty when he kills the bird that comes back to him; Tip, the frightened adolescent, sees a dragon in the approaching figure of his grandmother. The woods are also enchanted; marvelous things happen there. Peter cries without knowing why and gains a semblance of a heart; Tommy meets Bonzo and the doll-makers who operate on him; and Sarah walks and even dances as she had never dared to before.

The woods still play an important part in *Godric*. Elric, the frightened anchorite, peoples them with demons, whereas Godric, who has come to terms with himself, no longer finds them threatening. He settles in a clearing to spend the end of his life there. In *The Book of Bebb*, this allegorical device is not used; to a certain extent it is replaced by tricks of light and darkness, as the narrator goes from the North to the South, and by images of the barren land through which Redpath and Antonio travel before reaching their goal.

All the novels are marked by constant traveling. As in medieval and Renaissance romances, traveling is the product of sin, but the traveling itself is a way toward mending. In *The Final Beast*, Rooney undertakes her journey to Muscadine with a clear sense of purpose. Nicolet, on the other hand, does not recognize his own need to travel but realizes his own emptiness on the way. Pilgrimage in *The Entrance to Porlock* is undertaken for the wrong reason, but the journey is beneficial to all. In *The Book of Bebb*, each of Bebb's moves to a new home is the result of his exposing himself, except that move he makes from Antonio and Sharon's house because their marriage is shaky. The journey is therefore the product of either one's own sin or that of others, but it is always a test and a grace. Antonio, who travels to the South to expose Bebb, finds a family and spiritual inspiration in the most unlikely place. The journey has broken the habit of his life, and he is free to find himself and be himself. Yet the journey is really what man makes of it; in Richard Hooker's phrase, it is "matter indifferent," like the woods. This is the view Buechner arrives at in *Godric*. Godric's earlier journeys, spent looting and thieving, are of no spiritual benefit to him. He is first dragged on a pilgrimage by his mother, and he attains self-knowledge in spite of himself on the road to Rome; his last journey to Jerusalem is the product of coincidence or providence, depending on one's point of view, since he was there for material profit but gained spiritual goods. The journey then becomes a spiritual journey, a return from evil-doing to the world of grace. In terms of medieval allegory, Godric has to conquer the dragon to gain the Holy Grail. But in Buechner, the dragon is no exterior phantasm but lurks within the saint's soul.

The path takes various forms. In *The Final Beast*, there is a contrast between the path of Irma Reinwasser—straight, geometrical, and lined with barbed wire—and that of Nicolet and Rooney, which meanders through woods and clearings. Eventually Irma's barren path flourishes with red roses until at the moment of her death it is finally set ablaze. In *The Entrance to Porlock*, the road includes a ferry and woods; both seem safe enough but happen to be full of surprises. In *The Book of Bebb*, the train is the link between the way of the North and that of the South. The path that Antonio takes is winding, whereas the paths of other characters follow a straighter line. It is significant that in his dream Antonio follows a straight line on a path that is so barren that it contains no distraction. Godric's path also meanders until he finds the straight-and-narrow path; though he has left for the high seas, two other poles of attraction still remain in his life: his parent's house and the island of Farne, his earthly home and his spiritual home. Eventually he finds both earthly and spiritual home in the vicinity of Durham under the protection of the Church. His journey is over the sea, across the barren land, across the waters, and into the woods where he can dwell safely, for having achieved some form of saintliness, Godric need no longer be a wanderer.

The sense of mystery and wonder is further enhanced by the presence of the marvelous. This was one of the standard features of Elizabethan and Jacobean pamphleteering: "Look up and see wonders." Marvelous and unexpected events occur in Buechner's novels. When tree-branches clack, peace is restored in the heart of the searching minister in *The Final Beast*. Bebb believes that silvers and goldens are messengers from God; and the fleeting appearances of Golden confirm the presence of some other reality, beyond tangible reality, of some caring presence whose ways are not ours. Trains do not run through mantle-shelves, as in Magritte's surrealist paintings, but they could. We are placed in the world of dreams.

Symbolical imagery of light and darkness, of colors and of the elements reinforce the allegorical message. We have already seen that in *The Final Beast*, the clearing in the woods is suffused with green and golden light, and that at the end of the path Rooney takes, light shines abundantly. The symbol recurs forcibly in *The Book of Bebb*, especially in *Lion Country*, where Antonio is constantly leaving the northern realm of death and drizzling November to go and gain some life from sun-flooded Florida. Many modern American writers have used this device, among them Updike, who often contrasts the North—White, ice-cold, and foggy—to the South—Black, warm, sunny, generous, and lively. Within *The Book of Bebb*, Buechner unites the two poles of American literature, opposing "paleface" ways of life with those of people with red or black skin.

Whereas sacred love is marked by the rays of the sun and clouds of glory, evil is a dark, Gothic affair. In *The Book of Bebb*, Babe offers dark chocolate cake and coffee. The narration of the Abbott and Costello film in *Lion Country* best exemplifies the attraction of darkness that overcomes man, slowly at first, then at greater and greater speed. Evil is set in a dark cave, and though man turns away with regret from the light, he can still be lured into the vampire's cave, where he will be blanched into a ghost. Also ghost-like are those who have been unable to choose between life and death: the Metzgers, Antonio, and Charlie Blaine of *The Book of Bebb*. The innocent and the youthful also become victims of vampires, among them Hedwic, the Lord de Granville's mistreated wife, whose cheeks have turned from pink to grey.

Although the contrast between light and darkness is clearly defined in Buechner's work, it is difficult to find any systematic use of colors. Unlike Flannery O'Connor, he does not paint with the liturgical palette. His colors have degrees of ambiguity and interact upon each other; he uses them dynamically.

Traditionally, blue is the color of heaven. And all of the ministers in Buechner's novels have blue eyes, as he does: Nicolet, Strasser, Antonio, Bebb, and Godric. Blue is also the color that Rooney sees after the storm of her own heart has been appeased and after the rain has dispelled the clouds. It is also the color of the sky that Peter Ringkoping sees when Strasser gives him back his land in *The Entrance to Porlock*. In *The Book of Bebb*, it is the symbol of heaven in the pilgrimages of Redpath and Antonio. But in *The Final Beast*, one of Poteat's colors is bottle-blue. Discouraged Bebb in *Love Feast* has turned blue. The lion-headed lady of *The Final Beast*, Madge Cusper, chooses to wear blue because she has given up on life. And Gertrude Conover has blue hair. What symbolism does Buechner intend in these characters? We are faced with the usual difficulty of deciding whether the imagery is descriptive or symbolic, but in Buechner's fiction there is not always a clear-cut way to decide which is intended.

Red is the color of the earth, painted on Herman Redpath's chest when he is on his way to heaven in *Open Heart*. But earthiness has its danger: in *The Final Beast*, the adulterous Rooney has red hair; in *Treasure Hunt*, the devilish Babe, who clings to his property, has spiky red hair, and in *Godric*, the worldly bishop Flambard also has a red mane. Buechner seems to be saying that those who love life are vampires who will spill the blood of others to quench their own insatiable thirst. Red is also the color of sacrifice. In *The Final Beast*, the carpet of the church is red, and the guilt-ridden Nicolet spills his own blood, as does Lyman Beecher in *Telling the Truth*. Man can also bleed in the presence of the holy, as Callaway does in *Treasure Hunt*. The earth needs to be sanctified.

Yellow, the color of light, seems to be Buechner's favorite color. His loose-limbed females are often dressed in yellow, as are Rooney in *The Final Beast* and Sharon in *The Book of Bebb*. His characters often have blond hair, and paintings are gilded by the light of the sun. In *The Final Beast*, Lillian Flagg, disappointed with her painting, brings it to life with streaks of yellow and lavender. In *The Entrance to Porlock*, Strasser makes the land valuable to Sarah by painting it with the colors of gold. Silvers and Goldens, angels of the Lord in *The Book of Bebb*, convey the riches of God's grace. Golden paints on the walls of Open Heart the image of Bebb's life in all its beauty and sordidness, but the image is suffused with yellow light.

Yellow and gold seem to be what give value to life, but, as in previous cases, it is also an ambiguous color. In *The Final Beast*, Poteat's eyes turn golden as he projects his evil thoughts on Irma and draws her into the circle of evil and destruction. When Nicolet and Rooney are in the clearing in the forest, the ferns are also golden, suggesting the possibility of new adultery. Bebb's greatest temptation is the possession of gold, and Godric succumbs to it as he sails the wide seas in search of more loot. Yellow and gold may be the colors of the most precious things in man's life, but they can also be symbolical of the lure of the satanic. Yet the clue comes from the direction of the light: light coming from above is sacred, contrasted in Buechner's pictures with the doubtful inner glow of things, which may be deceitful.

Red, yellow, and blue are combined in the color of fire, which often symbolizes the presence of the Holy Spirit. As she is about to minister to Nicolet in *The Final Beast*, Lillian Flagg wears a flame-blue dress. Whenever Nicolet is about to preach, a combination of red, blue, and yellow in the shape of flames appears in the church's stained-glass windows. Red and blue are the essential components of man's life, and they are painted on Herman Redpath's chest to insure him a safe trip to the happy hunting ground.

Colors are essential to life, but they are as mixed as human motives. Hope is expressed by green, often triggered by love. In *The Final Beast*, Poteat makes love for the first time on a pile of green ponchos, and Irma Reinwasser wears a green hat when Nicolet jokingly addresses her as "my true love." Children draw with green pens, and lovers sit among green ferns and green leaves. In *The*

Book of Bebb, the congregation starts putting out new leaves as they hear the gracious Word of God. But green is also the color of jealousy that grips the heart of Poteat in *The Final Beast* and of Antonio and Babe in *The Book of Bebb*.

The same ambiguity applies to white, the color of purity and of death. In *The Final Beast*, the children's upper lips are sometimes white with milk, and the Church of the Communion of Saints is white. On the other hand, Irma, who is about to be killed and has sacrificed herself, sits on a white horse with a red mane; is Buechner's message that purity can be attained only through death? Nicolet announces the coming of the white horse of the Apocalypse; Roy, Nicolet's father, has white hair and a powdery white complexion, features common to all hypochondriacs in Buechner's novels. In *Love Feast*, a Christmastime snowfall brings the tormented Antonio peace and joy; but at the time Antonio is attracted to the cold, and his love for snow is a death-wish, which is also an essential part of the human experience.[9]

One can deduce some of Buechner's philosophy from his use of color imagery. To live is to be garish, cruel, and bloodthirsty; to do less than truly live is to be pale, wan, and half-dead. There are no lilies of the field in Buechner's depiction of humanity. We are simply foul and doomed to be in the wrong in God's eyes. Only grace can save us from sin.

In Buechner's restless cloudland of sky, colors are as dynamic as characters; they change as characters change. Bebb turns from blue to pink as Gertrude Conover coaxes him into new life. In *The Final Beast*, when Rooney arrives in the parish, her hair is the color of sand; after she commits adultery, it is red; as she mourns for her sin, she covers her hair with a black scarf; when she is forgiven she wears a yellow band. Both Irma and Poteat are associated with green by the inspiration of love. Clem, who is dressed in khakis in both summer and winter, paints the floor of his shop yellow for the love of Rooney, who often wears this color; when he is recon-

---

9. It is expressed by Godric, who plunges into the Wear and becomes numb with cold. He praises God for all that is cold and dark, because it is the end of suffering.

ciled with her, he orders bright straw hats from the West Indies. Lillian Flagg uses all the colors of life in her house, but gradually they, like her, are being bleached by the sun and by age.

This symbolism of colors in the characters' lives creates dynamic movement, as does the interaction of colors. We have already mentioned the image of the vampire, who draws his life from others' blood. The same seems to be true, to some extent, of certain characters. When Rooney commits adultery, her hair changes from sable to red, but Poteat, her lover, who had for a moment turned from grey to green, becomes black. In *Godric*, we find two examples of the same device: the ruddy De Granville sucks the blood out of his young wife Hedwic, whom he maltreats out of anger over his own impotence; and Flambard, the flaming red bishop, sows black death upon the land. He stains the snow with the blood coming from his horse's mouth, held too tight in a bit. Thus abundant and unruled life brings out its contrary, death.

Like the images of the woods or of travel, the hues are finally "matter indifferent," neither sacred nor profane, potentially good or evil. Colors are no longer a static symbol, and their interaction gives us a glimpse of some of the dynamism that is typical of Buechner's mobile world. When he uses film techniques, as we shall see, his pictures are always in technicolor. With the bright colors he uses, Buechner reminds us of Fernand Léger, but his characters are not mechanical. The varieties of hues and shades he employs could link him to Chagall, except that Buechner's pictures are three-dimensional, not flat. He is strongly influenced by surrealism, but Paul Delvaux never uses as bright a palette, and Magritte sometimes paints in monochrome. Nevertheless, the end of *The Entrance to Porlock* can be compared to Magritte's work. Like Magritte (and Strasser in the novel), Buechner likes to paint a picture within a picture, both representing the same reality.

Before I discuss the cinematic techniques Buechner employs, I should say a few words about elemental imagery, which along with the images of color and the bestiary is an essential component of Buechner's symbolism. Buechner's elemental imagery is apparently derived from two sources: when applied to characters, it is related to the theories of the humors, and whenever it is meteorological, it is inspired by Shakespeare's plays—particularly by *The Tempest*, which forms the background of *The Entrance to Porlock*, and *King Lear*, which is essential to the understanding of *The Book of Bebb*. Both plays are mentioned in the course of the novels.

In all his books, Buechner tends to relate characters to the elements, the well-adjusted character being one in whom the elements are found in the right proportions. Fathers are usually associated with air and lack of substance: this is true of Roy in *The Final Beast*, of Peter Ringkoping in *The Entrance to Porlock*, of Antonio (but not of Bebb) in *The Book of Bebb*, and of Aedlward in *Godric*. These men are married to earth mothers: Sarah in *The Entrance to Porlock*, Sharon or Billie Kling, consort to the hypochondriac Charlie Blaine, in *The Book of Bebb*, and Aedwen in *Godric*. Other characters, the dramatic destroyers, are linked with consuming fires: the young man who burns Irma in *The Final Beast*, Golden in *The Book of Bebb*, and Flambard in *Godric*. Others still represent the void: they are the hypochondriacs of Buechner's novels. The action really depends on the unity of the first two elements. Thus Buechner's marriages are based upon this association of heaven and earth, and well-rounded characters like Lillian Flagg and Nicolet in *The Final Beast*, Strasser in *The Entrance to Porlock*, Bebb in *The Book of Bebb*, and Godric and Ailred in *Godric* have come to terms with the elements.

Water also plays an essential part in Buechner's fiction. The sea in all its treachery is contrasted with the cleansing and beneficial pool.[10] In *Open Heart* and *Love Feast*, the unity of the family is depicted as a protective boat; whenever it is destroyed, all the characters are at sea, at a loss. They then dream of tropical islands on which to land and be secure. In *Godric*, the pirate is tossed upon the seas until he finds his home in God, whereas his companion Mouse is shattered by the sea when it turns into a killer. Until *Godric*, one could have contrasted saltwater and rainwater in Buechner's imagery; but with *Godric*, the river with its eddy, the treacherous Wear, is also dangerous. Neither can one contrast still waters with moving waters, for if the pool is the central image of baptism and

10. See Edward A. Armstrong, *Shakespeare's Imagination* (Lincoln, Neb.: University of Nebraska Press, 1946), who reminds us at the same time that nakedness, bathing, and the pool of light were essential to the Romantic imagination of Wordsworth and Coleridge.

redemption for Buechner, so is the rain. Men avoid pools or puddles or rain, but they are mistaken to do so. Rain and pools water the soul, relieve dryness and barrenness, cleanse the spirit that is thus renewed. Antonio in *The Book of Bebb* dreams of splashing in the pool, and Godric bathes in the Jordan with great enthusiasm.

Buechner's meteorological imagery uses the traditional images of the storm and the rain. Electricity crackles in the background and relationships or characters are tense until the beneficial rain falls. Examples can be found in *The Final Beast*: it rains as Rooney and Nicolet approach Muscadine, and at the end of the picnic in *Myron*. A rainstorm breaks as the characters make their way through the forest in *The Entrance to Porlock*, and all are drenched. The storm rumbles in the kitchen in *Open Heart* as Tony and Sharon have one of their lovers' quarrels, and rumbles on until a wet and naked Tony finally confesses to Antonio that he has slept with Sharon. Finally, as Godric leaves Farne with his treasure and travels over the moors and through the woods to Bishop Auckland, he is caught in a ''bitter winter rain.'' As in *King Lear*, the rain reminds the proud of the poor, naked wretches that they are, and of their solidarity with other human beings. Godric decides to leave his loot for the poor and unsheltered. The storm indicates that all is not well among and within human beings, but the rain both reduces and elevates them to mere humanity.

Man has to face the warring elements of the sin that is within him, but Buechner insists that there is peace in the eye of the storm: the island can be found; the boat, if the crew pulls together, will be able to endure the seas. Thus all characters find a haven at Strasser's place in *The Entrance to Porlock*, Antonio and Sharon go back together on their raft in *Love Feast*, and in *Treasure Hunt* all the characters find peace in Brownie's motel room, in which hangs the picture of the boy fishing in the pool. Godric reaches the church of Bishop Auckland and finds both work and shelter from the storm. Thus stillness and contentment always follow the storms in Buechner's novels. The rain is followed by the sun's rays and a pure, clean sky.

Even more dangerous than the storm is the mist that settles over the land. Camus used this image most felicitously in *The Fall*. Buechner appropriately uses it to depict the world of the twentieth century. Land and sky are rendered indistinguishable because of this mixture of the elements of air and water. Antonio in *The Book of Bebb* lives in this nondescript state, in the mists of November, confused and unattuned to the rhythm of the earth. But mist can also provide the benefit of blurring the past. Godric, having retrieved his belongings from Farne, leaves it forever, and as he does so a mist settles over it. The dream island has had its use, but now Godric must go on with the reality of his new life.

As in Shakespeare, Buechner's imaginative thought starts with the realization of life's duality. There is often an oscillating movement from one image to its contrary—from the beast of prey to sheep or cattle, from light to darkness, from colors to black and white, from the earth to the sky. As in dreams or in paintings, each image serves as a foil to the other, either enhancing it or blurring it or negating its impact. The poles of life and death are set against each other, but the work gives an impression of fluidity, of life in death and of death in life. As Buechner develops as a writer, the images intensify emotions in a relevant way. *The Entrance to Porlock* is an incredible mixture of archetypal images, symbols, and fairy tale. Buechner comes out of the woods again in *The Book of Bebb* in his parody of the young writer who uses imagery for adornment or forces literary references and symbols upon his thoughts. He uses images based on the physical realities of daily life: the home and the kitchen, natural bodily functions. In *Godric*, images are so adeptly interwoven into the story that they are unnoticeable; the elements, colors, and flora and fauna are part of the narrative, combining to point out the occult in the most natural fashion. The craftsman is no longer to be detected in the painting of his picture, but the atmosphere remains unmistakably his.

Movement, Buechner points out in *The Alphabet of Grace* and *The Book of Bebb*, is a succession of stills. In all of Buechner's fiction there are some unforgettable stills, when the air is motionless and the reader holds his breath: Rooney and Nicolet, for instance, in the clearing in *The Final Beast*; the four male characters eating lunch in the woods in *The Entrance to Porlock*; Gertrude Conover holding Jimmy Bob Luby in front of the door of the trailer in *Treasure Hunt*; Godric and Ailred (in *Godric*) perched like birds on the roof of his shack as the waters of the Wear overrun their banks. Time is suspended and so is movement.

At other times Buechner paints pictures full of the animation of life, but they are still tableaux vivants. Such is, for instance, the torture scene in which Irma Reinwasser's feet are deformed by reveling Nazis, which is depicted with the vividness and horror with which Franz Hals paints debauchery. In *The Entrance to Porlock*, one could choose the scene with the doll-makers at the center of the woods. In *Lion Country*, the confession scene at Revenoc has the same quality of animated stillness, and *Godric* is constructed like a medieval polyptych.

The Apostle Paul proclaimed, "I am become all things to all men, that I may by all means save some" (I Cor. 9:22b). Nor does the all-encompassing Buechner spurn any of the forms of the media to convey his message. His successions of stills are sometimes like comic strips which he eventually animates and turns into cartoons. Nathanael West had thought of subtitling his book *Miss Lonelyhearts* "a novel in the form of the comic strip." Buechner also uses the comic strip in *The Book of Bebb*, mainly to depict Lucille Bebb, a lonely character indeed.

As Buechner knows, the comic strip suggests more than it actually depicts; balloons are partial clues to what is happening. Lucille's speech is always laconic, and her silences suggest the contents of the balloons. Herman Redpath appears as a comic-strip Indian. Antonio himself sometimes becomes a comic-strip character —in *Love Feast* when he is standing next to the discarded Christmas tree near the compost heap, and in *Treasure Hunt* when he is waiting outside a nursery where Bebb's friends hope to find his reincarnation. A girl who had met Antonio previously at the store where he was inquiring about Bebb's house, but whom he does not recognize, asks him whether he found what he was looking for. Unable to know which of his two quests she is referring to, Antonio philosophizes:

> The other thing was the oracular utterance that had just come out of her moist little mouth like a comic strip balloon which seemed to confirm the reality of a world where messages from outer space were transmitted dentally and dead evangelists turned up in diapers to have their fingers pricked.[11]

---

11. Buechner, *The Book of Bebb*, p. 463.

Is this providence or coincidence? We are left to decide for ourselves.

In *Open Heart*, Buechner uses the comic-strip technique to depict the quarrel between the illicit lovers, Sharon and Tony. The first picture shows a happy family at breakfast; the second shows Chris's downcast face when Tony tells Sharon she is turning Chris into a homosexual, and a balloon appears. The third focuses on the "rain" falling in the kitchen as Sharon throws a glass of water at Tony. The fourth shows Sharon brandishing a banana at Tony, and the series closes on Chris's downcast face. By using the comic-strip technique, Buechner has contracted time to give us the bare story line, which he will expand and develop later on in the novel.

Buechner uses the comic-strip technique in his novels for two main reasons. Tragedies in comic strips are not real tragedies, but the balloons are pregnant with meaning. Like allegory, the comic strip points both at itself and at an unexpressed or inexpressible reality within the framework of a given technique.

Cartoonists animate the comic-strip stills, each frame of which suggests a story and movement. Buechner uses the same technique in his alternation of stills and slow motion. Animated and tottering on her French heels, Lucille becomes a cartoon character, but by the time she commits suicide she has developed into a real human being. Both Sharon in *The Book of Bebb* and Godric's fellow pirate in *Godric* are compared to the king of the early cartoon, Mickey Mouse, who in American lore is the epitome of the insignificant character. Both of these characters dance on the surface of their lives, taking incredible risks, unconscious of the dangers that await them, until they start looking around. At this point they crash and either die in the fall or are miraculously rescued. Mouse dies in *Godric*, while in *The Book of Bebb*, Sharon is given a new lease on life. Just as the characters in early cartoons are never totally sure of what is happening to them, so the characters who "wash up" on Parr island at Lucille's death are unsure. Sharon, Antonio, the two nephews, and Bebb all end up living in the same household, but they have all lost the meaning of their lives. They are both together and separated.

Besides the comic strip and the cartoon, Buechner employs successive photographic stills and movies, either silent reels or talkies. The combination of the still and the movie camera, of sound and

silence is employed nowadays by the *cineastes* themselves. One of
the latest films of Alain Resnais, *Mon Oncle d'Amérique*, comes to
mind. It is only in his latest novels that Buechner uses all these
techniques in conjunction. For an author whose philosophy is primarily dynamic, the use of modern cinematic technology comes as
a matter of course. All modern writers have been influenced to a
certain extent by the movies, a change that was predicted by Tolstoi.
James Joyce and Virginia Woolf used it to depict the stream of consciousness; John Dos Passos used it to develop imagism and im-
pressionism; F. Scott Fitzgerald, Nathanael West, and William
Faulkner all had a love/hate relationship with Hollywood; and
Ernest Hemingway and Graham Greene integrated filmic methods
with the more novelistic techniques of interior, discursive, and
abstract writing.[12]

But too much can be attributed to film techniques. Writers did,
after all, use close-ups before movies existed. In *The Canterbury Tales*,
Chaucer scans the pilgrims before he focuses on each of them, drawing "characters" before Bishop Hall's ever came into fashion. And
Balzac in the nineteenth century certainly used the technique of
panning: with a lingering look, he took in the relevant details of
a house, a room, a dining table. So in literary criticism, as well
as in the drawing of relationships between the arts, one must be
careful not to attribute to novelty what is mere ignorance of the past.

What enables us to speak of Buechner's cinematic imagination
is his own awareness of the fact. Scenes from movies occur in *The
Hungering Dark* and in "The Face in the Sky," a sermon. In *The
Alphabet of Grace*, he compares his life to a home movie, and the minister to a performer in the theatre.[13] In *The Book of Bebb*, Antonio,
who has been given a super-eight movie camera, expands on the
theme: "A comic-strip, an arrow in flight, a life, like a movie, they
are all a succession of stills, a parade of unmoving moments that
only seem to move."[14] This is the point of view of Antonio the
aesthete. Bebb would offer a different philosophy, if he was given

---

12. See Keith Cohen, *Film and Fiction: The Dynamics of Exchange* (New
Haven, Conn.: Yale University Press, 1979).

13. Buechner, *The Alphabet of Grace*, pp. 15, 43.

14. Buechner, *The Book of Bebb*, pp. 249, 283, and 380.

to philosophizing, since he often compares human beings to organic matter.

It is undeniable that in his tetralogy as well as in *Peculiar Treasures*, Buechner has derived much from the film tradition of American comedy. In *Love Feast*, Antonio gives a clue to Bebb's character when he says that Bebb reminds him of W. C. Fields. In *The Final Beast* and *The Entrance to Porlock*, Buechner refers to the minister and the wizard (a minister in disguise) as showmen. Nicolet winks at God, and Strasser puts on magic shows. Bebb is also a theatrical performer similar to Fields in a variety of ways. Like Fields, he grew up poor and hungry and is afraid of rainy days. His fight with the Internal Revenue Service also echoes Fields' struggles against the bankers. Both men are condemned by public opinion but both are characters one can feel sorry for; both hate the establishment; both meet their audience with radical honesty and are the masters of ceremonies. In addition, both have a tendency to court disaster, and both play gags involving ice-cream cones, elevators, and planes. In *Never Give a Sucker an Even Break*, Fields plunges out of an airplane to retrieve his bottle. Similarly, at the end of *Love Feast*, Bebb flies over the Princeton Parade (the Annual Parade of Alumni and Alumnae) with a banner that reads, ''Here's to Jesus, here's to you.'' In *Treasure Hunt*, Gertrude Conover sees a reincarnation of Bebb in a baby who looks like W. C. Fields. Buechner has borrowed some gags from Fields and invented others for Bebb which are in character. And just as George Moran and Leon Errol serve as foil and background to Fields' personality, so Herman Redpath, Harry Hocktaw, and the Joking Cousin are the foils in the Bebb saga.[15] Yet Bebb is not Fields: he does not have Fields' bitter bite, nor does he share Fields' hatred of women and children, and his fondness for liquor.

Buechner borrows other features from American comedy as well. One is the figure of the con man, which almost always gladdens the hearts of Americans but saddens that of Europeans. Pitted against him is the desperately earnest fellow who can't see beyond

15. See Donald Deschner, *The Films of W. C. Fields* (Secaucus, N.J.: Citadel Press, 1973), and W. K. Everson, *The Art of W. C. Fields* (Indianapolis: Bobbs-Merrill, 1967).

the tip of his nose. Such a pair is formed by Bebb and Antonio in
The Book of Bebb, and by Jacob and Esau and others in *Peculiar
Treasures*. Buechner laughs with rather than at the con man. He
also laughs at wives rather than at women in *The Book of Bebb*,
another feature which links his work to the comic tradition of cinematography. There are no harridans in his novels, but Sharon is
the typical Amazonian wife serving her husband cold toast for breakfast. Lucille is not even capable of doing that, and Brownie replaces
her as housewife. In this situation we get double laughs, both at
the incompetent wife and at the homosexual. These treatments
might tempt a reader to call Buechner sexist if it were not for the
men included in this general laughter at incompetence and role
reversal. The inhibited Antonio almost has to be propositioned by
any girl he meets—it takes that much to summon up some life and
sexual desire in him. He is deliberately frozen, unlike the overactive
and scheming Bebb, who has too many irons in the fire.

Antonio cannot be related to any particular character in film comedies, though he does have some traits that were popular in the
old films. The ineffectual young man, sincere and clumsy, appears
in the Keystone movies and is played by Buster Keaton, the man
with "the great stone face" (today the character is played by Jerry
Lewis). Speed was of the essence in these comedies as the characters
attempted to cope with their lives. Antonio's life, however, moves
imperceptibly; things happen to him despite himself. Like Keaton,
he has a face that hardly moves. He is surprised at his own tears,
the only sign of emotion that ever betrays his poker face. The sort
of comic ploys he uses also bears some resemblance to that of the
Marx Brothers; in their films characters often step away from the
action to converse in asides with the audience. Antonio bores us
with his endless rationalizations and philosophizing, and leaves the
scene of the Bebbsian rebellion to go and relieve himself in Mur-
ray Dodge Hall. Hopelessly closed within himself, Antonio would
make a great satirical portrait of twentieth-century man, himself
surprised.

Although *The Book of Bebb* is Buechner's most comprehensive attempt at uniting literary and cinematic comedy, characters in other
novels are also inspired by the early movies. In *The Entrance to Porlock*,
Tommy is a little like Stan Laurel, slender and unsure of himself

and always doing the wrong thing. He is the joker, the trickster, the clown who hides his sadness behind a mask of practical joking. He is pitted against his pompous father, Peter Ringkoping, who, like Hardy, the tin man in the 1925 version of *The Wizard of Oz*, is exasperated by the companions of the trip. In fact, Hardy is referred to at the end of *Treasure Hunt*, when Babe, disguised as his wife Bert, expresses his hatred of Bebb's family and friends by destroying their car: "Like Oliver Hardy demolishing a Model T, she jumped up and down on it with her arm flung wide, her head bent low, her legs pumping" (*BB*, p. 504).

Although lightheartedness triumphs in *The Book of Bebb*, as it does in *The Final Beast* and *The Entrance to Porlock*, it is not unmixed with terror. The mixture of comedy and terror is mainly derived from the topsy-turviness of Buechner's world. Special effects are inspired both by several specific films—*Abbott and Costello Meet the Wolf Man, Frankenstein, Dr. Jekyll and Mr. Hyde*—and by Hitchcock's movies. Every man, Buechner assumes, is Dr. Jekyll and Mr. Hyde—even Nicolet, the young minister of *The Final Beast*—a theme Buechner develops particularly in *Treasure Hunt*. Antonio, confused, suffers from double vision, and comes to suspect even his friends, as his perception of Brownie suggests: "The whole smile dropped about an inch, and suddenly it was not Brownie any more but Lon Chaney changing from Dr. Jekyll to Mr. Hyde with his terrible maw of fangs hanging out over his lower lip" (*BB*, p. 483).

The theme of the puzzled hero caught up in bewildering events recurs throughout the whole of *The Book of Bebb*, a theme shaped with more determination in *Treasure Hunt*. As in *Shadow of a Doubt*, the action is set in a small town and deals with the growth of suspicion. Antonio's suspicion is both well-founded and ill-founded, since his vision is blurred. Buechner develops suspense by tracking the action as if with a camera, using cutting and montage, chases and superimposition. The first process is used notably when Babe, consumed by jealousy, looks at his wife and the black man Callaway hanging out the wash together. His camera eye goes from one to the other and then embraces both in a shot, while the spy is in turn spied upon by the narrator Antonio. Antonio, also influenced by his past, superimposes several images on the picture of Bert and Callaway: he sees her as concubine or great mare and him as

Pharaoh, or as laundry: "he a long black stocking, she a sheet ballooning out in the summer" (*BB*, p. 472).

The chase is used in *Love Feast* when Sharon and Antonio follow Golden to find Bebb's hiding place. Steps follow sonorous steps, and taxi chases taxi; the contact is momentarily lost, then recovered, and clues indicate the path to follow. In *Treasure Hunt*, cross-cutting between dream sequences suggests that Bebb and Babe may look alike but that they are in fact two totally different persons with different ideals. Smiles are crooked or appear when they should not, unexplained. Alternating montages of sight and sound feature both Babe and Bebb until both are revealed for what they truly are: the crook and the saint in the making. Finally, vision clears, even for Antonio, and the solution to the mystery is unraveled. Despite Brownie's death, *Treasure Hunt* ends on a happy note, since righteousness has been restored and the sinner discovered and forgiven.

For many of his effects Buechner relies on the cinematic world, which clearly fascinates him. Zooming, editing, cross-cutting, montage and editing, superimpositions and dissolves, special effects, the alternation of long shots and rapid cutting—all have their place in his novels. They are particularly evident in *The Book of Bebb*, in which scenes shaped by these techniques alternate with photographic stills.

Stills present reality at a given moment. They also enable the author to condense reminiscences in Proustian fashion. In *The Book of Bebb*, Bebb, for instance, appears in many shots: exposing himself to the children in Miami, taking a picture of coupling lions, eating an ice-cream cone at the Eiffel Tower, holding on to his daughter as he feels the end is coming. These pictures express the complexity of the man, and can be summoned at will. Whenever Antonio thinks of Bebb's courage, the picture of the lions is superimposed by a trick of the camera; whenever he misses the Sharon he first met, he remembers the scene at the Salamander Motel.

Memories need not be static; they can also be animated. In *The Final Beast*, shots of Irma Reinwasser's past life in the concentration camp develop into animated scenes. In his bedroom in Muscadine, Nicolet relives in a flashback the conversation he had with the young man who gave him a ride; through a dissolve this recalls the even more distant past of preconversion and conversion times. In *The Entrance to Porlock*, Nels gradually reveals the whole of his career as Dean of Students up to the present time and his confrontation with Mullavey, the young boy who commits suicide. The autobiographies that constitute Buechner's latest fiction use this device constantly, but there is a slight difference between *The Book of Bebb* and *Godric*. The tetralogy unwinds like film on a reel, whereas *Godric* gives us the impression of reading an illuminated book of life. Walt Disney used this process: the book was presented, and suddenly the camera stopped at one point and moved in for a close-up on the page; the viewer became absorbed by the image, which then became animated. This is the way Godric reminisces, flitting from one page to another, unsequentially.

Flashbacks are not typical only of the cinematic technique. The Canterbury pilgrims, for instance, reminisced about their past. Buechner often uses flashbacks to explain the circumstances of his characters. In *The Book of Bebb*, it is also a unitive device which creates a bridge from one novel to the next. What *is* cinematic, however, is the use of flashback together with cutting and superimposition to create cinematic montages. Buechner uses this device with particular felicity in two novels: *The Final Beast* and *Treasure Hunt*. In *The Final Beast*, Irma's present life and past life are intermingled through cross-cutting. The pain and embarrassment she feels at Nicolet's flight from home is juxtaposed with the pain she experienced at the hands of her Nazi lover and torturer Heinz Taffel; images and sequences follow each other until both men are one in her mind; she dreams about Heinz Taffel's funeral, and in spite of herself she betrays Nicolet to his enemy Poteat. Forgiveness is harder than she had imagined, and through cross-cutting and flashbacks Buechner suggests that this woman who wants so much to forgive secretly hates all men. A novelistic technique would have explained all this in a single flashback. The succession of flashbacks shows that Irma is morbidly haunted by the past; the cross-cutting shows how it affects her present view of life; the superimposition reveals the demonic possession that turns all good into bad. Irma has to be exorcised.

The battle between good and evil in *Treasure Hunt* is depicted in a similar fashion, but this time good triumphs in Antonio's mind. The flashbacks of Bebb are cross-cut with the actions of Babe, who disguises evil as good. There is constant confusion in Antonio's mind because Babe's actions are mainly superimposed on his mental screen in sight-and-sound montages. Truth for Antonio becomes a vision seen through a stereopticon slide and is no longer three-dimensional (*BB,* p. 460).

Cross-cutting is an essential component of Buechner's art. In *The Entrance to Porlock*, the psychology of Nels is developed through short shots, medium shots, and sequences of the cat on the road, the office of the Dean, and his dream of the hospital. The breakdown of characters is echoed by the breakdown of the two cars. Alice has alternate visions of the ideal home and of death. In *The Book of Bebb*, Antonio's character is depicted in a similar fashion. In *Lion Country*, cross-cutting shots of his cat, his art, the dying Miriam and the living Sharon, orchestrated to music, give a good clue to his dual nature and his youth. In *Open Heart*, art and hypochondria are interwoven. In *Godric*, similar juxtaposition of the far past, the near past, and the present show the evolution or regression of the old man's soul.

The repetition of such images or sequences gives stability to the characters. But the alteration of any element in them gives an impression of movement. For instance, when Sharon remembers, in *Open Heart*, the scene in the Salamander Motel, she realizes how things have changed between her and Antonio. In *Love Feast*, Antonio remembers the same scene when he is about to patch things up with Sharon. In this sense the repetition of the same visual image of the past emphasizes the changing aspect of life. On the other hand, the five encounters between Antonio and Laura Fleischman in different settings indicate the changes in their relationship: at first teacher and student, they explore the possibility of being lovers, and then plan, realize, and discard their romance.

The complexity of life is also described by cinematic techniques. Superimposition, used by the Surrealist painters, was taken over by novelists and filmmakers. In *The Entrance to Porlock*, Nels's thoughts are commented on by caption, a technique Joyce used in "Cyclops." This time, Buechner uses a montage of both sight and sound. What Tip and his grandfather read aloud from Strasser's pamphlet is meant to pacify Nels's roaring and tumultuous thoughts: "We are all of us pilgrims."[16] In *The Book of Bebb*, televi-

---

16. Frederick Buechner, *The Entrance to Porlock* (New York: Atheneum, 1970), p. 49.

sion is a kind of commentary on the conversation between Antonio and Lucille, Bebb's embittered wife. During that time Brownie is watching a commercial "which showed the vapors rising from an acid stomach into the esophagus and causing heartburn" (*BB*, p. 42). In *Lion Country*, Buechner uses superimposition several times. Later, when Miriam, who is dying of cancer, listens to her son's summary of *Abbott and Costello Meet Frankenstein and the Wolf Man*, she superimposes the story on her own situation: she too has resisted the vampire for a long time, but now she is longing for death (*BB*, p. 87). Antonio's jealousy is projected by the superimposition of the flaming vision of a buck with horns on the smoke rising from burning toast. When he looks at his wife in bed, he sees a vision of Laura Fleischman seized by a buck.

Many more examples could be given, especially from *Treasure Hunt*. Buechner also makes use of the Schufftau process. In the haven of peace of Brownie's bedroom, there hangs a picture of a boy fishing in a millpond. All the while the Bebbsian group are conversing, Antonio's attention is focused on this picture, which is so reassuring amid the turmoil and anguish of the friends (*BB*, p. 456). At the end of the book, Antonio, looking at the poor blind child Jimmy Bob Luby, superimposes the vision of the Lone Ranger coming to save those in distress.

Sometimes superimpositions exist for the flicker of an instant, as transition between scenes to suggest a lapse of time or a change of location. In *The Entrance to Porlock*, the connection between Strasser and the preciousness of Peter's land is indicated by a dissolve. In *The Book of Bebb*, dissolves occur at the time of telephone conversations, bringing worlds together, people together, and then making them slowly disappear. In *Lion Country*, Antonio oscillates between life and death. When he is in the South, he telephones his dying sister Miriam and summons the world of death, whereas when he is in the North he telephones Bebb, hoping to hear about Sharon, the epitome of life.

But smooth transitions are mostly effected by fade-ins and fade-outs. In *The Entrance to Porlock*, Buechner thus emphasizes the fluidity of the objective and the subjective by making the two constantly interpenetrate each other, as the characters live both in the exterior moment and their own interior dreams. Flashbacks, fade-ins, fade-outs, and focusing follow the natural mental processes in *The Book of Bebb*, a device also used by Joyce in *Ulysses*. In *Lion Country*, when Antonio is attending his sister on her deathbed, he tells her the current news of the world she can no longer share in; his attention lags, and he falls into a daydream in which he remembers them as children. He comes back to reality to realize that she too has escaped into some world of her own and, partly because of pain or exhaustion, has not been listening to him. Finally, fade-outs also emphasize resolution and choice. In *Love Feast*, Buechner's camera encompasses both the house of Revenoc, where the Love Feast is prepared, and the outside world of Princeton. As night falls, lights gradually dim in the cold outside world and the camera concentrates solely on the joy of the feast in the lighted house, a device much used in the theatre. Antonio, who has been saddened by his separation from Sharon and made particularly sensitive to the misery of humanity, resolutely decides that for this evening at least, he will participate in the rejoicing.

The rapid cutting Buechner employs indicates the wealth of an individual's psychological resources and the variety of his experiences. Thus in *Open Heart*, Bebb's psychological make-up is suggested through short takes of his past and his present dreams: his desires for money and power are thus associated with his family's poverty and his memory of wasted peaches lying on the roadside. In *Love Feast*, Bebb, hiding in a fireproof basement, announces his death, Sharon's pregnancy and the sex of the baby, and his anxiety and faith. Sometimes Buechner employs a short series of sequences. When Bebb visits Antonio in *Love Feast*, he suggests the problems of Bebb's life in three short sequences: he depicts Bebb and the IRS, Bebb and the Princeton authorities, and Bebb and the insurance company. Laura Fleischman's richness is evoked in the same manner. We see her as a student, as a dental assistant, as a housewife, and as a lover. In *Godric*, the saint's make-up is revealed in the same way. Through rapid cutting Buechner endeavors to suggest the infinite potentialities of human beings.

Subjective and objective views of characters alternate; the camera pursues them with long shots and wide angles or lingers on them in close-ups. Buechner, whose gift for delineating people with his pen is quite extraordinary, probes faces in detail. In *Treasure Hunt*, he even uses the modern device of showing only part of the Joking Cousin's face instead of all of it (*BB*, p. 420). His camera eye is mobile, zooming, scanning, or shooting from various angles.

Editing and montage are essential to the construction of a novel or a film, as they are to the recollection of one's life. As in Buechner's novels, the montage is not only visual but also auditory, the silences speaking as loudly as sounds and speech. The good editor, like the comic-strip creator, knows what should remain unexpressed, left to be theorized by the reader or audience. In the tape he leaves for his heirs in *Treasure Hunt*, Bebb says only what is essential. The very much alive Bebb is suggested by sounds—the shuffling of papers, the muttering of TV, the honking of car horns. The strangeness of Babe's house is suggested as much by sound as it is by pictures and movement: the rhythmical noise of the swatting of flies echoes the sound of the rattle of death in the previous novels of the tetralogy.

For Buechner, as for movie directors, pace and timing are of the essence of his success. In *The Book of Bebb*, Antonio's slow motion is always contrasted with Bebb's energetic appearances and Sharon's endless attempts to cope with her own life. Life *is* motion, and characters are often divided into pale and static and colorful and mobile. Examples of speeded-up action are to be found particularly in *Love Feast*, in which Buechner uses the device that the pioneering film director D. W. Griffith used: alternating inner abstract themes with historical action. Antonio provides the thematic pauses, and Bebb is launched like a general into action. Like an army commander, he deploys his forces to fight or to trick the enemy. In a mock-heroic way, Bebb's fight against the Princeton authorities is likened to the Battle of Princeton (in the War of Independence), and as the Bebbsian followers fight against the atheists, action is speeded up.

Thus accelerated action and slowed action pace Buechner's novels. In *Lion Country*, Sharon's seductions of Antonio occur in slow motion, whereas Redpath's ordination causes a whirlwind that interrupts the lovers' *joyeux ébats*. On the other hand, love is also portrayed in stormy encounters, shopping sprees, and fast chases. Speed is an essential component of magic, because one thing is substituted for another within the very few minutes that the audience's attention is distracted. Speed is thus a part of the action in *Treasure*

Hunt when Babe, impersonating his wife, goes about his destructive work.

Speed was not one of the essential components of Buechner's early novels, which he wrote in a more meditative mood. In *The Book of Bebb* and *Godric*, accelerated action and slowed action are happily contrasted. Time and space montages are also the products of Buechner's growth as an artist, indicators of his becoming well-versed in the techniques of cinematography. In time montages, space is fixed but the interior monologue progresses through flashbacks and superimpositions. Buechner's most recent novel, *Godric*, is essentially such a montage. From his cell Godric tells the story of his life unsequentially. In space montages, on the other hand, time is fixed but spatial elements change. When Antonio phones Laura from his rented quarters at Mrs. Gunther's, he is aware of what everyone he loves or is connected with is doing at that moment, although they are miles apart: Sharon, Bebb, Nancy, Bill's secretary, his brother-in-law, his dentist. . . . Life has gained such an intensity through his hoping to get a date with Laura that he is unlike his usual self; Antonio the lover can take in the bustle of the world's activities. Buechner also creates special effects of time and space with trains and cars; these vehicles make all places seem to be one, and the innermost parts of consciousness are released.

Buechner often uses special effects in his novels with the surrealistic purpose of divulging inexpressible truth. He uses two main devices: the blurring and distorting of the image, and the blending of sound and silence. Emotion is visually represented. In *The Entrance to Porlock*, Nels, the rationalist and the judge who does not believe in emotions, perceives his family through throbbing or "bent" air, a perception that effectively shows that his judgments are influenced by the physical change that his propensity for anger triggers in him.[17] Another character who denies his own emotivity is Antonio. In *The Book of Bebb*, he realizes that he is crying because the images he perceives are being distorted by the film of tears over his eyes (*BB*, pp. 395, 413).

---

17. Buechner, *The Entrance to Porlock*, pp. 8, 20, 65, etc. See also *The Book of Bebb*, pp. 8, 295.

Other of Buechner's effects are influenced by surrealism. Dutch painters sometimes included a mirror in their pictures to show what was not in the room they were rendering and thus added a dimension to reality. The Belgian artist Magritte often painted the picture of a picture of a landscape. Modern filmmakers have used both these devices in stills or sequences of movement, and both appear in Buechner's *The Entrance to Porlock*. As the psychological climate becomes more oppressive, clouds are reflected in Nels's glasses. Later, and dynamically this time, Peter Ringkoping perceives the gathering clouds in the window of the car moving at high speed. Buechner achieves a surrealistic effect similar to that of Magritte's *The Liberator* when Peter is daydreaming: Strasser, opening his shirt, reveals his chest and shows Peter a picture of his land rising toward the sky. When he looks at himself, Peter sees an old man with white clouds (instead of hair) racing by. By a double trick of the camera, Strasser has been superimposed on the landscape viewed from the car, which reminds Peter of his land and makes it dear to him for the first time. Then, through a dissolve, the image of Strasser disappears and Peter comes to consciousness; he then realizes that his own shiftiness is reflected in the car window, although what he sees is only external objective reality. Ingmar Bergman has created similar effects with similar results in *Wild Strawberries*, a film about an artist also preoccupied with his inner turmoil.

Buechner also experiments with special sound effects in *The Book of Bebb*. The alternation of speech and silence is mainly literary in *The Final Beast* and *The Entrance to Porlock*, while it is mainly documentary in *Godric*. In *The Book of Bebb*, Buechner orchestrates the narration. In *Lion Country*, the over-educated Antonio particularly enjoys opera, which, according to the eighteenth-century philosopher Diderot, is both instructive and emotionally fulfilling, since it combines imaginative visual effects and auditory perceptions. Thus, as in Gilbert and Sullivan's operettas, we hear in the background strains of Verdi when Antonio wants to skin Bebb alive, and of Mozart's *Don Giovanni* when he depicts Christ as the Great Lover. Antonio even orchestrates Dr. James's *Apocryphal Gospel* according to Mozart's canon. Such taste is amusingly contrasted with that of Sharon, who delights in popular music. The death rattle punctuates the whole story in *Open Heart*, which does indeed deal with the death of human beings—Herman Redpath and Lucille Bebb—and the death of personal relationships, as the marriage between Antonio and Sharon is increasingly rocky. *Treasure Hunt* is the loudest novel of all: the cassette recordings and electronic sounds that punctuate it make it an eerie work, interrupted only by the panicky squawking of chickens; it is a fiction of suspense and terror.

Sound often enhances the reality of life for Buechner, but it may also distort it. In *Open Heart*, the noise of a racing train stops Antonio from hearing Golden's message in a scene comparable to one in Godard's *Deux ou Trois Choses Que Je Sais d'Elle*. Buechner, more visual than auditory, sees the truth as T.V. news with the sound turned off. Miming and silent scenes are part of his technique. During the Love Feast at Revenoc, there are times when Antonio switches off the sound of Bebb's voice and watches the scene and Bebb's energetic movements in silence: ''The room flickered like the scratched print of an old newsreel, the hands of Bebb jerky as Woodrow Wilson laying a wreath on the tomb of the Unknown Soldier. Shadows. Faces. Afros like puff balls of dust under beds, more air than hair. Grainy, light-struck blizzarding of old film'' (*BB*, p. 307).

Later, the feast develops like a silent movie as the kiss of peace is passed on, and finishes on a comic note as Buechner accelerates the tempo. The silence is then interrupted by Nancy Oglethorpe's wail—''Jesus''—and her solo confession. If sound is restored to the first part of the scene, then what we hear is the orchestration of a negro spiritual. Both renderings are possible, and neither would betray the author's artistry.

Miming is also part of *The Book of Bebb*. Most of the part played by the Joking Cousin is mime. Callaway, the black, whose speech can be interpreted only by the most astute, resorts to miming to defend himself from accusations of lasciviousness: he tears up the note found in his room expressing the racial prejudice of the South. At the most sacred of life's moments, it seems that Buechner prefers silence to sound.

Like films which transport the spectator entirely into their world, Buechner's novels have something in common with the realist trend of the nineteenth-century novel. Insofar as he creates a reality which transcends basic perceptions, he is a disciple of the surrealists. Both real and surreal truth co-exist in Buechner's novels, but there is no question that he believes that to opt for only one is to be a reductionist. To be faithful to the Truth, Buechner uses the confluence of all arts, but his imagination is largely visual. Consecutiveness and singleness of viewpoint are for him outmoded. Buechner prefers simultaneity, multiple perspectives, and montage. People, like objects, can be viewed from inside or outside. Temporal distortions occur. Perspective is mobile, and paralipsis makes montage of consciousness possible.[18] By placing his characters against a studio background, by using the visual and auditory arts from both past and present, Buechner is reinforcing his message of unity and universality.

Buechner thus demonstrates himself to be a thoroughly modern man. He uses techniques from both talkies and silent films, comics and cartoons. He appreciates Jungian psychological insights and existentialism as a dynamic subjective philosophy. He integrates all this within a Christian vision which is yet tolerant enough to empathize with Gertrude Conover's Theosophy. His own far-reaching ecumenism embraces within Christianity the liberal Nicolet; the conservative evangelical Bebb, his most rounded Christian character; and the lean and ascetic mystic, Godric. His return to Christianity may seem to a superficial observer his least modern characteristic. But in fact it is his recognition that a world utterly relativistic and without values has a God-shaped blank that makes his writing profoundly relevant and prophetically modern.

---

18. See Keith Cohen, *Film and Fiction*.

Conclusion

When Mr. Calverley, a young English poet who managed to be expelled from both Oxford and Cambridge, sat for the compulsory entrance examination in theology, he was asked what he thought about the Decalogue. Ignorant but shrewd, he replied, ''I have feelings of awe, not unmingled with admiration.'' A similar attitude toward the works of Frederick Buechner inspired me to write this book. As the child in *Love Feast* explores his unfamiliar father's face with his hands, so the critic traces the contours of an author's thought, searching ''for something buried there, for secret treasure he maybe even half knew was a clue to the secret of himself,'' or at least of the world to which he belongs.[1]

E. C. Bentley once wrote: ''Geography is about maps/But biography is about chaps.'' In this instance, Buechner is his own biographer; I am merely the geographer. The drawback that a map-maker like myself encounters is that there is little time to scrutinize with telescope and microscope. Thus remote corners of the landscape are ignored and some of the details of the artistry overlooked. The pioneer must be content with tracing a possible way to approach the land, recording faithfully the flora and fauna.

In the making of this book, I have not ended as I began. On the one hand, I have had to develop some areas that were not part of my original plan. The book, for example, was to have had only five chapters, and I never intended to deal with Buechner's cinematic imagination. But suddenly the latter imposed itself on me as a must if I was to do justice to the artist's technique. On the other hand, I have had to set aside some parallels in Buechner that particularly fascinated me, such as his kinship with Cervantes, Erasmus, and Rabelais. I have also had to forego examining the ways in which his style has been influenced by G. K. Chesterton and Mark Twain, and by the tradition of

---

1. Frederick Buechner, *The Book of Bebb* (New York: Atheneum, 1979), pp. 377-378.

the confidence man in American literature. It must suffice that I have delineated a face, as honestly as possible, without substituting mine, hoping that others will peer more deeply into it. In so doing, it is my hope that none of us confuses the part for the whole of this extremely complex, thoughtful, and sensitive author. It is with his vision that I now wish to conclude.

There are two ways of viewing man in the creation. One is to bemoan his destructiveness, concentrate on his foibles, stoically harden oneself against the inevitable damage, and perhaps appeal to God for mercy. The other is to rejoice in the achievements of human beings, in the part they have played in the creation, to express a guarded satisfaction. Buechner seems to have little time for human achievements. His Christianity is not based on chirpy optimism or the positive thinking of Pelagianism. Behind the laughter lies the deep sadness caused by the folly of mankind. Buechner often wants us to face our vomit. He does not, however, want us to drown in it. He has moved from bitterness to humorous concern for humanity. *The Book of Bebb* still depicts a conscience-stricken view of the world, like *King Lear* without a Kent or a Cordelia, as no character is unblemished. But in *Godric*, despite the self-laceration of some characters, the grey clouds in the sky part here and there to reveal some patches of blue: Perkin is still incorrupt, and Ailred, the abbot of Rievaulx, has kept his integrity. Agitation has subsided. There is both time for contemplation and time for friendship. Buechner seems to be emerging from the troubled clouds in the valley, to have reached a more serene view of life. Like Moses, he glimpses the Promised Land.

Two basic responses also characterize those who are concerned with the existing world. Some think it should be shaken; others believe that it should be left to the tooth of time. Wines are best when, after bottling, they are aged in a cave, turned over at rare intervals, and served in a steady container that will allow few dregs to reach the surface. Does Buechner belong to the shakers of mankind? He does and he doesn't. The active youth in him attempts to shake the world out of its torpor, the middle-aged man acts indirectly by playing psychological games, and the older man, it seems, senses the vanity of it all and believes that, ultimately, all lies in the hands of God.

It is a tribute to the Reverend Mr. Buechner that during the years from 1970 to 1980 he has progressed both as thinker and as artist, refusing to rest on his laurels. His style, once an intricate design, has become simpler, while his thought has veered in the opposite direction, toward greater complexity. One has to respect the capacity of this man to take in new thoughts and new techniques, absorb them, and then reproduce them in the most inventive ways. To use Levi-Strauss's distinction, nothing is ever raw in Buechner's works; all is perfectly cooked and tastefully presented on the platter. It is an essentially civilized cuisine that he prepares. His work unites body and spirit, the secular and the sacred, the horizontal and the vertical in a successful attempt at an organic view of life and art. He writes like a man who has brushed away his tears to recall the great laughter at the heart of the universe and to live in ''Eternity's sunrise.''

Bibliography

Primary Sources

1. Books

The Alphabet of Grace. New York: Seabury Press, 1970.

The Book of Bebb. New York: Atheneum, 1979.

The Entrance to Porlock. New York: Atheneum, 1970.

The Final Beast. New York: Atheneum, 1965.

Godric. New York: Atheneum, 1981.

The Hungering Dark. New York: Seabury Press, 1969.

Lion Country. New York: Atheneum, 1970.

A Long Day's Dying. New York: Knopf, 1950.

Love Feast. New York: Atheneum, 1972.

The Magnificent Defeat. New York: Seabury Press, 1966.

Now and Then. New York: Harper and Row, 1983.

Open Heart. New York: Atheneum, 1972.

Peculiar Treasures. New York: Harper and Row, 1979.

The Return of Ansel Gibbs. New York: Knopf, 1958.

The Sacred Journey. New York: Harper and Row, 1982.

The Seasons' Difference. New York: Knopf, 1952.

Telling the Truth: The Gospel as Tragedy, Comedy and Fairy Tale. New York: Harper and Row, 1977.

Treasure Hunt. New York: Atheneum, 1977.

Wishful Thinking: A Theological ABC. New York: Harper and Row, 1973.

2. Other Publications

"Air for Two Voices," in *To God Be the Glory: Sermons in Honor of George Arthur Buttrick*. Ed. Theodore A. Gill. New York: Abingdon Press, 1973, pp. 131-139.

"All's Lost, All's Found." *The Christian Century*, March 12, 1980, pp. 282-285.

"Behold, the Lamb of God." *The Christian Century*, March 14, 1979, pp. 271-272.

"Comfort for a Sorrowing Mother." *The Christian Century*, March 5, 1969, p. 309.

"Despair in the Final Hour." *The Christian Century*, March 12, 1969, p. 340.

"The Face in the Sky." *Presbyterian Life*, Jan. 1, 1969, pp. 5-7.

"Family Scenes" (poems). *The Quarterly Review of Literature* (Princeton), XIX (1974).

"The Fat Man's Prescriptions, I-IV." *Poetry*, LXIX (Nov. 1946).

"The Fat Man's Prescriptions, I-IX," in *Ten Poets Anthology*. Ed. Anthony
Harrigan. East Dorset, Vt.: n.p., 1950, pp. 6-7.

"Finality & Completion." *The Christian Century*, March 26, 1969, p. 396.

"Forgiveness for Failed Saints." *The Christian Century*, Feb. 19, 1969, p. 244.

"If Not God, Old Scratch." *The New York Times Book Review*, May 6, 1973,
pp. 3, 14, 16.

"A Little While & You Will Not See Me." *The Christian Century*, March 7,
1979, p. 238.

"The Marriage at Cana" (poem). *The Anglican Theological Review*, LXII (April
1980), 152.

"Of Whipples, Wheels and Posy." *Blair & Ketchum's Country Journal*, 3 (Jan.
1976), 26-35.

"Promise of Paradise." *The Christian Century*, Feb. 26, 1969, p. 276.

"Sermon for the Rededication of Phillips Church." *Bulletin of Phillips Exeter
Academy*, Summer 1981, pp. 57-61.

"The Speaking & Writing of Words." *The Alumni Bulletin*, Bangor Theological
Seminary, LIV (Fall/Winter 1979-80), 3-17.

"Summons to Pilgrimage." *New York Times Book Review*, March 16, 1969,
pp. 25-26.

"Surrender to Infinite Grace." *The Christian Century*, April 2, 1969, p. 436.

"Thirst for Fulfillment." *The Christian Century*, March 19, 1969, p. 364.

"The Two Stories." *The Open Door*, Bangor Theological Seminary, Summer
1980, pp. 6-7.

Secondary Sources

1. Interpretations

Myers, Nancy B. *Sanctifying the Profane: Religious Themes in the Fiction of Frederick
Buechner*. Dissertation North Texas State University 1976.

Parker, Harry J. *The Nature of Faith in the Fiction of Frederick Buechner, 1965-1979*.
Senior Thesis Princeton University 1980.

Thompson, Stacey Webb. *The Rediscovery of Wonder: A Critical Introduction to
the Novels of Frederick Buechner*. Dissertation Michigan State University
1979.

2. General Works

Armstrong, Edward A. *Shakespeare's Imagination*. Lincoln, Neb.: University
of Nebraska Press, 1946.

Bailey, J. E., and Axon, W. E. A. *The Collected Sermons of Thomas Fuller D. D.,
1631-1659*. 2 vols. London: Unwin, 1891.

Bromiley, Geoffrey W. *An Introduction to the Theology of Karl Barth*. Grand Rapids, Mich.: Eerdmans, 1979.

Cohen, Keith. *Film and Fiction: The Dynamics of Exchange*. New Haven, Conn.: Yale University Press, 1979.

Colie, Rosalie L. *Paradoxica Epidemica: The Renaissance Tradition of Paradox*. Princeton, N.J.: Princeton University Press, 1966.

Crocker, Lionel G. *H.W. Beecher's Art of Preaching*. Chicago: University of Chicago Press, 1934.

Davies, Horton. *A Mirror of the Ministry in Modern Novels*. New York: Oxford University Press, 1959.

De Rougemont, Denis. *Love in the Western World*. New York: Harcourt Brace, 1940.

Deschner, Donald. *The Films of W.C. Fields*. Secaucus, N.J.: Citadel Press, 1973.

Everson, W. K. *The Art of W.C. Fields*. Indianapolis: Bobbs-Merrill, 1967.

Fordham, Frieda. *An Introduction to Jung's Psychology*. Harmondsworth, Middlesex: Penguin Books, 1953.

Jarrett-Kerr, Martin. *Studies in Literature and Belief*. London: Rockliff, 1954.

Jung, Carl G. *Memories, Dreams and Reflections*. 3rd ed. New York: Pantheon Books, 1963.

Kellogg, Jean. *Dark Prophets of Hope—Dostoievski, Sartre, Camus, Faulkner*. Chicago: Loyola University Press, 1975.

Kern, Edith G. *Existential Thought and Fictional Technique: Kierkegaard, Sartre, Beckett*. New Haven, Conn.: Yale University Press, 1970.

Kierkegaard, Søren. *Edifying Discourses*. Minneapolis: Augsburg Publishing House, 1950.

_____. *Fear and Trembling*. 1941; rpt. New York: Anchor Books, 1954.

Kurrick, Maire Jaanus. *Literature and Negation*. New York: Columbia University Press, 1979.

Lewalski, Barbara. *Protestant Poetics and the Seventeenth-Century Religious Lyric*. Princeton, N.J.: Princeton University Press, 1979.

Lewis, C. S. *Mere Christianity*. New York: Macmillan, 1957.

Lindauer, Martin S. *The Psychological Study of Literature*. Chicago: Nelson Hall, 1974.

Lynch, W., S.J. *Christ and Apollo: The Dimensions of the Literary Imagination*. South Bend, Ind.: University of Notre Dame Press, 1975.

Mackintosh, H. R. *Types of Modern Theology: Schleiermacher to Barth*. New York: Scribners, 1937.

Mitchell, W. Fraser. *English Pulpit Oratory from Andrewes to Tillotson*. New York and Toronto: Macmillan, 1932.

Ong, Walter, S.J. *Rhetoric, Romance and Technology: Studies in the Interaction of Expression and Culture*. Ithaca and London: Cornell University Press, 1971.

Plantinga, Theodore. *Learning to Live with Evil*. Grand Rapids, Mich.: Eerdmans, 1982.

Romberg, Bertil. *Studies in the Narrative Technique of the First-Person Novel*. Stockholm: Almquist, 1962.

Scott, Nathan A., Jr. *The Broken Center: Studies in the Theological Horizon of Modern Literature*. New Haven, Conn.: Yale University Press, 1966.

_____, ed. *The New Orpheus: Essays toward a Christian Poetics*. New York: Sheed & Ward, 1964.

_____. *The Unquiet Vision: Mirrors of Man in Existentialism*. New York and Cleveland: World Publishing, 1969.

Tavard, George. *Paul Tillich and the Christian Message*. New York: Scribners, 1962.

Tillich, Paul. *Systematic Theology*. 3 vols. Chicago: University of Chicago Press, 1951-63.

3. Articles

Davies, Horton. ''Frederick Buechner and the Strange Work of Grace.'' *Theology Today,* July 1979, pp. 186-193.

_____ and Marie-Hélène Davies. ''The God of Storm and Stillness: The Fiction of Flannery O'Connor and Frederick Buechner.'' *Religion in Life,* Summer 1979, pp. 188-196.

Interview with Frederick Buechner. *The Wittenburg Door*, Jan. 1980.